Workshop on Sense, Concept and Entity Representations and their Applications (SENSE 2017)

Valencia, Spain
4 April 2017

ISBN: 978-1-5108-3870-3

Organizers:

Jose Camacho-Collados, Sapienza University of Rome
Mohammad Taher Pilehvar, University of Cambridge

Program Committee:

Eneko Agirre, University of the Basque Country
Claudio Delli Bovi, Sapienza University of Rome
Luis Espinosa-Anke, Pompeu Fabra University
Lucie Flekova, Darmstadt University of Technology
Graeme Hirst, University of Toronto
Eduard Hovy, Carnegie Mellon University
Ignacio Iacobacci, Sapienza University of Rome
Richard Johansson, University of Gothenburg
David Jurgens, Stanford University
Omer Levy, University of Washington
Andrea Moro, Microsoft
Roberto Navigli, Sapienza University of Rome
Arvind Neelakantan, University of Massachusetts Amherst
Luis Nieto Piña, University of Gothenburg
Siva Reddy, University of Edinburgh
Horacio Saggion, Pompeu Fabra University
Hinrich Schütze, University of Munich
Piek Vossen, University of Amsterdam
Ivan Vulić, University of Cambridge
Torsten Zesch, University of Duisburg-Essen
Jianwen Zhang, Microsoft Research

Invited Speakers:

Roberto Navigli, Sapienza University of Rome
Hinrich Schütze, University of Munich

Table of Contents

Workshop Program

8:30 - 9:30 Registration

9:30 - 11:00 Session 1

- 9:30-9:40 - Opening Remarks

- 9:40-10:00 - Short paper presentations

  Improving Verb Metaphor Detection by Propagating Abstractness to Words, Phrases and Individual Senses
  Maximilian Köper and Sabine Schulte im Walde

  Using Linked Disambiguated Distributional Networks for Word Sense Disambiguation
  Alexander Panchenko, Stefano Faralli, Simone Paolo Ponzetto and Chris Biemann

- 10:00-11:00 - Invited talk by Roberto Navigli (Sapienza University)

11:00 - 11:30 Coffee break

11:30 - 13:00 Session 2

- 11:30-11:45 - Lightning talks (posters)

  Compositional Semantics using Feature-Based Models from WordNet
  Pablo Gamallo and Martín Pereira-Fariña

  Automated WordNet Construction Using Word Embeddings
  Mikhail Khodak, Andrej Risteski, Christiane Fellbaum and Sanjeev Arora

  Classifying Lexical-semantic Relationships by Exploiting Sense/Concept Representations
  Kentaro Kanada, Tetsunori Kobayashi and Yoshihiko Hayashi

  Supervised and unsupervised approaches to measuring usage similarity
  Milton King and Paul Cook

  Lexical Disambiguation of Igbo using Diacritic Restoration
  Ignatius Ezeani, Mark Hepple and Ikechukwu Onyenwe

Creating and Validating Multilingual Semantic Representations for Six Languages: Expert versus Non-Expert Crowds
Mahmoud El-Haj, Paul Rayson, Scott Piao and Stephen Wattam

Elucidating Conceptual Properties from Word Embeddings
Kyoung-Rok Jang and Sung-Hyon Myaeng

TTCS`e: a Vectorial Resource for Computing Conceptual Similarity
Enrico Mensa, Daniele P. Radicioni and Antonio Lieto

Measuring the Italian-English lexical gap for action verbs and its impact on translation
Lorenzo Gregori and Alessandro Panunzi

Supervised and Unsupervised Word Sense Disambiguation on Word Embedding Vectors of Unambigous Synonyms
Aleksander Wawer and Agnieszka Mykowiecka

- 11:45-13:00 - Poster session

13:00 - 14:30 Lunch

14:30 - 16:00 Session 3

- 14:30-15:00 - Invited talk by Hinrich Schütze (University of Munich)
- 15:00-16:00 - Presentations of the best paper award candidates

Improving Clinical Diagnosis Inference through Integration of Structured and Unstructured Knowledge
Yuan Ling, Yuan An and Sadid Hasan

One Representation per Word - Does it make Sense for Composition?
Thomas Kober, Julie Weeds, John Wilkie, Jeremy Reffin and David Weir

Word Sense Filtering Improves Embedding-Based Lexical Substitution
Anne Cocos, Marianna Apidianaki and Chris Callison-Burch

16:00 - 16:30 Coffee break

16:30 - 17:15 Session 4

- 16:30-17:15 - Open discussion, best paper award and closing remarks

Compositional Semantics using Feature-Based Models from WordNet

Pablo Gamallo
Centro Singular de Investigación en
Tecnoloxías da Información (CiTIUS)
Universidade de Santiago de Compostela
Galiza, Spain
pablo.gamallo@usc.es

Martín Pereira-Fariña
Centre for Argument
Technology (ARG-tech)
University of Dundee
Dundee, DD1 4HN, Scotland (UK)
m.z.pereirafarina@dundee.ac.uk
Departamento de Filosofía e Antropoloxía
Universidade de Santiago de Compostela
Pz. de Mazarelos, 15782, Galiza, Spain
martin.pereira@usc.es

Abstract

This article describes a method to build semantic representations of composite expressions in a compositional way by using WordNet relations to represent the meaning of words. The meaning of a target word is modelled as a vector in which its semantically related words are assigned weights according to both the type of the relationship and the distance to the target word. Word vectors are compositionally combined by syntactic dependencies. Each syntactic dependency triggers two complementary compositional functions: the named *head function* and *dependent function*. The experiments show that the proposed compositional method performs as the state-of-the-art for subject-verb expressions, and clearly outperforms the best system for transitive subject-verb-object constructions.

1 Introduction

The principle of compositionality (Partee, 1984) states that the meaning of a complex expression is a function of the meaning of its constituent parts and of the mode of their combination. In the recent years, different distributional semantic models endowed with a compositional component have been proposed. Most of them define words as high-dimensional vectors where dimensions represent co-occurring context words. This distributional semantic representation makes it possible to combine vectors using simple arithmetic operations such as addition and multiplication, or more advanced compositional methods such as learning functional words as tensors and composing constituents through inner product operations.

Notwithstanding, these models are usually qualified as black box systems because they are usually not interpretable by humans. Currently, the field of interpretable computational models is gaining relevance[1] and, therefore, the development of more explainable and understandable models in compositional semantics is also an open challenge. in this field. On the other hand, distributional semantic models, given the size of the vectors, needs significant resources and they are dependent on particular corpus, which can generate some biases in their application to different languages.

Thus, in this paper, we will pay attention to compositional approaches which employ other kind of word semantic models, such as those based on the WordNet relationships; i.e., synsets, hypernyms, hyponyms, etc. Only in (Faruqui and Dyer, 2015) we can find a proposal for word vector representation using hand-crafted linguistic resources (WordNet, FrameNet, etc.), although a compositional frame is not explicitly adopted. Therefore, to the best of our knowledge, this is the first work using WordNet to build compositional semantic interpretations. Thus, in this article, we propose a method to compositionally build the semantic representation of composite expressions using a feature-based approach (Hadj Taieb et al., 2014): constituent elements are induced by WordNet relationships.

However, this proposal raises a serious problem: the semantic representation of two syntactically related words (e.g. the verb *run* and the noun *computer* in *"the computer runs"*) encodes incompatible information and there is no direct way of combining the features used to represent the meaning of the two words. On the one hand, the verb

---

[1] http://www.darpa.mil/program/explainable-artificial-intelligence

Proceedings of the 1st Workshop on Sense, Concept and Entity Representations and their Applications, pages 1–11,
Valencia, Spain, April 4 2017. ©2017 Association for Computational Linguistics

run is related by synonymy, hypernym, hyponym and entailment to other verbs and, on the other, the noun *computer* is put in relation with other nouns by synonymy, hypernym, hyponym, and so on.

In order to solve this drawback, on the basis of previous work on dependency-based distributional compositionality (Thater et al., 2010; Erk and Padó, 2008), we distinguish between direct denotation and selectional preferences within a dependency relation. More precisely, when two words are syntactically related, for instance *computer* and the verb *run* by the subject relation, we build two contextualized senses: the contextualized sense of *computer* given the requirements of *run* and the contextualized sense of *run* given *computer*.

The sense of *computer* is built by combining the semantic features of the noun (its direct denotation) with the selectional preferences imposed by the verb. The features of the noun are built from the set of words linked to *computer* in WordNet, while the selectional preferences of *run* in the subject position are obtained by combining the features of all the nouns that can be the nominal subject of the verb (i.e. the features of *runners*). Then, the two sets of features are combined and the resulting new set represents the specific sense of the noun *computer* as nominal subject of *run*. The sense of the verb given the noun is built in a analogous way: the semantic features of the verb are combined with the (inverse) selectional preferences imposed by the noun, resulting in a new compositional representation of the verb *run* when it is combined with *computer* at the subject position. The two new compositional feature sets represent the contextualized senses of the two related words. During the contextualization process, ambiguous or polysemous words may be disambiguated in order to obtain the right representation.

For dealing with any sequence with N (lexical) words (e.g., *"the coach runs the team"*), the semantic process can be applied in two different ways: from left-to-right and from right-to-left. In the first case, it is applied $N-1$ times dependency-by-dependency in order to obtain N contextualized senses, one per lexical word. Thus, firstly, the subject dependency builds two contextualized senses: that of *run* given the noun *coach* and that of the noun given the verb. Then, the direct object dependency is applied on the already contextualized sense of the verb in order to contextualize it

again given *team* at the direct object position. This dependency also yields the contextualized sense of the object given the verb and its nominal subject (*coach+run*). At the end of the interpretation process, we obtain three fully contextualized senses. In the second case, from right-to-left, the semantic process process is applied in a similar way, being contextualized (and disambiguated) using the restrictions imposed by the verb and its nominal object (*run+team*). As in the first case, three slightly different word senses are also obtained.

Lastly, word sense disambiguation is out of the aim of this paper. Here, we only use WordNet for extracting semantic information from words, but not to identify word senses.

The article is organized as follow: In the next section (2), different approaches on ontological feature-based representations and compositional semantics are introduced and discussed. Then, sections 3 and 4 respectively describe our feature-based semantic representation and compositional strategy. In Section 5, some experiments are performed to evaluate the quality of the word models and compositional word vectors. Finally, relevant conclusions are reported in Section 6.

2 Related Work

Our approach relies on two tasks: to build feature-based representations using WordNet relations, and to build compositional vectors using the WordNet representations. In this section, we will examine work related to these two tasks.

2.1 Feature-Based Approaches

Tversky (1977), in order to define a similarity measure, assumes that any object can be represented as a collection (set) of features or properties. Therefore, a similarity metric is a feature-matching process between two objects. This consists of a linear combination of the measures of their common and distinctive features. It is worth noting that this is a non-symmetric measure.

In the particular case of semantic similarity metrics, each word or concept is featured by means of a set of words (Hadj Taieb et al., 2014). Framed into an ontology such as WordNet, these sets of words are obtained from taxonomic (hypernym, hyponym, etc.) and non-taxonomic (synsets, glosses, meronyms, etc.) properties (Meng et al., 2013), although these last ones are classified as secondary in many cases (Slimani, 2013). The main objective of this approach is to capture the semantic knowledge induced by ontological relationships.

Our model is partly inspired by that defined in (Rodríguez and Egenhofer, 2003). It proposes that the set of properties that characterizes a word may be stratified into three groups: i) *synsets*; ii) *features* (e.g., meronyms, attributes, hyponym, etc.), and, iii) *neighbor concepts* (those linked via semantic pointers). Each one of these strata is weighted according to its contribution to the representation of the concept. The measure analyzes the overlapping among the three strata between the two terms under comparison.

2.2 Compositional Strategies

Several models for compositionality in vector spaces have been proposed in recent years, and most of them use bag-of-words as basic distributional representations of word contexts. The basic approach to composition, explored by Mitchell and Lapata (2008; 2009; 2010), is to combine vectors of two syntactically related words with arithmetic operations: addition and component-wise multiplication. The additive model produces a sort of union of word contexts, whereas multiplication has an intersective effect. According to Mitchell and Lapata (2008), component-wise multiplication performs better than the additive model. However, in (Mitchell and Lapata, 2009; Mitchell and Lapata, 2010), these authors explore weighted additive models giving more weight to some constituents in specific word combinations. For instance, in a noun-subject-verb combination, the verb is provided with higher weight because the whole construction is closer to the verb than to the noun. Other weighted additive models are described in (Guevara, 2010) and (Zanzotto et al., 2010). All these models have in common the fact of defining composition operations for just word pairs. Their main drawback is that they do not propose a more systematic model accounting for all types of semantic composition. They do not focus on the logical aspects of the functional approach underlying compositionality.

Other distributional approaches develop sound compositional models of meaning inspired by Montagovian semantics, which induce the compositional meaning of the functional words from examples adopting regression techniques commonly used in machine learning (Krishnamurthy and Mitchell, 2013; Baroni and Zamparelli, 2010; Baroni, 2013; Baroni et al., 2014). In our approach, by contrast, compositional functions, which are driven by dependencies and not by functional words, are just basic arithmetic operations on vectors as in (Mitchell and Lapata, 2008). Arithmetic approaches are easy to implement and produce high-quality compositional vectors, which makes them a good choice for practical applications (Baroni et al., 2014).

Other compositional approaches based on Categorial Grammar use tensor products for composition (Grefenstette et al., 2011; Coecke et al., 2010). A neural network-based method with tensor factorization for learning the embeddings of transitive clauses has been introduced in (Hashimoto and Tsuruoka, 2015). Two problems arise with tensor products. First, they result in an information scalability problem, since tensor representations grow exponentially as the phrases grow longer (Turney, 2013). And second, tensor products did not perform as well as component-wise multiplication in Mitchell and Lapata's (2010) experiments.

There are also works focused on the notion of sense contextualization, e.g., Dinu and Lapata (2010) work on context-sensitive representations for lexical substitution. Reddy et al. (2011) work on dynamic prototypes for composing the semantics of noun-noun compounds and evaluate their approach on a compositionality-based similarity task.

So far, all the cited works are based on bag-of-words to represent vector contexts and, then, word senses. However, there are a few works using vector spaces structured with syntactic information. Thater et al. (2010) distinguish between *first-order* and *second-order* vectors in order to allow two syntactically incompatible vectors to be combined. This work is inspired by that described in (Erk and Padó, 2008). Erk and Padó (2008) propose a method in which the combination of two words, *a* and *b*, returns two vectors: a vector *a'* representing the sense of *a* given the selectional preferences imposed by *b*, and a vector *b'* standing for the sense of *b* given the (inverse) selectional preferences imposed by *a*. A similar strategy is reported in Gamallo (2017). Our approach is an attempt to join the main ideas of these syntax-based models (namely, second-order vectors, selectional preferences and two returning words per combination) in order to apply them to WordNet-based word representations.

3 Semantic Features from WordNet

A word meaning is described as a feature-value structure. The *features* are the words with which the target word is related to in the ontology (e.g., in WordNet, hypernym, hyponym, etc.) and the *values* correspond to weights computed taking into account two parameters: the relation type and the edge-counting distance between the target word and each word feature (i.e. the number of relations required to achieve the feature from the target word) (Rada et al., 1989).

The algorithm to set the feature values is the following. Given a target word w_1 and the feature set F, where $w_i \in F$ if w_i is a word semantically related to w_1 in WordNet, the weight for the relation between w_1 and w_i is computed by equation 1:

$$weight(w_1, w_i) = \sum_{j=1}^{R} \frac{1}{length(w_1, w_i, r_j)} \quad (1)$$

where R is the number of different semantic relations (e.g. synonymy/synset, hyperonymy, hyponymy, etc) that WordNet defines for the part-of-speech of the target word. For instance, nouns have five different relations, verbs four and adjectives just two. $length(w_1, w_i, r_j)$ is the length of the path from the target word w_1 to its feature w_i in relation r_j. $length(w_1, w_i, r_j) = 1$ when r_j stands for the synonymy relationship, i.e. when w_1 and w_i belong to the same synset; $length(w_1, w_i, r_j) = 2$ if w_i is at the first level within the hierarchy associated to relation r_j.

For instance, the length value of a direct hypernym is 2 because there is a distance of two arcs with regard to the target word: the first arc goes from the target word to a synset and the second one is the hyperonymy relation between the direct hypernym and the synset. The length value increases in one unit as the hierarchy level goes up, so at level 4, the length score is 5 and then the partial weight is $1/5 = 0.2$. For some non-taxonomic relations, namely meronymy, holonymy and coordinates, there is only one level in WordNet, but the distance is 3 since the target word and the word feature (part, whole or coordinate term) are separated by a synset and a hypernym.

As a feature word w_i may be related to the target w_1 *via* different semantic relations (without distinguishing between different word senses), the final weight is the addition of all partial weights. For instance, take the noun *car*. It is related to *automobile* through two different relationships: they belong to the same synset and the latter is a direct hypernym of the former, so $weight(car, automobile) = 1/1 + 1/2 = 1.5$.

To compute compositional operations on words, the feature-value structure associated to each word is modeled as a vector, where features are dimensions, words are objects, and weights the values for each object/dimension position.

4 Compositional Semantics

4.1 Syntactic Dependencies As Compositional Functions

Our approach is also inspired in (Erk and Padó, 2008). Here, semantic composition is modeled in terms of function application driven by binary dependencies. A dependency is associated in the semantic space with two compositional functions on word vectors: the head and the dependent functions. To explain how they work, let us take the direct object relation ($dobj$) between the verb *run* and the noun *team* in the expression *"run a team"*. The head function, $dobj_\uparrow$, combines the vector of the head verb $\vec{run}$ with the selectional preferences imposed by the noun, which is also a vector of WordNet features, and noted $\vec{team}°$. This combination is performed by component-wise multiplication and results in a new vector $\vec{run}_{dobj\uparrow}$, which represents the contextualized sense of *run* given *team* in the $dobj$ relation:

$$dobj_\uparrow(\vec{run}, \vec{team}°) = \vec{run} \odot \vec{team}° = \vec{run}_{dobj\uparrow}$$

To build the (inverse) selectional preferences imposed by the dependent word *team* as direct object on the verb, we require a reference corpus to extract all those verbs of which *team* is the direct object. The selectional preferences of *team* as direct object of a verb, and noted $\vec{team}°$, is a new vector obtained by component-wise addition of the vectors of all those verbs (e.g. *create, support, help*, etc) that are in $dobj$ relation with the noun *team*:

$$\vec{team}° = \sum_{\vec{v} \in T} \vec{v}$$

where T is the vector set of verbs having *team* as direct object (except *run*). T is thus included in the subspace of verb vectors. Component-wise addition has an union effect.

Similarly, the dependent function, $dobj_\downarrow$, combines the noun vector $\vec{team}$ with the selectional preferences imposed by the verb, noted $\vec{run}^\circ$, by component-wise multiplication. Such a combinations builds the new vector of $\vec{team}_{dobj\downarrow}$, which stands for the contextualized sense of *team* given *run* in the $dobj$ relation:

$$dobj_\downarrow(\vec{run}^\circ, \vec{team}) = \vec{team} \odot \vec{run}^\circ = \vec{team}_{dobj\downarrow}$$

The selectional preferences imposed by the head word *run* to its direct object are represented by the vector $\vec{run}^\circ$, which is obtained by adding the vectors of all those nouns (e.g. *company*, *project, marathon*, etc) which are in relation $dobj$ with the verb *run*:

$$\vec{run}^\circ = \sum_{\vec{v} \in \boldsymbol{R}} \vec{v}$$

where $\boldsymbol{R}$ is the vector set of nouns playing the direct object role of *run* (except *team*). $\boldsymbol{R}$ is included in the subspace of nominal vectors.

Each multiplicative operation results in a compositional vector of a contextualized word. Component-wise multiplication has an intersective effect. The vector standing for the selectional preferences restricts the vector of the target word by assigning weight 0 to those WordNet features that are not shared by both vectors. The new compositional vector as well as the two constituents all belong to the same vector subspace (the subspace of nouns, verbs, or adjectives).

Notice that, in approaches to computational semantics inspired by Combinatory Categorial Grammar (Steedman, 1996) and Montagovian semantics (Montague, 1970), the interpretation process for composite expressions such as "*run a team*" or "*electric coach*" relies on rigid function-argument structures: relational expressions, like verbs and adjectives, are used as predicates while nouns and nominals are their arguments. In the composition process, each word is supposed to play a rigid and fixed role: the relational word is semantically represented as a selective function imposing constraints on the denotations of the words it combines with, while non-relational words are in turn seen as arguments filling the constraints imposed by the function. For instance, *run*

and *electric* would denote functions while *team* and *coach* would be their arguments.

By contrast, we deny the rigid "predicate-argument" structure. In our compositional approach, dependencies are the active functions that control and rule the selectional requirements imposed by the two related words. Thus, each constituent word imposes its selectional preferences on the other within a dependency-based construction. This is in accordance with non-standard linguistic research which assumes that the words involved in a composite expression impose semantic restrictions on each other (Pustejovsky, 1995; Gamallo et al., 2005; Gamallo, 2008).

4.2 Recursive Compositional Application

In our approach, the consecutive application of the syntactic dependencies found in a sentence is actually the process of building the contextualized sense of all the lexical words which constitute it. Thus, the whole sentence is not assigned to an unique meaning (which could be the contextualized sense of the *root* word), but one sense per lemma, being the sense of the *root* just one of them.

This incremental process may have two directions: from left-to-right and vice versa (i.e., from right-to-left). Figure 1 illustrates the incremental process of building the sense of words dependency-by-dependency from left-to-right. Thus, given the composite expression "*the coach runs the team*" and its dependency analysis depicted in the first row of the figure, two compositional processes are driven by the two dependencies involved in the analysis ($nsubj$ and $dobj$). Each dependency is decomposed into two functions: head ($nsubj_\uparrow$ and $dobj_\uparrow$) and dependent ($nsubj_\downarrow$ and $dobj_\downarrow$) functions.[2] The first compositional process applies, on the one hand, the head function $nsubj_\uparrow$ on the denotation of the head verb ($\vec{run}$) and on the selectional preferences required by *coach* ($\vec{coach}^\circ$), in order to build a contextualized sense of the verb: $\vec{run}_{nsubj\uparrow}$. On the other hand, the dependent function $nsubj_\downarrow$ builds the sense of *coach* as nominal subject of *run*: $\vec{coach}_{nsubj\downarrow}$. Then, the contextualized head vector is involved in the compositional process driven by $dobj$. At this level of semantic composition, the selectional preferences imposed on the noun *team*

---

[2] We do not consider the meaning of determiners, auxiliary verbs, or tense affixes. Quantificational issues associated to them are also beyond the scope of this work.

stand for the semantic features of all those nouns which may be the direct object of *coach+run*. At the end of the process, we have not obtained one single sense for the whole expression, but one contextualized sense per lexical word: $\overrightarrow{coach}_{nsubj\downarrow}$, $\overrightarrow{run}_{nsubj\uparrow+dobj\uparrow}$ and $\overrightarrow{team}_{dobj\downarrow}$.

In other case, from right-to-left, the verb *run* is first restricted by *team* at the direct object position, and then by its subject *coach*. In addition, this noun is now restricted by the selectional preferences imposed by *run* and *team*, that is, it is combined with the semantic features of all those nouns that may be the nominal subject of *run+team*.

5 Experiments

We have performed several similarity-based experiments using the semantic word model defined in Section 3 and the compositional algorithm described in 4.[3] First, in Subsection 5.1, we evaluate just word similarity without composition. Then, in Subsection 5.2, we evaluate the simple compositional approach by making use of a dataset with similar noun-verb pairs (NV constructions). Finally, the recursive application of compositional functions is evaluated in Subsection 5.3, by making use of a dataset with similar noun-verb-noun pairs (NVN constructions).

In all experiments, we made use of datasets suited for the task at hand, and compare our results with those obtained by the best systems for the corresponding dataset. Moreover, in order to build the selectional preferences of the syntactically related words, we used the British National Corpus (BNC). Syntactic analysis on BNC was performed with the dependency parser DepPattern (Gamallo and González, 2011; Gamallo, 2015), previously PoS tagged with Tree-Tagger (Schmid, 1994).

5.1 Word Similarity

Recently, the use of word similarity methods has been criticised as a reliable technique for evaluating distributional semantic models (Batchkarov et al., 2016), given the small size of the datasets and the limitation of context information as well. However, given this procedure still is widely accepted, we have performed two different kinds of experiments: rating by similarity and synonym detection with multiple-choice questions.

---

[3]Both the software and the semantic word model are freely available at `http://fegalaz.usc.es/~gamallo/resources/CompWordNet.tar.gz`.

5.1.1 Rating by Similarity

In the first experiment, we use the WordSim353 dataset (Finkelstein et al., 2002), which was constructed by asking humans to rate the degree of semantic similarity between two words on a numerical scale. This is a small dataset with 353 word pairs. The performance of a computational system is measured in terms of correlation (Spearman) between the scores assigned by humans to the word pairs and the similarity Dice coefficient assigned by our system (*WN*) built with the WordNet-based model space.

Table 1 compares the Spearman correlation obtained by our model, *WN*, with that obtained by the corpus-based system described in (Halawi et al., 2012), which is the highest score reached so far on that dataset. Even if our results were clearly outperformed by that corpus-based method, *WN* seems to behave well if compared with the state-of-the-art knowledge-based (unsupervised) strategy reported in (Agirre et al., 2009).

Systems	ρ	Method
WN	0.69	knowledge
(Hassan and Mihalcea, 2011)	0.62	knowledge
(Agirre et al., 2009)	0.66	knowledge
(Halawi et al., 2012)	**0.81**	corpus

Table 1: Spearman correlation between the Word-Sim353 dataset and the rating obtained by our knowledge-based system *WN* and the state-of-the-art for both knowledge and corpus-based strategies.

5.1.2 Synonym Detection with Multiple-Choice Questions

In this evaluation task, a target word is presented with four synonym candidates, one of them being the correct synonym of the target. For instance, for the target *deserve*, the system must choose between *merit* (the correct one), *need*, *want*, and *expect*. Accuracy is the number of correct answers divided by the total number of words in the

Systems	Noun	Adj	Verb	All
WN	**0.85**	**0.85**	**0.75**	0.80
(Freitag et al., 2005)	0.76	0.76	0.64	0.72
(Zhu, 2015)	0.71	0.71	0.63	0.69
(Kiela et al., 2015)	-	-	-	**0.88**

Table 2: Accuracy of three systems on the WBST test (synonym detection on nouns, adjectives, and verbs)

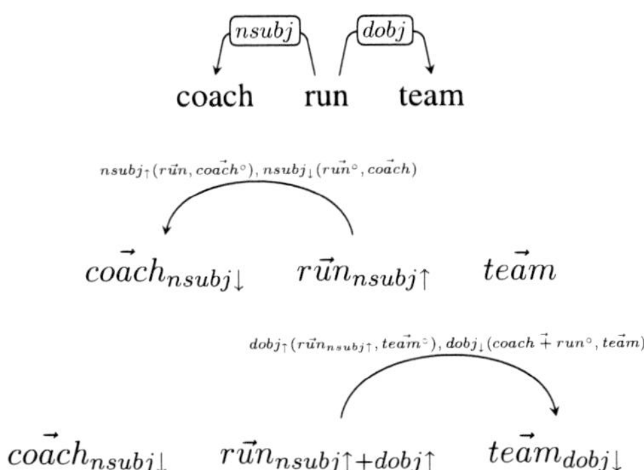

Figure 1: Syntactic analysis of the expression *"the coach runs the team"* and left-to-right construction of the word senses.

dataset.

The dataset is an extended TOEFL test, called the WordNet-based Synonymy Test (WBST) proposed in (Freitag et al., 2005). WBST was produced by generating automatically a large set of TOEFL-like questions from the synonyms in WordNet. In total, this procedure yields 9,887 noun, 7,398 verb, and 5,824 adjective questions, a total of 23,509 questions, which is a very large dataset. Table 2 shows the results. In this case, the accuracy obtained by *WN* for the three syntactic categories is close to state-of-the-art corpus-based method for this task (Kiela et al., 2015), which is a neural network trained with a huge corpus containing 8 billion words from English Wikipedia and newswire texts.

5.2 Noun-Verb Composition

The first experiment aimed at evaluating our compositional strategy uses the test dataset by Mitchell and Lapata (2008), which comprises a total of 3,600 human similarity judgments. Each item consists of an intransitive verb and a subject noun, which are compared to another noun-verb pair (NV) combining the same noun with a synonym of the verb that is chosen to be either similar o dissimilar to the verb in the context of the given subject. For instance, *"child stray"* is related to *"child roam"*, being *roam* a synonym of *stray*. The dataset was constructed by extracting NV composite expressions from the British National Corpus (BNC) and verb synonyms from WordNet. In order to evaluate the results of the tested systems, Spearman correlation is computed between individual human similarity scores and the systems' predictions.

In this experiment, we compute the similarity between the contextualized heads of two NV composites and between their contextualized dependent expressions. For instance, we compute the similarity between *"eye flare"* vs *"eye flame"* by comparing first the verbs *flare* and *flame* when combined with *eye* in the subject position (head function), and by comparing how (dis)similar is the noun *eye* when combined with both the verbs *flare* and *flame* (dependent function). In addition, as we are provided with two similarities (head and dep) for each pair of compared expressions, it is possible to compute a new similarity score by averaging the results of head and dependent functions (head+dep).

Table 3 shows the Spearman's correlation values (ρ) obtained by the three versions of *WN*: only head function (head), only dependent function (dep) and average of both (head+dep). The latter score value is comparable to the state-of-the-art system for this dataset, reported in (Erk and Padó, 2008). It is also very similar to the most recent results described in (Dinu et al., 2013), where the authors made use of the compositional strategy defined in (Baroni and Zamparelli, 2010).

Systems	ρ
WN (head+dep)	**0.29**
WN (head)	0.26
WN (dep)	0.14
(Erk and Padó, 2008)	0.27
(Dinu et al., 2013)	0.26

Table 3: Spearman correlation for intransitive expressions using the benchmark by Mitchell and Lapata (2008)

5.3 Noun-Verb-Noun Composition

The last experiment consists in evaluating the quality of compositional vectors built by means of the consecutive application of head and dependency functions associated with nominal subject and direct object. The experiment is performed on the dataset developed in (Grefenstette and Sadrzadeh, 2011a). The dataset was built using the same guidelines as Mitchell and Lapata (2008), using transitive verbs paired with subjects and direct objects: NVN composites.

Given our compositional strategy, we are able to compositional build several vectors that somehow represent the meaning of the whole NVN composite expression. In order to known which is the best compositional strategy and be exhaustive and complete, we evaluate all of them; i.e., both left-to-right and right-to-left strategies. Thus, take again the expression *"the coach runs the team"*. If we follow the left-to-right strategy (noted nv-n), at the end of the compositional process, we obtain two fully contextualized senses:

nv-n_head The sense of the head *run*, as a result of being contextualized first by the preferences imposed by the subject and then by the preferences required by the direct object. We note nv-n_head) the final sense of the head in a NVN composite expression following the left-to-right strategy.

nv-n_dep The sense of the object *team*, as a result of being contextualized by the preferences imposed by *run* previously combined with the subject *coach*. We note nv-n_dep the final sense of the direct object in a NVN composite expression following the left-to-right strategy.

If we follow the right-to-left strategy (noted n-vn), at the end of the compositional process, we obtain two fully contextualized senses:

n-nv_head The sense of the head *run* as a result of being contextualized first by the preferences imposed by the object and then by the subject.

n-nv_dep The sense of the subject *coach*, as a result of being contextualized by the preferences imposed by *run* previously combined with the object *team*.

Systems	ρ
WN (nv-n_head+dep)	0.35
WN (nv-n_head)	0.34
WN (nv-n_dep)	0.13
WN (n-vn_head+dep)	**0.50**
WN (n-vn_head)	0.35
WN (n-vn_dep)	0.44
WN (n-vn+nv-n)	0.47
(Grefenstette and Sadrzadeh, 2011b)*	0.28
(Van De Cruys et al., 2013)*	0.37
(Tsubaki et al., 2013)*	0.44
(Milajevs et al., 2014)	0.46
(Polajnar et al., 2015)	0.35
(Hashimoto et al., 2014)	0.48
(Hashimoto and Tsuruoka, 2015)	0.48
Human agreement	0.75

Table 4: Spearman correlation for transitive expressions using the benchmark by Grefenstette and Sadrzadeh (2011)

Table 4 shows the Spearman's correlation values (ρ) obtained by all the different versions built from our model *WN*. The best score was achieved by averaging the head and dependent similarity values derived from the n-vn (right-to-left) strategy. Let us note that, for NVN composite expressions, the left-to-right strategy seems to build less reliable compositional vectors than the right-to-left counterpart. Besides, the combination of the two strategies (n-vn+nv-n) does not improve the results of the best one (n-vn).[4]. The score values obtained by the different versions of the right-to-left strategy outperform other systems for this dataset (see results reported below in the table). Our best strategy ($\rho = 0.50$) also outperforms the neural network strategy described in (Hashimoto and Tsuruoka, 2015), which achieved 0.48 without considering extra linguistic information not included in the dataset. The (ρ) scores for this task are reported for averaged human ratings. This is due to a disagreement in previous work regarding which metric to use when reporting results. We mark with asterisk those systems reporting (ρ) scores based on non-averaged human ratings.

6 Conclusions

In this paper, we described a compositional model based on WordNet features and dependency-based functions on those features. It is a recursive proposal since it can be repeated from left-to-right or from right-to-left and the sense of each constituent word is performed in a recursive way.

---

[4] *n-vn+nv-n* is computed by averaging the similarities of both *n-vn_head+dep* and *nv-n_head+dep*

Our compositional model tackles the problem of *information scalability*. This problem states that the size of semantic representations should not grow exponentially, but proportionally; and, information must not be loss using fixed size of compositional vectors. In our approach, however, even if the size of the compositional vectors is fixed, there is no information loss since each word of the composite expression is associated to a compositional vector representing its context-sensitive sense. In addition, the compositional vectors do not grow exponentially since their size is fixed by the vector space: they are all first-order (or direct) vectors. Finally, the number of vectors increases in proportion to the number of constituent words found in the composite expression. So, both points are successfully solved.

In future work, we will try to design a compositional model based on word semantic representations combining WordNet-based features with syntactic-based distributional contexts as well as extend our model to full sentences instead of the simple ones described in this paper.

Acknowledgements

We would like to thank the anonymous reviewers for helpful comments and suggestions. This work was supported by a 2016 BBVA Foundation Grant for Researchers and Cultural Creators, and by project TELPARES (FFI2014-51978-C2-1-R) and grant TIN2014-56633-C3-1-R, Ministry of Economy and Competitiveness. It has received financial support from the Consellería de Cultura, Educación e Ordenación Universitaria (Postdoctoral Training Grants 2016 and Centro Singular de Investigación de Galicia accreditation 2016-2019, ED431G/08) and the European Regional Development Fund (ERDF).

References

Eneko Agirre, Enrique Alfonseca, Keith Hall, Jana Kravalova, Marius Paşca, and Aitor Soroa. 2009. A study on similarity and relatedness using distributional and wordnet-based approaches. In *Proceedings of Human Language Technologies: The 2009 Annual Conference of the North American Chapter of the Association for Computational Linguistics*, NAACL '09, pages 19–27, Stroudsburg, PA, USA. Association for Computational Linguistics.

Marco Baroni and Roberto Zamparelli. 2010. Nouns are vectors, adjectives are matrices: Representing adjective-noun constructions in semantic space. In *Proceedings of the 2010 Conference on Empirical Methods in Natural Language Processing*, EMNLP'10, pages 1183–1193, Stroudsburg, PA, USA.

Marco Baroni, Raffaella Bernardi, and Roberto Zamparelli. 2014. Frege in space: A program for compositional distributional semantics. *LiLT*, 9:241–346.

Marco Baroni. 2013. Composition in distributional semantics. *Language and Linguistics Compass*, 7:511–522.

Miroslav Batchkarov, Thomas Kober, Jeremy Reffin, Julie Weeds, and David Weir. 2016. A critique of word similarity as a method for evaluating distributional semantic models. In *Proceedings of the ACL Workshop on Evaluating Vector Space Representations for NLP*, Berlin, Germany.

B. Coecke, M. Sadrzadeh, and S. Clark. 2010. Mathematical foundations for a compositional distributional model of meaning. *Linguistic Analysis*, 36(1-4):345–384.

Georgiana Dinu and Mirella Lapata. 2010. Measuring distributional similarity in context. In *Proceedings of the 2010 Conference on Empirical Methods in Natural Language Processing*, pages 1162–1172, Cambridge, MA, October. Association for Computational Linguistics.

G. Dinu, N. Pham, and M. Baroni. 2013. General estimation and evaluation of compositional distributional semantic models. In *ACL 2013 Workshop on Continuous Vector Space Models and their Compositionality (CVSC 2013)*, pages 50–58, East Stroudsburg PA.

Katrin Erk and Sebastian Padó. 2008. A structured vector space model for word meaning in context. In *Proceedings of EMNLP*, Honolulu, HI.

Manaal Faruqui and Chris Dyer. 2015. Non-distributional word vector representations. In *Proceedings of ACL*.

Lev Finkelstein, Evgeniy Gabrilovich, Yossi Matias, Ehud Rivlin, Zach Solan, Gadi Wolfman, and Eytan Ruppin. 2002. Placing search in context: the concept revisited. *ACM Trans. Inf. Syst.*, 20(1):116–131.

Dayne Freitag, Matthias Blume, John Byrnes, Edmond Chow, Sadik Kapadia, Richard Rohwer, and Zhiqiang Wang. 2005. New experiments in distributional representations of synonymy. In *Proceedings of the Ninth Conference on Computational Natural Language Learning*, pages 25–32.

Pablo Gamallo and Isaac González. 2011. A grammatical formalism based on patterns of part-of-speech tags. *International Journal of Corpus Linguistics*, 16(1):45–71.

Pablo Gamallo, Alexandre Agustini, and Gabriel Lopes. 2005. Clustering Syntactic Positions with Similar Semantic Requirements. *Computational Linguistics*, 31(1):107–146.

Pablo Gamallo. 2008. The meaning of syntactic dependencies. *Linguistik OnLine*, 35(3):33–53.

Pablo Gamallo. 2015. Dependency parsing with compression rules. In *International Workshop on Parsing Technology (IWPT 2015)*, Bilbao, Spain.

Pablo Gamallo. 2017. The role of syntactic dependencies in compositional distributional semantics. *Corpus Linguistics and Linguistic Theory*.

Edward Grefenstette and Mehrnoosh Sadrzadeh. 2011a. Experimental support for a categorical compositional distributional model of meaning. In *Conference on Empirical Methods in Natural Language Processing*.

Edward Grefenstette and Mehrnoosh Sadrzadeh. 2011b. Experimenting with transitive verbs in a discocat. In *Workshop on Geometrical Models of Natural Language Semantics (EMNLP-2011)*.

Edward Grefenstette, Mehrnoosh Sadrzadeh, Stephen Clark, Bob Coecke, and Stephen Pulman. 2011. Concrete sentence spaces for compositional distributional models of meaning. In *Proceedings of the Ninth International Conference on Computational Semantics*, IWCS '11, pages 125–134.

Emiliano Guevara. 2010. A regression model of adjective-noun compositionality in distributional semantics. In *Proceedings of the 2010 Workshop on GEometrical Models of Natural Language Semantics*, GEMS '10.

M. A. Hadj Taieb, M. Ben Aouicha, and A. Ben Hamadou. 2014. Ontology-based approach for measuring semantic similarity. *Engineering Applications of Artificial Intelligence*, 36:238–261.

Guy Halawi, Gideon Dror, Evgeniy Gabrilovich, and Yehuda Koren. 2012. Large-scale learning of word relatedness with constraints. In *Proceedings of the 18th ACM SIGKDD International Conference on Knowledge Discovery and Data Mining*, KDD '12, pages 1406–1414.

Kazuma Hashimoto and Yoshimasa Tsuruoka. 2015. Learning embeddings for transitive verb disambiguation by implicit tensor factorization. In *Proceedings of the 3rd Workshop on Continuous Vector Space Models and their Compositionality*, pages 1–11, Beijing, China, July. Association for Computational Linguistics.

Kazuma Hashimoto, Pontus Stenetorp, Makoto Miwa, and Yoshimasa Tsuruoka. 2014. Jointly learning word representations and composition functions using predicate-argument structures. In *Proceedings of the 2014 Conference on Empirical Methods in Natural Language Processing (EMNLP)*, pages 1544–1555, Doha, Qatar, October. Association for Computational Linguistics.

S. Hassan and R. Mihalcea. 2011. Semantic relatedness using salient semantic analysis. In *Proceedings of AAAI Conference on Artificial Intelligence*.

Douwe Kiela, Felix Hill, and Stephen Clark. 2015. Specializing word embeddings for similarity or relatedness. In Lluís Màrquez, Chris Callison-Burch, Jian Su, Daniele Pighin, and Yuval Marton, editors, *EMNLP*, pages 2044–2048. The Association for Computational Linguistics.

Jayant Krishnamurthy and Tom Mitchell, 2013. *Proceedings of the Workshop on Continuous Vector Space Models and their Compositionality*, chapter Vector Space Semantic Parsing: A Framework for Compositional Vector Space Models, pages 1–10. Association for Computational Linguistics.

Lingling Meng, Runquing Huang, and Junzhong Gu. 2013. A review of semantic similarity measures in wordnet. *International Journal of Hybrid Information Technology*, 6(1).

Dmitrijs Milajevs, Dimitri Kartsaklis, Mehrnoosh Sadrzadeh, and Matthew Purver. 2014. Evaluating neural word representations in tensor-based compositional settings. In Alessandro Moschitti, Bo Pang, and Walter Daelemans, editors, *EMNLP*, pages 708–719. ACL.

Jeff Mitchell and Mirella Lapata. 2008. Vector-based models of semantic composition. In *Proceedings of ACL-08: HLT*, pages 236–244.

Jeff Mitchell and Mirella Lapata. 2009. Language models based on semantic composition. In *Proceedings of EMNLP*, pages 430–439.

Jeff Mitchell and Mirella Lapata. 2010. Composition in distributional models of semantics. *Cognitive Science*, 34(8):1388–1439.

Richard Montague. 1970. Universal grammar. theoria. *Theoria*, 36:373–398.

Barbara Partee. 1984. Compositionality. In Frank Landman and Frank Veltman, editors, *Varieties of Formal Semantics*, pages 281–312. Dordrecht: Foris.

Tamara Polajnar, Laura Rimell, and Stephen Clark. 2015. An exploration of discourse-based sentence spaces for compositional distributional semantics. In *Proceedings of the First Workshop on Linking Computational Models of Lexical, Sentential and Discourse-level Semantics*, pages 1–11, Lisbon, Portugal, September. Association for Computational Linguistics.

James Pustejovsky. 1995. *The Generative Lexicon*. MIT Press, Cambridge.

R. Rada, H. Mili, E. Bicknell, and M. Blettner. 1989. Development and application of a metric on semantic nets. *Systems, Man and Cybernetics, IEEE Transactions on*, 19(1):17–30.

Siva Reddy, Ioannis P. Klapaftis, Diana McCarthy, and Suresh Manandhar. 2011. Dynamic and static prototype vectors for semantic composition. In *Fifth International Joint Conference on Natural Language Processing, IJCNLP 2011, Chiang Mai, Thailand, November 8-13, 2011*, pages 705–713.

M. Andrea Rodríguez and Max J. Egenhofer. 2003. Determining semantic similarity among entity classes from different ontologies. *IEEE Trans. Knowl. Data Eng.*, 15(2):442–456.

H. Schmid. 1994. Probabilistic part-of-speech tagging using decision trees. In *International Conference on New Methods in Language Processing*.

Thabet Slimani. 2013. Description and evaluation of semantic similarity measures approaches. *International Journal of Computer Applications*, 80(1):25–33.

Mark Steedman. 1996. *Surface Structure and Interpretation*. The MIT Press.

Stefan Thater, Hagen Fürstenau, and Manfred Pinkal. 2010. Contextualizing semantic representations using syntactically enriched vector models. In *Proceedings of the 48th Annual Meeting of the Association for Computational Linguistics*, pages 948–957, Stroudsburg, PA, USA.

Masashi Tsubaki, Kevin Duh, Masashi Shimbo, and Yuji Matsumoto. 2013. Modeling and learning semantic co-compositionality through prototype projections and neural networks. In *EMNLP*, pages 130–140. ACL.

Peter D. Turney. 2013. Domain and function: A dual-space model of semantic relations and compositions. *Journal of Artificial Intelligence Research (JAIR)*, 44:533–585.

A. Tversky. 1977. Features of similarity. *Psichological Review*, 84(4).

Tim Van De Cruys, Thierry Poibeau, and Anna Korhonen. 2013. A Tensor-based Factorization Model of Semantic Compositionality. In *Conference of the North American Chapter of the Association of Computational Linguistics (HTL-NAACL)*, pages 1142–1151, Atlanta, United States, June.

Fabio Massimo Zanzotto, Ioannis Korkontzelos, Francesca Fallucchi, and Suresh Manandhar. 2010. Estimating linear models for compositional distributional semantics. In *Proceedings of the 23rd International Conference on Computational Linguistics*, COLING '10, pages 1263–1271.

Peng Zhu. 2015. N-grams based linguistic search engine. *International Journal of Computational Linguistics Research*, 6(1):1–7.

Automated WordNet Construction Using Word Embeddings

**Mikhail Khodak, Andrej Risteski, Christiane Fellbaum and
Sanjeev Arora**

Computer Science Department, Princeton University, 35 Olden St., Princeton, New Jersey 08540

{mkhodak,risteski,fellbaum,arora}@cs.princeton.edu

Abstract

We present a fully unsupervised method for automated construction of WordNets based upon recent advances in distributional representations of sentences and word-senses combined with readily available machine translation tools. The approach requires very few linguistic resources and is thus extensible to multiple target languages. To evaluate our method we construct two 600-word test sets for word-to-synset matching in French and Russian using native speakers and evaluate the performance of our method along with several other recent approaches. Our method exceeds the best language-specific and multi-lingual automated WordNets in F-score for both languages. The databases we construct for French and Russian, both languages without large publicly available manually constructed WordNets, will be publicly released along with the test sets.

1 Introduction

A *WordNet* is a lexical database for languages based upon a structure introduced by the Princeton WordNet (PWN) for English in which sets of cognitive synonyms, or synsets, are interconnected with arcs standing for semantic and lexical relations between them (Fellbaum, 1972). WordNets are widely used in computational linguistics, information retrieval, and machine translation. Constructing one by hand is time-consuming and difficult, motivating a search for automated or semi-automated methods. We present an unsupervised method based on word embeddings and word-sense induction and build and evaluate WordNets for French and Russian. Our approach needs only a large unannotated corpus like Wikipedia in the target language and machine translation (MT) between that language and English.

A standard minimal WordNet design is to have synsets connected by hyponym-hypernym relations and linked back to PWN (Global WordNet Association, 2017). This allows for applications to cross-lingual tasks and rests on the assumption that synsets and their relations are invariant across languages (Sagot and Fišer, 2008). For example, while all senses of English word *tie* may not line up with all senses of French word *cravate*, the sense "necktie" will exist in both languages and be represented by the same synset.

Thus MT is often used for automated Word-Nets to generate a set of candidate synsets for each word w in the target language by getting a set of English translations of w and using them to query PWN (we will refer to this as MT+PWN). The number of candidate synsets produced may not be small, even as large as a hundred for some polysemous verbs. Thus one needs a way to select from the candidates of w those synsets that are its true senses. The main contributions of this paper is a new *word embedding*-based method for matching words to synsets and the release of two large word-synset matching test sets for French and Russian.[1]

Though there has been some work using word-vectors for WordNets (see Section 2), the resulting databases have been small, containing less than 1000 words. Using embeddings for this task is challenging due to the need for good ways to use PWN synset information and account for the breakdown of cosine-similarity for polysemous words. We approach the first issue by representing synset information using recent work on sentence-embeddings by Arora et al. (2017). To handle polysemy we devise a sense clustering scheme based on Word Sense Induction (WSI) via linear alge-

---

[1] https://github.com/mkhodak/pawn

12

Proceedings of the 1st Workshop on Sense, Concept and Entity Representations and their Applications, pages 12–23,
Valencia, Spain, April 4 2017. ©2017 Association for Computational Linguistics

bra over word-vectors (Arora et al., 2016a). We demonstrate how this *sense purification* procedure effectively combines clustering with embeddings, thus being applicable to many word-sense disambiguation (WSD) and induction-related tasks. Using both techniques yields a WordNet method that outperforms other language-independent methods as well as language-specific approaches such as WOLF, the French WordNet used by the Natural Language ToolKit (Sagot and Fišer, 2008; Bond and Foster, 2013; Bird et al., 2009).

Our second contribution is the creation of two new 600-word test sets in French and Russian that are larger and more comprehensive than any currently available, containing 200 each of nouns, verbs, and adjectives. They are constructed by presenting native speakers with all candidate synsets produced as above by MT+PWN and treating the senses they pick out as "ground truth" for measuring precision and recall. The motivation behind separating by part-of-speech (POS) is that nouns are often easier than adjectives and verbs, so reporting one number — as done by some past work — allows high noun performance to mask low performance on adjectives and verbs.

Using these test sets, we can begin addressing the difficulties of evaluation for non-English automated WordNets due to the use of different and unreported test data, incompatible metrics (e.g. matching synsets to words vs. retrieving words for synsets), and differing cross-lingual dictionaries. In this paper we use the test sets to evaluate our method and several other automated WordNets.

2 Related Work

There have been many language-specific approaches for building automated WordNets, notably for Korean (Lee et al., 2000), French (Sagot and Fišer, 2008; Pradet et al., 2013), and Persian (Montazery and Falll, 2010). These approaches also use MT+PWN to get candidate word-synset pairs, but often use further resources — such as bilingual corpora, expert knowledge, or WordNets in related languages — to select correct senses.

The Korean construction depends on a classifier trained on 3260 word-sense matchings that yields 93.6% precision and 77.1% recall, albeit only on nouns. The Persian WordNet uses a scoring function based on related words between languages (requiring expert knowledge and parallel corpora) and achieves 82.6% precision, though without reporting recall and POS-separated statistics.

The most comparable results to ours are from the Wordnet Libre du Français (WOLF) of Sagot and Fišer (2008), which leverages multiple European WordNet projects. Our best method exceeds this approach on our test set and benefits from having far fewer resource requirements. The Wordnet du Français (WoNeF) of Pradet et al. (2013) depends on combining linguistic models by a voting scheme. Their performance is found to be generally below WOLF's, so we compare to the latter.

There has also been work on multi-language WordNets, specifically the Extended Open Multilingual Wordnet (OMW) (Bond and Foster, 2013), which scraped Wiktionary, and the Universal Multilingual Wordnet (UWN) (de Melo and Weikum, 2009), which used multiple translations to rate word-sense matches. In our evaluation both produce high-precision/low-coverage WordNets.

Finally, there have been recent vector approaches for an Arabic WordNet (Tarouti and Kalita, 2016) and a Bengali WordNet (Nasiruddin et al., 2014). The Arabic effort uses a cosine-similarity threshold for correcting direct translation and reports a precision of 78.4% on synonym matching, although its small size (943 synsets) indicates a poor precision/recall trade-off. The Bengali WordNet paper examines WSI on word vectors, evaluating clustering methods on seven words and achieving F_1-scores of at best 52.1%. It is likely that standard clustering techniques are insufficient when one needs many thousands of clusters, an issue we address via sparse coding.

Our use of distributional word embeddings to construct WordNets is the latest in a long line of their applications, e.g. approximating word similarity and solving word-analogies (Mikolov et al., 2013). The latter discovery was cited as the inspiration for the theoretical model in Arora et al. (2016b), whose Squared-Norm (SN) vectors we use; the computation is similar in form and performance to GloVe (Pennington et al., 2014).

3 Methods for WordNet Construction

The basic WordNet method is as follows. Given a target word w, we use a bilingual dictionary to get its translations in English and let its set of candidate synsets be all PWN senses of the translations (MT+PWN). We then assign a score to each synset and accept as correct all synsets with score above a threshold α If no synset is above the cutoff we

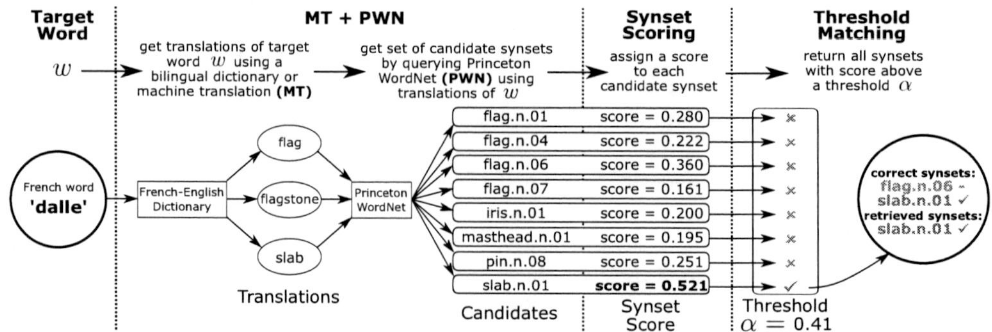

Figure 1: The score-threshold procedure for French word $w = dalle$ (flagstone, slab). Candidate synsets generated by MT+PWN are given a score and matched to w if the score is above a threshold α.

accept only the highest-scoring synset. This *score-threshold* method is illustrated in Figure 1.

Thus we need methods to assign high scores to correct candidate synsets of w and low scores to incorrect ones. We use unsupervised word vectors in the target language computed from a large text corpus (e.g. Wikipedia). Section 3.1 presents a simple baseline that improves upon MT+PWN via a cosine-similarity metric between w and each synset's lemmas. A more sophisticated *synset representation* method using sentence-embeddings is described in Section 3.2. Finally, in Section 3.3 we discuss WSI-based procedures for improving the score-threshold method for words with fine sense distinctions or poorly-annotated synsets.

In this section we assume a vocabulary V of target language words with associated d-dimensional unit word-vectors $v_w \in \mathbb{R}^d$ for $d \ll |V|$ (e.g. $d = 300$ for vocabulary size 50000) trained on a large text corpus. Each word $w \in V$ also has a set of candidate synsets found by MT+PWN. We call synsets S, S' in PWN *related*, denoted $S \sim S'$, if one is a hyponym, meronym, antonym, or attribute of the other, if they share a verb group, or $S = S'$.

3.1 Baseline: Average Similarity Method

This method for scoring synsets can be seen as a simple baseline. Given a candidate synset S, we define $T_S \subset V$ as the set of translations of its lemmas from English to the target language. The score of S is then $\frac{1}{|T_S|}\sum_{w' \in T_S} v_w \cdot v_{w'}$, the average cosine similarity between w and the translated lemmas of S. Although straightforward, this scoring method is quite noisy, as averaging word-vectors dilutes similarity performance, and does not use all synset information provided by PWN.

3.2 Method 1: Synset Representation

To improve upon this baseline we need a better vector representation of S to score S via cosine similarity with v_w. Previous efforts in synset and sense embeddings (Iacobacci et al., 2015; Rothe and Schütze, 2015) often use extra resources such as WordNet or BabelNet for the target language (Navigli and Ponzetto, 2012). As such databases are not always available, we propose a synset representation u_S that is unsupervised, needing no extra resources beyond MT and PWN, and leverages recent work on sentence embeddings.

This new representation combines embeddings of synset information given by PWN, e.g. synset relations, definitions, and example sentences. To create these embeddings we first consider the question of how to represent a list of words L as a vector in $\mathbb{R}^d$. One way is to simply take the normalized sum $\hat{v}_L^{(SUM)}$ of their word-vectors, where

$$v_L^{(SUM)} = \sum_{w' \in L} v_{w'}$$

Potentially more useful is to compute a vector $\hat{v}_L^{(SIF)}$ via the sentence embedding formula of Arora et al. (2017), based on *smooth inverse frequency* (SIF) weighting, which (for $a = 10^{-4}$ and before normalization) is expressed as

$$v_L^{(SIF)} = \sum_{w' \in L} \frac{a}{a + \mathbb{P}\{w'\}} v_{w'}$$

SIF is similar in spirit to TF-IDF (Salton and Buckley, 1988) and builds on work of Wieting et al. (2016); it has been found to perform well on other similarity tasks (Arora et al., 2017).

We find that SIF improves performance on sentences but not on translated lemma lists (Figure 2),

14

likely because sentences contain many distractor words that SIF will weight lower while the presence of distractors among lemmas is independent of word frequency. Thus to compute the synset score $u_S \cdot v_w$ we make the vector representation u_S of S the element-wise average of:

- $\hat{v}_{T_S}^{(SUM)}$ — T_S is the set of translations of lemmas of S (as in Section 3.1).

- $\hat{v}_{R_S}^{(SUM)}$ — $R_S = \left(\bigcup_{S' \sim S} T_{S'} \right) \setminus T_S$ is the set of lemma translations of synsets S' related to S.

- $\hat{v}_{D_S}^{(SIF)}$ — D_S is the list of tokens in the translated definition of S.

- $\dfrac{1}{|\mathcal{E}_s|} \sum_{E \in \mathcal{E}_S} \hat{v}_E^{(SIF)}$ — $\mathcal{E}_S$ contains the lists of tokens in the translated example sentences of S (excluded if S has no example sentences).

3.3 Method 2: Better Matching Using WSI

We found through examination that the score-threshold method we have used so far performs poorly in two main cases:

(a) the word w has no candidate synset with score high-enough to clear the threshold.

(b) w has multiple closely related synsets that are all correct matches but some of which have a much lower score than others.

Here we address both issues by using sense information found by applying a word-sense induction method first introduced in Arora et al. (2016a).

We summarize their WSI-model – referred to henceforth as *Linear-WSI* — in Section 3.3.1. Then in Section 3.3.2 we devise a *sense purification* procedure for constructing a word-cluster for each induced sense of a word. Applying this procedure to construct word-cluster representations of candidates synsets provides an additional metric for the correctness of word-synset matches that can be used to devise a w-specific threshold α_w to ameliorate problem (a). Meanwhile, using Linear-WSI to associate similar candidate synsets of w to each other provides a way to address problem (b). We explain these methodologies in Section 3.3.3.

3.3.1 Summary of Linear-WSI Model

In Arora et al. (2016a) the authors posit that the vector of a polysemous word can be linearly decomposed into vectors associated to its senses.

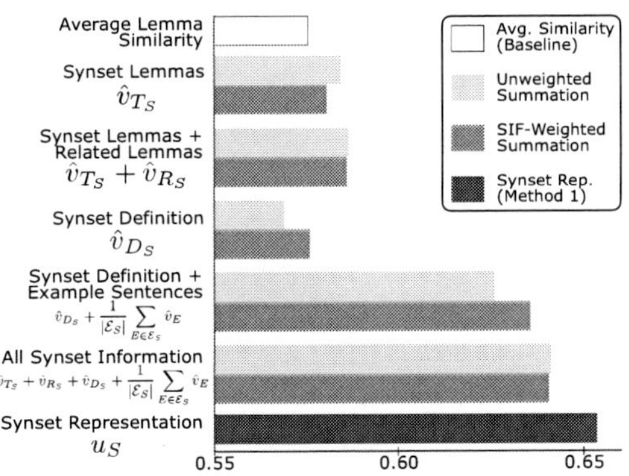

Figure 2: F-score comparison between using unweighted summation and SIF-weighted summation for embedding PWN synset information.

Thus for $w = tie$ — which can be an article of clothing, a drawn match, and so on — we would have $v_w \approx a v_{w(clothing)} + b v_{w(match)} + \ldots$ for $a, b \in \mathbb{R}$. It is unclear how to find such sense-vectors, but one expects different words to have closely related sense-vectors, e.g. for $w' = bow$ the vector $v_{w'(clothing)}$ would be close to the vector $v_{w(clothing)}$ of *tie*. Thus the Linear-WSI model proposes using sparse coding, namely finding a set of unit basis vectors $a_1, \ldots, a_k \in \mathbb{R}^d$ s.t. $\forall\, w \in V$,

$$v_w = \sum_{i=1}^{k} R_{wi} a_i + \eta_w, \qquad (1)$$

for $k > d$, η_w a noise vector, and at most s coefficients R_{wi} nonzero. The hope is that the sense-vector $v_{w(clothing)}$ of *tie* is in the neighborhood of a vector a_i s.t. $R_{wi} > 0$. Indeed, for $k = 2000$ and $s = 5$, Arora et al. (2016a) report that solving (1) represents English word-senses as well as a competent non-native speaker and significantly better than older clustering methods for WSI.

3.3.2 Sense Purification

While (1) is a good WSI method, its use for building WordNets is hampered by its inability to produce more than a few thousand senses a_i, as setting a large k yields repetitive rather than different senses. As this is far fewer than the number of synsets in PWN, we use sense purification to address this by extracting a cluster of words related to a_i as well as w to represent each sense. In addition to w and a_i, the procedure takes as input a search-space $V' \subset V$ and set size n. Then we find

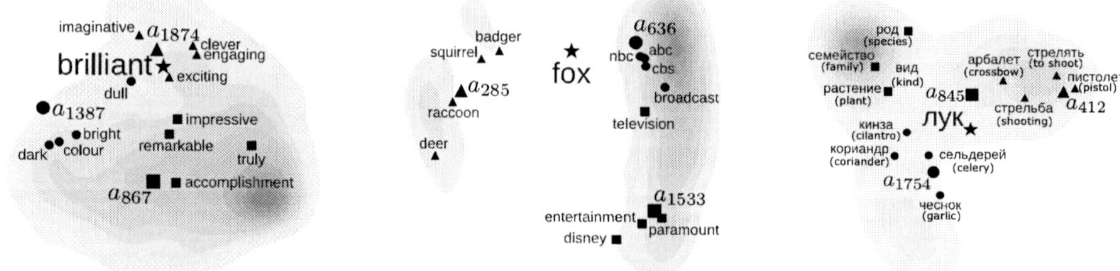

Figure 3: Isometric mapping of sense-cluster vectors for $w = brilliant, fox$, and лук (bow, onion). w is marked by a star and each sense a_i of w, shown by a large marker, has an associated cluster of words with the same marker shape. Contours are densities of vectors close to w and at least one sense a_i.

$C \subset V'$ of size n containing w that maximizes

$$f = \min_{\substack{x = a_i \text{ or} \\ x = v_{w'} : w' \in C}} \text{Median}\{x \cdot v_{w'} : w' \in C\} \quad (2)$$

A cluster C maximizing this must ensure that neither a_i nor any word $w' \in C$ (including $w' = w$) has low average cosine similarity with cluster-words, resulting in a dense cluster close to both w and a_i. We explain this further in Appendix A.

We illustrate this method in Figure 3 by purifying the senses of English words *brilliant* and *fox* and Russian word лук, which has the senses "bow" (weapon), "onion" (vegetable), and "onion" (plant). Note how correct senses are recovered across POS and language and for proper and common noun senses.

3.3.3 Applying WSI to Synset Matching

The problem addressed by sense purification is that senses a_i induced by Linear-WSI have too many related words; purification solves this by extracting a cluster of words related to w from the words close to a_i. When translating WordNet synsets, we have a similar problem in that translations of a synset's lemmas may not be relevant to the synset itself. Thus we can try to create a purified representation of each candidate synset S of w by extracting a cluster of translated lemmas close to w and one of its induced senses. We run purification on every sense a_i in the sparse representation (1) of w, using as a search-space $V' = V_S$ the set of translations of all lemmas of synsets S' related to S in PWN (i.e. $S' \sim S$ as defined in Section 3). To each synset S we associate the sense a_S and corresponding cluster C_S that are optimal in the objective (2) among all senses a_i of w.

Although we find a sense a_S and purified representation C_S for each candidate synset of w, we note that an incorrect synset is likely to have a lower objective value (2) than a correct synset as it likely has fewer words related to w in its search-space V_S. However, using $f_S = f(w, a_S, C_S)$ as a synset score is difficult as some synsets have very small search-spaces, leading to inconsistent scoring even for correct synsets.

Instead we use f_S as part of a w-specific threshold $\alpha_w = \min\{\alpha, u_{S^*} \cdot v_w\}$, where u_S is the vector representation of S from Section 3.2 and $S^* = \arg\max f_S + u_S \cdot v_w$. This attempts to address problem (a) of the score-threshold method — that some words have no synsets above the cut-off α and returning only the highest-scoring synset in such cases will not retrieve multiple sense for polysemous words. By the construction of α_w, if w is polysemous, a synset other than the one with the highest score $u_S \cdot v_w$ may have a better value of f_S and thus found to be S^*; then all synsets with higher scores will be matched to w, allowing for multiple matches even if no synset clears the cut-off α. Otherwise if w is monosemous, we expect the correct synset S to have the highest value for both $u_S \cdot v_w$ and f_S, making $S^* = S$. Then if no synset has score greater than α the threshold will be set to $u_S \cdot v_w$, the highest synset-score, so only the highest scoring synset will be matched to w.

To address problem (b) of the threshold method — that w might have multiple correct and closely related candidate synsets of which only some clear the cutoff — we observe that closely related synsets of w will have similar search-spaces V_S and so are likely to be associated to the same sense a_i. For example, in Figure 4 the candidates of *dalle* related to its correct meanings as a flagstone or slab are associated to the same sense a_{892} while distractor synsets related to the incorrect sense as a

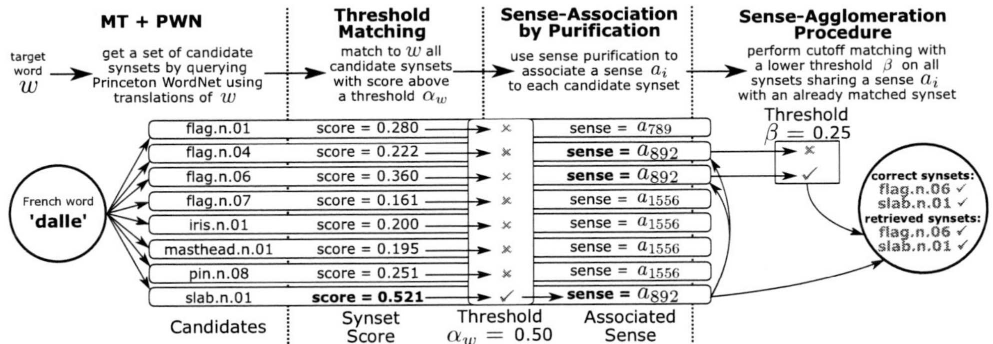

Figure 4: The score-threshold and sense-agglomeration procedure for French word $w = dalle$ (flagstone, slab). Candidate synsets are given a score and matched to w if they clear a high threshold α_w (as in Section 3.2). If an unmatched synset shares a sense a_i with a matched synset, it is compared to a low threshold β (the sense-agglomeration procedure in Section 3.3.3).

flag are mostly matched to other senses. This motivates the *sense agglomeration* procedure, which uses threshold-clearing synsets to match synsets with the same sense below the score-threshold. For $\beta < \alpha$, the procedure is roughly as follows:

1. Run score-threshold method with cutoff α_w.

2. For each synset S with score $u_S \cdot v_w$ below the threshold, check for a synset S' with score $u_{S'} \cdot v_w$ above the threshold and $a_{S'} = a_S$.

3. If $u_S \cdot v_w \geq \beta$ and the clusters $C_S, C_{S'}$ satisfy a cluster similarity condition, match S to w.

We include the lower cutoff β because even similar synsets may not both be senses of the same word. The cluster similarity condition, available in Appendix B.2, ensures the relatedness of synsets sharing a sense a_i, as an erroneous synset S' may be associated to the same sense as a correct one.

In summary, the improved synset matching approach has two steps: 1-conduct score-threshold matching using the modified threshold α_w; 2-run the sense-agglomeration procedure on all senses a_i of w having at least one threshold-clearing synset S. Although for fixed α both steps focus on improving the recall of the threshold method, in practice they allow α to be higher, so that both precision and recall are improved. For example, note the recovery of a correct synset left unmatched by the score-threshold method in the simplified depiction of sense-agglomeration shown in Figure 4.

4 Evaluation of Methods

We evaluate our method's accuracy and coverage by constructing and testing WordNets for French and Russian. For both we train 300-dimensional SN word embeddings (Arora et al., 2016b) on co-occurrences of words occurring at least 1000 times, or having candidate PWN synsets and occurring at least 100 times, in the lemmatized Wikipedia corpus. This yields $|V| \approx 50000$. For Linear-WSI we run sparse coding with sparsity $s = 4$ and basis-size $k = 2000$ and use set-size $n = 5$ for purification. To get candidate synsets we use Google and Microsoft Translators and the dictionary of the translation company ECTACO, while for sentence-length MT we use Microsoft.

4.1 Testsets

A common way to evaluate accuracy of an automated WordNet is to compare its synsets or word matchings to a manually-constructed one. However, the existing ELRA French Wordnet [2] is not public and half the size of ours while Russian WordNets are either even smaller and not linked to PWN[3] or obtained via direct translation[4].

Instead we construct test sets for each language that allow for evaluation of our methods and others. We randomly chose 200 each of adjectives, nouns, and verbs from the set of target language words whose English translations appear in the synsets of the Core WordNet. Their "ground truth"

---

[2] http://catalog.elra.info/product_info.php?products_id=550
[3] http://project.phil.spbu.ru/RussNet/
[4] http://wordnet.ru/

Method	POS	$F_{.5}$-Score[*]	F_1-Score[*]	Precision[*]	Recall[*]	Coverage	Synsets	α	β
Direct Translation (MT + PWN)	Adj.	50.3	59.3	46.1	100.0	99.9	11271		
	Noun	56.2	64.6	52.2	100.0	100.0	74477		
	Verb	41.4	51.3	37.0	100.0	100.0	13017		
	Total	49.3	58.4	45.1	100.0	100.0	100174[†]		
Wordnet Libre du Français (WOLF) (Sagot and Fišer, 2008)	Adj.	66.3	58.6	78.1	53.4	84.8	6865		
	Noun	68.6	58.7	83.2	51.5	95.0	36667		
	Verb	60.8	48.4	81.0	39.6	88.2	7671		
	Total	65.2	55.2	80.8	48.2	92.2	52757[†]		
Universal Wordnet (de Melo and Weikum, 2009)	Adj.	64.5	51.5	88.3	42.3	69.2	7407		
	Noun	67.5	52.2	94.1	40.8	75.9	24670		
	Verb	55.4	39.5	88.0	28.5	76.2	5624		
	Total	62.5	47.7	90.1	37.2	75.0	39497[†]		
Extended Open Multilingual Wordnet (Bond and Foster, 2013)	Adj.	58.4	40.8	**90.9**	28.4	54.7	2689		
	Noun	61.3	43.8	**96.5**	31.7	66.6	14936		
	Verb	47.8	29.4	**95.9**	18.6	57.7	2331		
	Total	55.9	38.0	**94.5**	26.2	63.2	20449[†]		
Baseline: Average Similarity (Section 3.1)	Adj.	62.8±0.0	62.6±0.0	65.3±0.0	**68.5**±0.0	88.7	9687	0.31	
	Noun	67.3±0.0	65.4±0.1	71.6±0.1	**69.0**±0.1	92.2	37970	0.27	
	Verb	51.8±0.0	50.8±0.1	55.9±0.1	**57.0**±0.1	83.5	10037	0.26	
	Total	60.6±0.0	59.6±0.0	64.3±0.0	**64.9**±0.0	90.0	58962[†]		
Method 1: Synset Representation (Section 3.2)	Adj.	65.9±0.0	60.4±0.0	75.9±0.1	59.5±0.1	85.1	8512	0.47	
	Noun	71.0±0.0	**67.3**±0.1	78.7±0.1	69.1±0.1	**96.7**	35663	0.41	
	Verb	61.6±0.0	53.0±0.0	78.7±0.1	49.8±0.1	89.9	8619	0.45	
	Total	66.2±0.0	60.2±0.0	77.8±0.0	59.5±0.1	**93.7**	53852[†]		
Method 2: Synset Representation + Linear-WSI (Section 3.3)	Adj.	**67.7**±0.0	**62.5**±0.1	76.9±0.1	62.6±0.1	**91.2**	8912	0.56	0.42
	Noun	**73.0**±0.0	66.0±0.1	83.7±0.1	62.0±0.2	90.9	34001	0.50	0.25
	Verb	**64.4**±0.0	**55.9**±0.0	79.3±0.0	51.5±0.1	**93.6**	9262	0.46	0.28
	Total	**68.4**±0.0	**61.5**±0.0	80.0±0.0	58.7±0.1	91.5	53208[†]		

[*] Micro-averages over a randomly held-out half of the data; parameters tuned on the other half. 95% asymptotic confidence intervals found with 10000 randomized trials.

[†] Includes adverb synsets. For the last three methods they are matched with the same parameter values (α and β) as for adjectives.

Table 1: French WordNet Results

word senses are picked by native speakers, who were asked to perform the same matching task described in Section 3, i.e. select correct synsets for a word given a set of candidates generated by MT + PWN. For example, the French word *foie* has one translation, *liver* with four PWN synsets: 1-"glandular organ"; 2-"liver used as meat"; 3-"person with a special life style"; 4-"someone living in a place." The first two align with senses of *foie* while the others do not, so the expert marks the first two as good and the others as negative. Two native speakers for each language were trained by an author with knowledge of WordNet and at least 10 years of experience in each language. Inconsistencies in the matchings of the two speakers were resolved by the same author.

We get 600 words and about 12000 candidate word-synset pairs for each language, with adjectives and nouns having on average about 15 candidates and verbs having about 30. These numbers makes the test set larger than many others,

with French, Korean, and Persian WordNets cited in Section 2 being evaluated on 183 pairs, 3260 pairs, and 500 words, respectively. Accuracy measured with respect to this ground truth estimates how well an algorithm does compared to humans.

A significant characteristic of this test set is its dependence on the machine translation system used to get candidate synsets. While this can leave out correct synset matches that the system did not propose, by providing both correct and incorrect candidate synsets we allow future authors to focus on the semantic challenge of selecting correct senses without worrying about finding the best bilingual dictionary. This allows dictionary-independent evaluation of automated WordNets, an important feature in an area where the specific translation systems used are rarely provided in full. When comparing the performance of our construction to that of previous efforts on this test set, we do not penalize word-synset matches in which the synset is not among the candidate synsets we generate for that word, negating the loss of precision incurred by other methods due to the use of different dictionaries. We also do not penalize other WordNets for test words they do not contain.

In addition to precision and recall, we report the *Coverage* statistic as the proportion of the Core set of most-used synsets, a semi-automatically constructed set of about 5000 PWN frequent senses, that are matched to at least one word (Fellbaum, 1972). While an imperfect metric given different sense usage by language, the synsets are universal-enough for it to be a good indicator of usability.

4.2 Evaluation Results

We report the evaluation of methods in Section 3 in Tables 1 & 2 alongside evaluations of UWN (de Melo and Weikum, 2009), OWM (Bond and Foster, 2013), and WOLF (Sagot and Fišer, 2008). Parameters α and β were tuned to maximize the micro-averaged $F_{.5}$-score $\frac{1.25 \cdot \text{Precision} \cdot \text{Recall}}{.25 \cdot \text{Precision} + \text{Recall}}$, used instead of F_1 to prioritize precision, which is often more important for application purposes.

Our synset representation method (Section 3.2) exceeds the similarity baseline by 6% in $F_{.5}$-score for French and 10% for Russian. For French it is competitive with the best other WordNet (WOLF) and in both languages exceeds both multi-lingual WordNets. Improving this method via Linear-WSI (Section 3.3) leads to 2% improvement in $F_{.5}$-score for French and 1% for Russian. Our methods also perform best in F_1-score and Core coverage.

As expected from a Wiktionary-scraping method, OMW achieves the best precision across languages, although it and UWN have low recall and Core coverage. The performance of our best method for French exceeds that of WOLF in $F_{.5}$-score across POS while achieving similar coverage. WOLF's recall performance is markedly lower than the evaluation in Sagot and Fišer (2008, Table 4); we believe this stems from our use of words matched to Core synsets, not random words, leading to a more difficult test set as common words are more-polysemous and have more synsets to retrieve. There is no comparable automated Russian-only WordNet, with only semi-automated and incomplete efforts (Yablonsky and Sukhonogov, 2006).

Comparing across POS, we do best on nouns and worst on verbs, likely due to the greater polysemy of verbs. Between languages, performance is similar for adjectives but slightly worse on Russian nouns and much worse on Russian verbs.

The discrepancy in verbs can be explained by a difference in treating the reflexive case and aspectual variants due to the grammatical complexity of Russian verbs. In French, making a verb reflexive requires adding a word while in Russian the verb itself changes, e.g. *to wash→to wash oneself* is *laver→se laver* in French but мыть→мыться in Russian. Thus we do not distinguish the reflexive case for French as the token found is the same but for Russian we do, so both мыть and мыться may appear and have distinct synset matches. Thus matching Russian verbs is challenging as the reflexive usage of a verb is often contextually similar to the non-reflexive usage. Another complication for Russian verbs is due to aspectual verb pairs; thus *to do* has aspects (делать, сделать) in Russian that are treated as distinct verbs while in French these are just different tenses of the verb *faire*. Both factors pose challenges for differentiating Russian verb senses by a distributional model.

Overall however the method is shown to be robust to how close the target language is to English, with nouns and adjectives performing well in both languages and the difference for verbs stemming from an intrinsic quality rather than dissimilarity with English. This can be further examined by testing the method on a non-European language.

5 Conclusion and Future Work

We have shown how to leverage recent advances in word embeddings for fully-automated WordNet construction. Our best approach combining sentence embeddings, and recent methods for WSI obtains performance 5-16% above the naive baseline in $F_{.5}$-score as well as outperforming previous language-specific and multi-lingual methods. A notable feature of our work is that we require only a large corpus in the target language and automated translation into/from English, both available for many languages lacking good WordNets.

We further contribute new 600-word human-annotated test sets split by POS for French and Russian that can be used to evaluate future automated WordNets. These larger test sets give a more accurate picture of a construction's strengths and weaknesses, revealing some limitations of past methods. With WordNets in French and Russian largely automated or incomplete, the WordNets we build also add an important tool for multi-lingual natural language processing.

Method	POS	$F_{.5}$-Score*	F_1-Score*	Precision*	Recall*	Coverage	Synsets	α	β
Direct Translation (MT + PWN)	Adj.	50.2	59.6	45.9	100.0	99.6	11412		
	Noun	41.2	50.2	37.1	100.0	100.0	73328		
	Verb	32.5	41.7	28.6	100.0	100.0	13185		
	Total	41.3	50.5	37.2	100.0	99.9	99470†		
Universal Wordnet (de Melo and Weikum, 2009)	Adj.	52.4	38.8	80.3	29.6	51.0	11412		
	Noun	65.0	53.0	87.5	45.1	71.1	19564		
	Verb	48.1	34.8	74.8	25.7	65.0	3981		
	Total	55.1	42.2	80.8	33.4	67.1	30015†		
Extended Open Multilingual Wordnet (Bond and Foster, 2013)	Adj.	58.7	41.3	**91.7**	29.2	55.3	2419		
	Noun	67.8	53.1	**93.5**	42.5	68.4	14968		
	Verb	51.1	34.8	**84.5**	23.9	56.6	2218		
	Total	59.2	43.1	**89.9**	31.9	64.2	19983†		
Baseline: Average Similarity (Section 3.1)	Adj.	61.4±0.0	64.6±0.1	60.9±0.0	**77.3**±0.1	92.1	10293	0.24	
	Noun	55.9±0.0	54.8±0.1	59.9±0.1	59.9±0.1	77.0	32919	0.29	
	Verb	46.3±0.0	46.5±0.1	49.0±0.1	**55.1**±0.1	84.1	9749	0.21	
	Total	54.5±0.0	55.3±0.0	56.6±0.0	**64.1**±0.1	80.5	54372†		
Method 1: Synset Representation (Section 3.2)	Adj.	69.5±0.0	64.1±0.0	78.1±0.0	61.7±0.1	84.2	8393	0.43	
	Noun	69.8±0.0	65.5±0.0	77.6±0.1	66.0±0.1	85.2	29076	0.46	
	Verb	54.2±0.0	**51.1**±0.1	63.3±0.1	57.4±0.1	91.2	8303	0.39	
	Total	64.5±0.0	60.2±0.0	73.0±0.0	61.7±0.1	86.3	46911†		
Method 2: Synset Representation + Linear-WSI (Section 3.3)	Adj.	**69.7**±0.0	**64.9**±0.1	77.3±0.0	63.6±0.1	**93.3**	9359	0.43	0.35
	Noun	**71.6**±0.0	**67.6**±0.0	78.1±0.0	**68.0**±0.1	**91.0**	31699	0.46	0.33
	Verb	**54.4**±0.0	49.7±0.1	64.9±0.1	52.6±0.2	**91.9**	8582	0.44	0.33
	Total	**65.2**±0.0	**60.7**±0.0	73.4±0.0	61.4±0.1	**91.5**	50850†		

* Micro-averages over a randomly held-out half of the data; parameters tuned on the other half. 95% asymptotic confidence intervals found with 10000 randomized trials.

† Includes adverb synsets. For the last three methods they are matched with the same parameter values (α and β) as for adjectives.

Table 2: Russian WordNet Results

Further improvement to our work may come from other methods in word-embeddings, such as multi-lingual word-vectors (Faruqui and Dyer, 2014). Our techniques can also be combined with others, both language-specific and multi-lingual, for automated WordNet construction. In addition, our method for associating multiple synsets to the same sense can contribute to efforts to improve PWN through sense clustering (Snow et al., 2007). Finally, our sense purification procedure, which uses word-vectors to extract clusters representing word-senses, likely has further WSI and WSD applications; such exploration is left to future work.

Acknowledgments

We thank Angel Chang and Yingyu Liang for helpful discussion at various stages of this paper. This work was supported in part by NSF grants CCF-1302518, CCF-1527371, Simons Investigator Award, Simons Collaboration Grant, and ONR-N00014-16-1-2329.

References

Michal Aharon, Michael Elad, and Alfred Bruckstein. 2006. K-svd: An algorithm for designing overcomplete dictionaries for sparse representation. *IEEE Transactions on Signal Processing*, 54(11).

Sanjeev Arora, Yuanzhi Li, Yingyu Liang, Tengyu Ma, and Andrej Risteski. 2016a. Linear algebraic structure of word sense, with applications to polysemy.

Sanjeev Arora, Yuanzhi Li, Yingyu Liang, Tengyu Ma, and Andrej Risteski. 2016b. Rand-walk: A latent variable model approach to word embeddings. *Transactions of the Association for Computational Linguistics*, 4:385–399.

Sanjeev Arora, Yingyu Liang, and Tengyu Ma. 2017. A simple but tough-to-beat baseline for sentence embeddings. In *International Conference on Learning Representations*. To Appear.

Steven Bird, Edward Loper, and Ewan Klein. 2009. *Natural Language Processing with Python*. O'Reilly Media Inc.

Francis Bond and Ryan Foster. 2013. Linking and extending an open multilingual wordnet. In *Proceedings of the 51st Annual Meeting of the Association for Computational Linguistics*.

Gerard de Melo and Gerhard Weikum. 2009. Towards a universal wordnet by learning from combined evidence. In *Proceedings of the 18th ACM Conference on Information and Knowledge Management*.

Manaal Faruqui and Chris Dyer. 2014. Improving vector space word representations using multilingual correlation. In *Proceedings of the 14th Conference of the European Chapter of the Association for Computational Linguistics*.

Christiane Fellbaum. 1972. *WordNet: An Electronic Lexical Database*. MIT Press, Cambridge, MA.

Global WordNet Association. 2017. Wordnets in the world.

Ignaci Iacobacci, Mohammad Taher Pilehvar, and Roberto Navigli. 2015. Sensembed: Learning sense embeddings for word and relational similarity. In *Proceedings of the 53rd Annual Meeting of the Association for Computational Linguistics*.

Changki Lee, Geunbae Lee, and Seo JungYun. 2000. Automated wordnet mapping using word sense disambiguation. In *Proceedings of the 2000 Joint SIGDAT Conference on Empirical Methods in Natural Language Processing and Very Large Corpora*.

Tomas Mikolov, Kai Chen, Greg Corrado, and Jeffrey Dean. 2013. Efficient estimation of word representations in vector space.

Mortaza Montazery and Heshaam Faili. 2010. Automatic persian wordnet construction. In *Proceedings of the 23rd International Conference on Computational Linguistics*.

Mohammad Nasiruddin, Didier Schwab, and Andon Tchechmedjiev. 2014. Induction de sens pour enrichir des ressources lexicales. In *21éme Traitement Automatique des Langues Naturelles*.

Roberto Navigli and Simone Paolo Ponzetto. 2012. Babelnet: The automatic construction, evaluation and application of a wide-coverage multilingual semantic network. *Artificial Intelligence*, 193.

Jeffrey Pennington, Richard Socher, and Christopher D. Manning. 2014. Glove: Global vectors for word representation. In *Proceedings of Empirical Methods in Natural Language Processing*.

Quentin Pradet, Gaël de Chalendar, and Jeanne Baguenier Desormeaux. 2013. Wonef, an improved, expanded and evaluated automatic french translation of wordnet. In *Proceedings of the Seventh Global Wordnet Conference*.

Sascha Rothe and Hinrich Schütze. 2015. Autoextend: Extending word embeddings to embeddings for synsets and lexemes. In *Proceedings of the 53rd Annual Meeting of the Association for Computational Linguistics*.

Benoît Sagot and Darja Fišer. 2008. Building a free french wordnet from multilingual resources. In *Proceedings of the Sixth International Language Resources and Evaluation Conference*.

Gerald Salton and Christopher Buckley. 1988. Term-weighting approaches in automatic text retrieval. *Information Processing & Management*, 24(5).

Rion Snow, Sushant Prakash, Daniel Jurafsky, and Andrew Y. Ng. 2007. Learning to merge word senses. In *Proceedings of the 2007 Joint Conference on Empirical Methods in Natural Language Processing and Computational Natural Language Learning*.

Feras Al Tarouti and Jugal Kalita. 2016. Enhancing automatic wordnet construction using word embeddings. In *Proceedings of the Workshop on Multilingual and Cross-lingual Methods in NLP*.

John Wieting, Mohit Bansal, Kevin Gimpel, and Karen Livescu. 2016. Towards universal paraphrastic sentence embeddings. In *International Conference on Learning Representations*.

Sergey Yablonsky and Andrej Sukhonogov. 2006. Semi-automated english-russian wordnet construction: Initial resources, software and methods of translation. In *Proceedings of the Global WordNet Conference*.

A Purification Procedure

As discussed in Section 3.3.1, the Linear-WSI model (Arora et al., 2016a) posits that there exists an *overcomplete basis* $a_1, \ldots, a_k \in \mathbb{R}^d$ of unit vectors such that each word $w \in V$ can be approximately represented by a linear combination of at most s basis vectors (see Equation 1). Finding the basis vectors a_i and their coefficients R_{wi} requires solving the optimization problem

$$\begin{aligned} \text{minimize} \quad & \|Y - RA\|_2 \\ \text{subject to} \quad & \|R_w\|_0 \leq s \ \forall \ w \in V \end{aligned}$$

where $Y \in \mathbb{R}^{|V| \times n}$ has word-vectors as its rows, $R \in \mathbb{R}^{|V| \times k}$ is the matrix of coefficients R_{wi}, and $A \in \mathbb{R}^{k \times d}$ has the overcomplete basis $a_1, \ldots, a_k$ as its rows. This problem is non-convex and can be solved approximately via the K-SVD algorithm (Aharon et al., 2006).

Given a word w, the purification procedure is a method for purifying the senses induced via Linear-WSI (the vectors a_i s.t. $R_{wi} \neq 0$) by representing them as word-clusters related to both the sense itself and the word. This is done so as to create a more fine-grained collection of senses, as Linear-WSI does not perform well for more than a few thousand basis vectors, far fewer than the number of word-senses (Arora et al., 2016a). The procedure is inspired by the hope that words related to each sense of w will form clusters near both v_w and one of its senses a_i. Given a fixed set-size n and a search-space $V' \subset V$, we realize this hope via the optimization problem

$$\underset{C \subset V'}{\text{maximize}} \quad \gamma$$

subject to

$$\gamma \leq \text{Median}\{v_x \cdot v_{w'} : w' \in C \backslash \{x\}\} \ \forall \ x \in C$$
$$\gamma \leq \text{Median}\{a_i \cdot v_{w'} : w' \in C\}$$
$$w \in C, \ |C| = n$$

This problem is equivalent to maximizing (2) with constraints $|C| = n$ and $w \in C \subset V'$. The objective value is constrained to be the lowest median cosine similarity between any word $x \in C$ or the sense a_i and the rest of C, so optimizing it ensures that the words in C are closely related to each other and to a_i. Forcing the cluster to contain w leads to the words in C being close to w as well.

For computational purposes we solve this problem approximately using a greedy algorithm that starts with $C = \{w\}$ and repeatedly adds the word in $V' \backslash C$ that results in the best objective value until $|C| = n$. Speed of computation is also a reason for using a search-space $V' \subset V$ rather than the entire vocabulary as a source of words for the cluster; we found that restricting V' to be all words w' s.t. $\min\{v_{w'} \cdot v_w, v_{w'} \cdot a_i\} \geq .2$ dramatically reduces processing time with little performance loss.

The purification procedure represents only one sense of w, so to perform WSI we generate clusters for all senses a_i s.t. $R_{wi} > 0$. If two senses have clusters that share a word other than w, only the cluster with the higher objective value is returned. To find the clusters displayed in Figure 3 we use this procedure with cluster size $n = 5$ on English and Russian SN vectors decomposed with basis size $k = 2000$ and sparsity $s = 4$.

B   Applying WSI to Synset Matching

We use the purification procedure to represent the candidate synsets of a word w by clusters of words related to w and one if its senses a_i. First, for each synset S we define the search-space

$$V_S = \bigcup_{S' \sim S} T_{S'}$$

where $T_{S'}$ is the set of translations of lemmas of S' as in Section 3.1. Then given a word w, one of its candidate synsets S, and a fixed set size n, we run the following procedure:

1. For each sense a_i in the sparse representation (1) of w let C_i be the output cluster of the purification procedure run on sense a_i with search-space $V' = V_S$.

2. Return the (sense, sense-cluster) pair (a_S, C_S) with the highest purification procedure objective value among senses a_i.

In the following methods we will assume that each candidate synset S of w has a sense a_S and sense-cluster C_S associated to it in this way. Examples of such clusters for the French word *dalle* (flagstone, slab) are provided in Table 3.

B.1   Word-Specific Threshold

One application of Linear-WSI is the creation of a word-specific threshold α_w to use in the score-threshold method instead of a global cutoff α. We do this by using the quality of the sense cluster C_S of each candidate synset S of w as an indicator of the correctness of that synset. Recalling that u_S is the synset representation of S as a vector (see Section 3.2) and letting $f_S = f(w, a_S, C_S)$ be the objective value (2), we find α_w as follows:

1. Find $S^* = \underset{S \text{ is a candidate of } w}{\arg\max} \ f_S + u_S \cdot v_w$.

2. Let $\alpha_w = \min\{\alpha, u_{S^*} \cdot v_w\}$.

As this modified threshold may be lower than more than one candidate synset of w it allows for multiple synset matches even when no synset has score high enough to clear the threshold α.

B.2   Sense-Agglomeration Procedure

We use Linear-WSI more explicitly through the sense-agglomeration procedure, which attempts to recover unmatched synsets using matched synsets sharing the same sense a_i of w. We define the *cluster similarity* ρ between word-clusters $C_1, C_2 \subset V$ as the median of all cosine-similarities of pairs of words in their set product, i.e.

$$\rho(C_1, C_2) = \text{Median}\{v_x \cdot v_y : x \in C_1, y \in C_2\}.$$

Then we say that two clusters C_1, C_2 are *similar* if

$$\rho(C_1, C_2) \geq \min\{\rho(C_1, C_1), \rho(C_2, C_2)\},$$

i.e. if their cluster similarity with each other exceeds at least one's cluster similarity with itself.

Synset	Associated Sense a_S	Purified Cluster Representation C_S	Objective Value $f(w, a_S, C_S)$
flag.n.01	a_{789}	poteau (goalpost), flèche (arrow), haut (high, top), mât (matte)	0.23
flag.n.04	a_{892}	flamme (flame), fanion (pennant), guidon, signal	0.06
flag.n.06	a_{892}	dallage (paving), carrelage (tiling), pavement, pavage (paving)	0.36
flag.n.07	a_{1556}	pan (section), empennage, queue, tail	0.14
iris.n.01	a_{1556}	bœuf (beef), usine (factory), plante (plant), puant (smelly)	0.07
masthead.n.01	a_{1556}	inscription, lettre (letter), catalogue (catalog), cotation (quotation)	0.10
pin.n.08	a_{1556}	trou (hole), tertre (mound), marais (marsh), pavillon (house, pavillion)	0.17
slab.n.01	a_{892}	carrelage (tiling), carreau (tile), tuile (tile), bâtiment (building)	0.27

Table 3: Purified Synset Representations of *dalle* (flagstone, slab). Note how the correct candidate synsets (bolded) have clusters of words closely related to the correct meaning while the other clusters have many unrelated words, leading to lower objective values.

Then given a global low threshold $\beta \leq \alpha$, for each sense a_i in the sparse representation (1), sense-agglomeration consists of the following algorithm:

1. Let M_i be the set of candidate synsets S of w that have $a_S = a_i$ and score above the threshold α_w. Stop if $M_i = \emptyset$.

2. Let U_i be the set of candidate synsets S of w that have $a_S = a_i$ and score below the threshold α_w. Stop if $U_i = \emptyset$.

3. For each synset $S \in U_i$, ordered by synset-score, check that C_S is similar (in the above sense) to all clusters $C_{S'}$ for $S' \in M_i$ and has score higher than β. If both are true, add S to M_i and remove S from U_i. Otherwise stop.

The sense-agglomeration procedure allows an unmatched synset S to be returned as a correct synset of w provided it shares a sense with a different matched synset S' and satisfies cluster similarity and score-threshold constraints.

Improving Verb Metaphor Detection by Propagating Abstractness to Words, Phrases and Individual Senses

Maximilian Köper and **Sabine Schulte im Walde**
Institut für Maschinelle Sprachverarbeitung
Universität Stuttgart, Germany
{maximilian.koeper,schulte}@ims.uni-stuttgart.de

Abstract

Abstract words refer to things that can not be seen, heard, felt, smelled, or tasted as opposed to concrete words. Among other applications, the degree of abstractness has been shown to be a useful information for metaphor detection. Our contribution to this topic are as follows: i) we compare supervised techniques to learn and extend abstractness ratings for huge vocabularies ii) we learn and investigate norms for multi-word units by propagating abstractness to verb-noun pairs which lead to better metaphor detection, iii) we overcome the limitation of learning a single rating per word and show that multi-sense abstractness ratings are potentially useful for metaphor detection. Finally, with this paper we publish automatically created abstractness norms for 3 million English words and multi-words as well as automatically created sense-specific abstractness ratings.

1 Introduction

The standard approach to studying abstractness is to place words on a scale ranging between abstractness and concreteness. Alternately, abstractness can also be given a taxonomic definition in which the abstractness of a word is determined by the number of subordinate words (Kammann and Streeter, 1971; Dunn, 2015).

In psycholinguistics abstractness is commonly used for concept classification (Barsalou and Wiemer-Hastings, 2005; Hill et al., 2014; Vigliocco et al., 2014). In computational work, abstractness has become an established information for the task of automatic detection of metaphorical language. So far metaphor detection has been carried out using a variety of features including selectional preferences (Martin, 1996; Shutova and Teufel, 2010; Shutova et al., 2010; Haagsma and Bjerva, 2016), word-level semantic similarity (Li and Sporleder, 2009; Li and Sporleder, 2010), topic models (Heintz et al., 2013), word embeddings (Dinh and Gurevych, 2016) and visual information (Shutova et al., 2016).

The underlying motivation of using abstractness in metaphor detection goes back to Lakoff and Johnson (1980), who argue that metaphor is a method for transferring knowledge from a concrete domain to an abstract domain. Abstractness was already applied successfully for the detection of metaphors across a variety of languages (Turney et al., 2011; Dunn, 2013; Tsvetkov et al., 2014; Beigman Klebanov et al., 2015; Köper and Schulte im Walde, 2016b).

The abstractness information itself is typically taken from a dictionary, created either by manual annotation or by extending manually collected ratings with the help of supervised learning techniques that rely on word representations. While potentially less reliable, automatically created norm-based abstractness ratings can easily cover huge dictionaries. Although some methods have been used to learn abstractness, literature lacks a comparison of these learning techniques.

We compare and evaluate different learning techniques. In addition we show and investigate the usefulness of extending abstractness ratings to phrases as well as individual word senses. We extrinsically evaluate these techniques on two verb metaphor detection tasks: (i) a type-based setting that makes use of phrase ratings, (ii) a token-based classification for multi-sense abstractness norms. Both settings benefit from our approach.

Proceedings of the 1st Workshop on Sense, Concept and Entity Representations and their Applications, pages 24–30,
Valencia, Spain, April 4 2017. ©2017 Association for Computational Linguistics

2 Experiments

2.1 Propagating Abstractness: A Comparison of Approaches & Ressources

2.1.1 Comparison of Approaches

Turney et al. (2011) first aproached to automatically create abstractness norms for 114 501 words, relying on manual ratings based on the MRC Psycholinguistic Database (Coltheart, 1981). The underlying algorithm (Turney and Littman, 2003) requires vector representation and annotated training samples of words. The algorithm itself performs a greedy forward search over the vocabulary to learn so-called paradigm words. Once paradigm words for both classes (abstract & concrete) are learned, a rating can be assigned to every word by comparing its vector representation against the vector representations of the paradigm words.

Köper and Schulte im Walde (2016a) used the same algorithm for a large collection of German lemmas, and in the same way additional created ratings for multiple norms including valency, arousal and imageability.

A different method that has been used to extend abstractness norms based on low-dimensional word embeddings and a Linear Regression classifier (Tsvetkov et al., 2013; Tsvetkov et al., 2014).

We compare approaches across different publicly available vector representations[1], to study potential differences across vector dimensionality we compare vectors between 50 and 300 dimensions. The Glove vectors (Pennington et al., 2014) have been trained on 6billion tokens of Wikipedia plus Gigaword (V=400K), while the word2vec cbow model (Mikolov et al., 2013) was trained on a Google internal news corpus with 100billion tokens (V=3million). For training and testing we relied on the ratings from Brysbaert et al. (2014), Dividing the ratings into 20% test (7 990) and 80% training (31 964) for tuning hyper parameters we took 1 000 ratings from the training data. We kept the ratio between word classes. Evaluation is done by comparing the new created ratings against the test (gold) ratings using Spearman's rank-order correlation. We first reimplemented the algorithm from Turney and Littman (2003) (T&L 03). Inspired by recent findings of Gupta et al. (2015) we apply the hypothesis that distributional vectors im-

[1]`http://nlp.stanford.edu/projects/glove/`
`https://code.google.com/archive/p/word2vec/`

plicitly encode attributes such as abstractness and directly feed the vector representation of a word into a classifier, either by using linear regression (L-Reg), a regression forest (Reg-F) or a fully connected feed forward neural network with up to two hidden layers (NN).[2]

	T&L 03	L-Reg.	Reg-F.	NN
Glove50	.76	.76	.78	**.79**
Glove100	.80	.79	.79	**.85**
Glove200	.78	.78	.76	**.84**
Glove300	.76	.78	.74	**.85**
W2V300	.83	.84	.79	**.90**

Table 1: Spearman's ρ for the test ratings. Comparing representations and regression methods.

Table 1 shows clearly that we can learn abstractness ratings with a very high correlation on the test data using the word representations from Google (W2V300) together with a neural network for regression (ρ=.90). The NN method significantly outperforms all other methods, using Steiger (1980)'s test ($p < 0.001$).

2.1.2 Comparison of Ressources

Based on the comparison of methods in the previous section we propagated abstractness ratings to the entire vocabulary of the W2V300 dataset (3million words) and compare the correlation with other existing norms of abstractness. For this comparison we use the common subset of two manually and one automatically created resource: MRC Psycholinguistic Database, ratings from Brysbaert et al. (2014) and the automatically created ratings from Turney et al. (2011). We map all existing ratings, as well as our newly created ratings, to the same interval using the method from Köper and Schulte im Walde (2016a). The mapping is performed using a continuous function, that maps the ratings to an interval ranging from very abstract (0) to very concrete (10). The common subset contains 3 665 ratings. Figure 1 shows the resulting pairwise correlation between all four resources. Despite being created automatically, we see that the newly created ratings provide a high correlation with both manually created collections (ρ for MRS=.91, Brysbaert=.93). In addition, the vocabulary of our ratings is much larger than any existing database. Thus this new collection might

[2]NN Implementation based on `https://github.com/amten/NeuralNetwork`

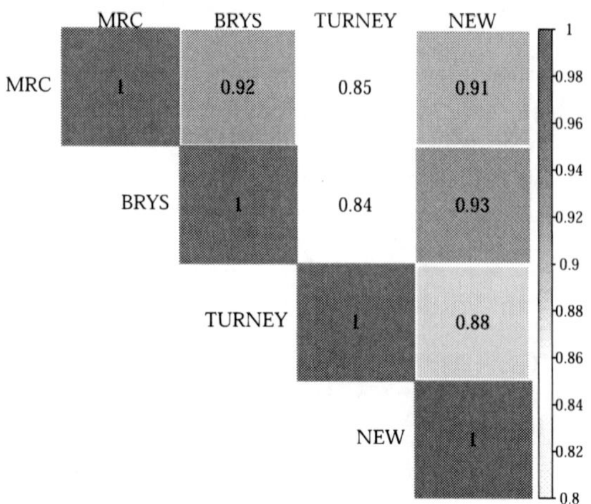

Figure 1: Pairwise Spearman's ρ on commonly covered subset. Red = high correlation.

be useful, especially for further research which requires large vocabulary coverage.[3]

2.2 Abstractness for Phrases

A potential advantage of our method is that abstractness can be learned for multi-word units as long as the representation of these units live in the same distributional vector space as the words required for the supervised training.

In this section we explore if ratings propagated to verb-noun phrases provide useful information for metaphor detection. As dataset we relied on the collection from Saif M. Mohammad and Turney (2016), who annotated different senses of WordNet verbs for metaphoricity (Fellbaum, 1998).

We used the same subset of verb–direct object and verb–subject relations as used in Shutova et al. (2016). As preprocessing step we concatenated verb-noun phrases by relying on dependency information based on a web corpus, the ENCOW14 corpus (Schäfer and Bildhauer, 2012; Schäfer, 2015). We removed words and phrases that appeared less than 50 times in our corpus, thus our selection covers 535 pairs, 238 of which were metaphorical and 297 literal.

Given a verb-noun phrase, such as stamp_person, we obtained vector representations using *word2vec* and the same hyper-parameters that were used for the *W2V300* embeddings (Section 2.1.1) together with the best learning

<hr>

[3]Ratings available at `http://www.ims.uni-stuttgart.de/data/en_abst_norms.html`

method (NN). The technique allows us to propagate abstractness to every vector, thus we learn abstractness ratings for all three constituents: verb, noun and the entire phrase.

For the metaphor classification experiment we use the rating score and apply the Area Under Curve (AUC) metric. AUC is a metric for binary classification. We assume that literal instances gain higher scores (= more concrete) than metaphorical word pairs. AUC considers all possible thresholds to divide the data into literal and metaphorical. In addition to the rating score we also show results based on cosine similarity and feature combinations (Table 2).

Feat.	Name	Type	AUC
-	Random	baseline	.50
1	V-NN	cosine	.75
2	V-Phrase	cosine	.70
3	NN-Phrase	cosine	.68
4	V	rating	.53
5	NN	rating	**.78**
6	Phrase	rating	.71
Comb	1+2+3	cosine	.75
Comb	4+5+6	rating	.74
Comb	all(1-6)	mixed	.80
Comb	1+5+6	best	**.84**

Table 2: AUC Score single features and combinations. Classifying literal and metaphorical phrases based on the Saif M. Mohammad and Turney (2016) dataset.

As shown in Table 2, the rating of the verb alone (AUC=.53) provides almost no useful information. The best performance based on a single feature is the abstractness value of the noun (.78) followed by the cosine between verb and noun vector representation (.75). The phrase rating alone performs moderate (.71). However when combining features we found that the best combinations are obtained by integrating the phrase rating. In more detail, combining noun and phrase rating (5+6) obtains a AUC of (.80). When adding the cosine (1) we obtain the best score of (.84). For comparison, the verb plus noun ratings (4+5) obtains a lower score (.72), this shows that the phrase rating provides complementary and useful information.

2.3 Sense-specific Abstractness Ratings

In this section we investigate if automatically learned multi-sense abstractness ratings, that is having different ratings per word sense, are potentially useful for the task of metaphor detection.

Recent advances in word representation learning led to the development of algorithms for non-parametric and unsupervised multi-sense representation learning (Neelakantan et al., 2014; Liu et al., 2015; Li and Jurafsky, 2015; Bartunov et al., 2016). Using these techniques one can learn a different vector representation per word sense. Such representations can be combined with our abstractness learning method from section 2.1.1.

While in theory any multi-sense learning technique can be applied, we decided for the one introduced by Pelevina et al. (2016), as it performs sense learning after single senses have been learned. Starting from the public W2V300 representations we apply the multi-sense learning technique using the default settings and learn sense-specific word representations. Finally we propagate abstractness to every newly created sense representation by using the exact same model and training data as in Section 1. For a given word in a sentence we can now disambiguate the word sense by comparing its sense-specific vector representation to all context words. The context words are represented using the (single sense) global representation. We always pick the sense representation that obtains the largest similarity, measured by cosine. The potential advantage of this method is that in a metaphor detection system we are now able to look up word-sense-specific abstractness ratings instead of globally obtained ratings.

For this experiment we use the VU Amsterdam Metaphor Corpus (Steen, 2010) (VUA), focusing on verb metaphors. The collection contains 23 113 verb tokens in running text, annotated as being used literally or metaphorically. In addition we present results for the TroFi metaphor dataset (Birke and Sarkar, 2006) containing 50 verbs and 3 737 labeled sentences. We pre-processed both recourses using *Stanford CoreNLP* (Manning et al., 2014) for lemmatization, part-of-speech tagging and dependency parsing.

We present results by applying ten-fold cross-validation over the entire data. For the VUA we additionally present results for the test data using the same training/test split as in Beigman Klebanov et al. (2016).

Abstractness norms are implemented using the same five feature dimensions as used by Turney et al. (2011) plus dimensions respectively for subject and object, thus we rely on the seven feature, namely:

1. Rating of the verbs subject

2. Rating of the verbs object

3. Average rating of all nouns (excluding proper names)

4. Average rating of all proper names

5. Average rating of all verbs, excluding the target verb

6. Average rating of all adjectives

7. Average rating of all adverbs

For classification we used a balanced Logistic Regression classifier following the findings from Beigman Klebanov et al. (2015). While this default setup tries to generalize over unseen verbs by only looking at a verb's context we further present results for a second setup that uses a 6th feature: namely the lemma of the target verb itself (+L). The purpose of the second system is to describe performance with respect to the state of the art (Beigman Klebanov et al., 2016), which among other features also uses the verb lemma.

Feat.	TroFi(10F)	VUA(10F)	VUA(Test)
1S	.72	.42	.44
MS	**.74**	**.44***	**.46**
1S(+L)	.74	**.61**	**.62**
MS(+L)	**.75**	**.61**	**.62**

Table 3: F-score (Metaphor). Classifying literal and metaphorical verbs based on the VUA and TroFi dataset. MS = multi-sense, 1S = single sense.

As shown in Table 3, the mutli-sense ratings constantly outperform the single-sense ratings in a direct comparison on all three sets. The difference in performance of single and multi-sense ratings is statistically significant on the full VUA dataset, using the χ^2 test and $*$ for $p < 0.05$. However we also notice that the effect vanishes as soon as we combine the ratings with the lemma of the verb, which is especially the case for the VUA dataset where the lemma increases the performance by a large margin. In contrast to related work, the system with the verb unigram (+UL) can be considered state-of-the-art. When applying the same evaluation as Beigman Klebanov et al. (2016), namely a macro-average over the four genres of VUA, we obtain an average f-score of .60 by using only eight feature dimensions and abstractness ratings as external resource.[4]

3 Conclusion

In this paper we compared supervised methods to propagate abstractness norms to words. We showed that a neural-network outperforms other methods. In addition we showed that norms for multi-words phrases can be beneficial for type based metaphor detection. Finally we showed how norms can be learned for sense representations and that sense specific norms show a clear tendency to improve token-based verb metaphor detection.

Acknowledgments

The research was supported by the DFG Collaborative Research Centre SFB 732 (Maximilian Köper) and the DFG Heisenberg Fellowship SCHU-2580/1 (Sabine Schulte im Walde).

References

Lawrence W Barsalou and Katja Wiemer-Hastings. 2005. Situating Abstract Concepts. *Grounding cognition: The role of perception and action in memory, language, and thought*, pages 129–163.

Sergey Bartunov, Dmitry Kondrashkin, Anton Osokin, and Dmitry Vetrov. 2016. Breaking Sticks and Ambiguities with Adaptive Skip-gram. In *Proceedings of the International Conference on Artificial Intelligence and Statistics*, pages 130–138, Cadiz, Spain.

Beata Beigman Klebanov, Chee Wee Leong, and Michael Flor. 2015. Supervised Word-level Metaphor Detection: Experiments with Concreteness and Reweighting of Examples. In *Proceedings of the Third Workshop on Metaphor in NLP*, pages 11–20, Denver, Colorado.

Beata Beigman Klebanov, Chee Wee Leong, E. Dario Gutierrez, Ekaterina Shutova, and Michael Flor. 2016. Semantic Classifications for Detection of Verb Metaphors. In *Proceedings of the h Annual Meeting of the Association for Computational Linguistics*, pages 101–106, Berlin, Germany.

Julia Birke and Anoop Sarkar. 2006. A Clustering Approach for the Nearly Unsupervised Recognition of Nonliteral Language. In *Proceedings of the 11th Conference of the European Chapter of the ACL*, pages 329–336, Trento, Italy.

Marc Brysbaert, AmyBeth Warriner, and Victor Kuperman. 2014. Concreteness Ratings for 40 Thousand Generally known English Word Lemmas. *Behavior Research Methods*, pages 904–911.

Max Coltheart. 1981. The MRC psycholinguistic database. *The Quarterly Journal of Experimental Psychology Section A*, 33(4):497–505.

Erik-Lân Do Dinh and Iryna Gurevych. 2016. Token-Level Metaphor Detection using Neural Networks. In *Proceedings of The Fourth Workshop on Metaphor in NLP*, pages 28–33, San Diego, CA, USA.

Jonathan Dunn. 2013. What Metaphor Identification Systems can tell us About Metaphor-in-language. In *Proceedings of the First Workshop on Metaphor in NLP*, pages 1–10, Atlanta, Georgia.

Jonathan Dunn. 2015. Modeling Abstractness and Metaphoricity. *Metaphor and Symbol*, pages 259–289.

Christiane Fellbaum. 1998. A Semantic Network of English Verbs. In Christiane Fellbaum, editor, *WordNet – An Electronic Lexical Database*, Language, Speech, and Communication. MIT Press, Cambridge, MA.

Abhijeet Gupta, Gemma Boleda, Marco Baroni, and Sebastian Padó. 2015. Distributional Vectors Encode Referential Attributes. In *Proceedings of Conference on Empirical Methods in Natural Language Processing*, pages 12–21, Lisbon, Portugal.

Hessel Haagsma and Johannes Bjerva. 2016. Detecting Novel Metaphor using Selectional Preference Information. In *Proceedings of The Fourth Workshop on Metaphor in NLP*, pages 10–17, San Diego, CA, USA.

Ilana Heintz, Ryan Gabbard, Mahesh Srivastava, Dave Barner, Donald Black, Majorie Friedman, and Ralph Weischedel. 2013. Automatic Extraction of Linguistic Metaphors with LDA Topic Modeling. In *Proceedings of the First Workshop on Metaphor in NLP*, pages 58–66, Atlanta, Georgia.

Felix Hill, Anna Korhonen, and Christian Bentz. 2014. A Quantitative Empirical Analysis of the Abstract/Concrete Distinction. *Cognitive Science*, 38:162–177.

Richard Kammann and Lynn Streeter. 1971. Two Meanings of Word Abstractness. *Journal of Verbal Learning and Verbal Behavior*, 10(3):303 – 306.

Maximilian Köper and Sabine Schulte im Walde. 2016a. Automatically Generated Affective Norms of Abstractness, Arousal, Imageability and Valence for 350 000 German Lemmas. In *Proceedings of the 10th International Conference on Language Resources and Evaluation*, pages 2595–2598, Portoroz, Slovenia.

---

[4]SOA results from Klebanov obtain also a score of .60

Maximilian Köper and Sabine Schulte im Walde. 2016b. Distinguishing Literal and Non-Literal Usage of German Particle Verbs. In *Proceedings of the Conference of the North American Chapter of the Association for Computational Linguistics: Human Language Technologies*, pages 353–362, San Diego, California.

George Lakoff and Mark Johnson. 1980. *Metaphors we live by*. University of Chicago Press.

Jiwei Li and Dan Jurafsky. 2015. Do Multi-Sense Embeddings Improve Natural Language Understanding? In *Proceedings of the Conference on Empirical Methods in Natural Language Processing*, pages 1722–1732, Lisbon, Portugal.

Linlin Li and Caroline Sporleder. 2009. Classifier Combination for Contextual Idiom Detection Without Labelled Data. In *Proceedings of the Conference on Empirical Methods in Natural Language Processing*, pages 315–323.

Linlin Li and Caroline Sporleder. 2010. Using Gaussian Mixture Models to Detect Figurative Language in Context. In *Proceedings of the Annual Conference of the North American Chapter of the Association for Computational Linguistics*, pages 297–300.

Pengfei Liu, Xipeng Qiu, and Xuanjing Huang. 2015. Learning Context-Sensitive Word Embeddings with Neural Tensor Skip-Gram Model. In *Proceedings of the Twenty-Fourth International Joint Conference on Artificial Intelligence*, pages 1284–1290, Buenos Aires, Argentina.

Christopher D. Manning, Mihai Surdeanu, John Bauer, Jenny Finkel, Steven J. Bethard, and David McClosky. 2014. The Stanford CoreNLP Natural Language Processing Toolkit. In *Proceedings of the Association for Computational Linguistics (ACL) System Demonstrations*, pages 55–60.

James H. Martin. 1996. Computational Approaches to Figurative Language. *Metaphor and Symbolic Activity*.

Tomas Mikolov, Ilya Sutskever, Kai Chen, Greg S Corrado, and Jeff Dean. 2013. Distributed Representations of Words and Phrases and their Compositionality. In C.J.C. Burges, L. Bottou, M. Welling, Z. Ghahramani, and K.Q. Weinberger, editors, *Advances in Neural Information Processing Systems 26*, pages 3111–3119.

Arvind Neelakantan, Jeevan Shankar, Alexandre Passos, and Andrew McCallum. 2014. Efficient Non-parametric Estimation of Multiple Embeddings per Word in Vector Space. In *Proceedings of the Conference on Empirical Methods in Natural Language Processing*, pages 1059–1069, Doha, Qatar.

Maria Pelevina, Nikolay Arefiev, Chris Biemann, and Alexander Panchenko. 2016. Making Sense of Word Embeddings. In *Proceedings of the 1st Workshop on Representation Learning for NLP*, pages 174–183, Berlin, Germany, August.

Jeffrey Pennington, Richard Socher, and Christopher D. Manning. 2014. Glove: Global Vectors for Word Representation. In *Proceedings of Conference on Empirical Methods in Natural Language Processing*, pages 1532–1543, Doha, Qatar.

Ekaterina Shutova Saif M. Mohammad and Peter D. Turney. 2016. Metaphor as a Medium for Emotion: An Empirical Study. In *Proceedings of the Fifth Joint Conference on Lexical and Computational Semantics (*Sem)*, pages 23–33, Berlin, Germany.

Roland Schäfer and Felix Bildhauer. 2012. Building Large Corpora from the Web Using a New Efficient Tool Chain. In *Proceedings of the 8th International Conference on Language Resources and Evaluation*, pages 486–493, Istanbul, Turkey.

Roland Schäfer. 2015. Processing and Querying Large Web Corpora with the COW14 Architecture. In Piotr Bański, Hanno Biber, Evelyn Breiteneder, Marc Kupietz, Harald Lüngen, and Andreas Witt, editors, *Proceedings of the 3rd Workshop on Challenges in the Management of Large Corpora*, pages 28–24, Lancaster.

Ekaterina Shutova and Simone Teufel. 2010. Metaphor Corpus Annotated for Source - Target Domain Mappings. In *Proceedings of the International Conference on Language Resources and Evaluation*, pages 3225–3261, Valletta, Malta.

Ekaterina Shutova, Lin Sun, and Anna Korhonen. 2010. Metaphor Identification Using Verb and Noun Clustering. In *Proceedings of the 23rd International Conference on Computational Linguistics*, pages 1002–1010.

Ekaterina Shutova, Douwe Kiela, and Jean Maillard. 2016. Black Holes and White Rabbits: Metaphor Identification with Visual Features. In *Proceedings of the Conference of the North American Chapter of the Association for Computational Linguistics: Human Language Technologies*, pages 160–170.

G. Steen. 2010. *A Method for Linguistic Metaphor Identification: From MIP to MIPVU*. Converging Evidence in Language and Communication Research. John Benjamins Publishing Company.

James H Steiger. 1980. Tests for Comparing Elements of a Correlation Matrix. *Psychological Bulletin*.

Yulia Tsvetkov, Elena Mukomel, and Anatole Gershman. 2013. Cross-lingual Metaphor Detection Using Common Semantic Features. In *Proceedings of the Workshop on Metaphor in NLP*, pages 45–51, Atlanta, USA.

Yulia Tsvetkov, Leonid Boytsov, Anatole Gershman, Eric Nyberg, and Chris Dyer. 2014. Metaphor Detection with Cross-Lingual Model Transfer. In *Proceedings of the 52nd Annual Meeting of the Association for Computational Linguistics*, pages 248–258.

Peter D. Turney and Michael L. Littman. 2003. Measuring Praise and Criticism: Inference of Semantic Orientation from Association. *ACM Transactions on Information Systems*, pages 315–346.

Peter Turney, Yair Neuman, Dan Assaf, and Yohai Cohen. 2011. Literal and Metaphorical Sense Identification through Concrete and Abstract Context. In *Proceedings of the Conference on Empirical Methods in Natural Language Processing*, pages 680–690, Edinburgh, UK.

Gabriella Vigliocco, Stavroula-Thaleia Kousta, Pasquale Anthony Della Rosa, David P Vinson, Marco Tettamanti, Joseph T Devlin, and Stefano F Cappa. 2014. The Neural Representation of Abstract Words: the Role of Emotion. *Cerebral Cortex*, pages 1767–1777.

Improving Clinical Diagnosis Inference through Integration of Structured and Unstructured Knowledge

Yuan Ling, Yuan An
College of Computing & Informatics
Drexel University
Philadelphia, PA, USA
{yl638,ya45}@drexel.edu

Sadid A. Hasan
Artificial Intelligence Laboratory
Philips Research North America
Cambridge, MA, USA
sadid.hasan@philips.com

Abstract

This paper presents a novel approach to the task of automatically inferring the most probable diagnosis from a given clinical narrative. Structured Knowledge Bases (KBs) can be useful for such complex tasks but not sufficient. Hence, we leverage a vast amount of unstructured free text to integrate with structured KBs. The key innovative ideas include building a concept graph from both structured and unstructured knowledge sources and ranking the diagnosis concepts using the enhanced word embedding vectors learned from integrated sources. Experiments on the TREC CDS and HumanDx datasets showed that our methods improved the results of clinical diagnosis inference.

1 Introduction and Related Work

Clinical diagnosis inference is the problem of automatically inferring the most probable diagnosis from a given clinical narrative. Many health-related information retrieval tasks can greatly benefit from the accurate results of clinical diagnosis inference. For example, in recent Text REtrieval Conference (TREC) Clinical Decision Support track (CDS[1]), diagnosis inference from medical narratives has improved the accuracy of retrieving relevant biomedical articles (Roberts et al., 2015; Hasan et al., 2015; Goodwin and Harabagiu, 2016).

Solutions to the clinical diagnostic inferencing problem require a significant amount of inputs from domain experts and a variety of sources (Ferrucci et al., 2013; Lally et al., 2014). To address such complex inference tasks, researchers (Yao and Van Durme, 2014; Bao et al., 2014; Dong et al., 2015) have utilized structured KBs

that store relevant information about various entity types and relation triples. Many large-scale KBs have been constructed over the years, such as WordNet (Miller, 1995), Yago (Suchanek et al., 2007), Freebase (Bollacker et al., 2008), DBpedia (Auer et al., 2007), NELL (Carlson et al., 2010), UMLS Metathesaurus (Bodenreider, 2004) etc. However, using KBs alone for inference tasks (Bordes et al., 2014) has certain limitations such as incompleteness of knowledge, sparsity, and fixed schema (Socher et al., 2013; West et al., 2014).

On the other hand, unstructured textual resources such as free texts from Wikipedia generally contain more information than structured KBs. As a supplementary knowledge to mitigate the limitations of structured KBs, unstructured text combined with structured KBs provides improved results for related tasks, for example, clinical question answering (Miller et al., 2016). For processing text, word embedding models (e.g. skip-gram model (Mikolov et al., 2013b; Mikolov et al., 2013a)) can efficiently discover and represent the underlying patterns of unstructured text. Word embedding models represent words and their relationships as continuous vectors. To improve word embedding models, previous works have also successfully leveraged structured KBs (Bordes et al., 2011; Weston et al., 2013; Wang et al., 2014; Zhou et al., 2015; Liu et al., 2015).

Motivated by the superior power of the integration of structured KBs and unstructured free text, we propose a novel approach to clinical diagnosis inference. The novelty lies in the ways of integrating structured KBs with unstructured text. Experiments showed that our methods improved clinical diagnosis inference from different aspects (Section 5.4). Previous work on diagnosis inference from clinical narratives either formulates the problem as a medical literature retrieval task (Zheng and Wan, 2016; Balaneshin-kordan and Kotov, 2016) or as a multiclass multilabel classi-

[1]http://www.trec-cds.org/

Proceedings of the 1st Workshop on Sense, Concept and Entity Representations and their Applications, pages 31–36,
Valencia, Spain, April 4 2017. ©2017 Association for Computational Linguistics

fication problem in a supervised setting (Hasan et al., 2016; Prakash et al., 2016). To the best of our knowledge, there is no work on diagnoses inference from clinical narratives conducted in an unsupervised way. Thus, we build such baselines for this task.

2 Overview of the Approach

Our approach includes four steps in general: 1) extracting source concepts, q, from clinical narratives, 2) iteratively identifying corresponding evidence concepts, a, from KBs and unstructured text, 3) representing both source and evidence concepts in a weighted graph via a regularizer-enhanced skip-gram model, and 4) ranking the relevant evidence concepts (i.e. diagnoses) based on their association with the source concepts, $S(q, a)$ (computed by weighted dot product of two vectors), to generate the final output. Figure 1 shows the overview using an illustrative example.

Given source concepts as input, we build an edge-weighted graph representing the connections among all the concepts by iteratively retrieving evidence concepts from both KBs and unstructured text. The weights of the edges represent the strengths of the relationships between concepts. Each concept is represented as a word embedding vector. We combine all the source concept vectors into a single vector representing a clinical scenario. Source concepts are differentiated according to the weighting scheme in Section 4.2. Evidence concepts are also represented as vectors and ranked according to their relevance to the source concepts. For each clinical case, we find the most probable diagnoses from the top-ranked evidence concepts.

3 Knowledge Sources of Evidence Concepts

In this study, we use UMLS Metathesaurus (Bodenreider, 2004) and Freebase (Bollacker et al., 2008) as the structured KBs. Both KBs provide semantic relation triples in the following format: <concept1, relation, concept2>. We select UMLS relation types that are relevant to the problem of clinical diagnosis inference. These types include disease-treatment, disease-prevention, disease-finding, sign or symptom, causes etc. Freebase contains a large number of triples from multiple domains. We select 61,243 triples from freebase that are classified as

medicine relation types. There are 19 such relation types in total. Most of them fall under the "medicine.disease" category.

For unstructured text, we use articles from Wikipedia and MayoClinic corpus as the supplementary knowledge source. Important clinical concepts mentioned in a Wikipedia/MayoClinic page can serve as a critical clue to a clinical diagnosis. For example, in Figure 1, we see that "dyspnea", "shortness of breath", "tachypnea" etc. are the related signs and symptoms of the "Pulmonary Embolism" diagnosis. We select 37,245 Wikipedia pages under the clinical diseases and medicine category in this study. Most of the page titles represent disease names. In addition, MayoClinic[2] disease corpus contains 1,117 pages, which include sections of Symptoms, Causes, Risk Factors, Treatments and Drugs, Prevention, etc.

4 Methodology

4.1 Building Weighted Concept Graph

Both the source and the evidence concepts are represented as nodes in a graph. A clinical case is represented as a set of source concept nodes: $q = \{q_1, q_2, \ldots\}$. We build a weighted concept graph from source concepts using Algorithm 1.

Algorithm 1: Build Concept Graph

```
Input  : source concept nodes q
Output : graph G = (V, E)
1  S = q and V = q;
2  while S ≠ ∅ do
3  |   for each q_i in S do
4  |   |   if distance(q_i, q) > 2 then
5  |   |   |   continue;
6  |   |   end
7  |   |   if triple < q_i, r, a_j > in KBs then
8  |   |   |   w_ij = 1;
9  |   |   |   e = (q_i, a_j) and e.value = w_ij;
10 |   |   |   insert a_j to V and S;
11 |   |   |   insert e to E;
12 |   |   end
13 |   |   Use q_i as query, search in Unstructured Text Corpora, get
   |   |     Result R;
14 |   |   for each page-similarity pair (p, s_ij) in R do
15 |   |   |   e = (q_i, title(p)) and e.value = s_ij;
16 |   |   |   insert title(p) to V and S;
17 |   |   |   insert e to E;
18 |   |   end
19 |   |   remove q_i from S;
20 |   end
21 end
```

Two kinds of evidence concept nodes are added to the graph: 1) the entities from KBs (UMLS and Freebase) (step 7-12 in Algorithm 1), and 2) the entities from unstructured text pages (step 13-18). If there exists a triple $< q_i, r, a_j >$ in KBs, where

---

[2]http://www.mayoclinic.org/diseases-conditions

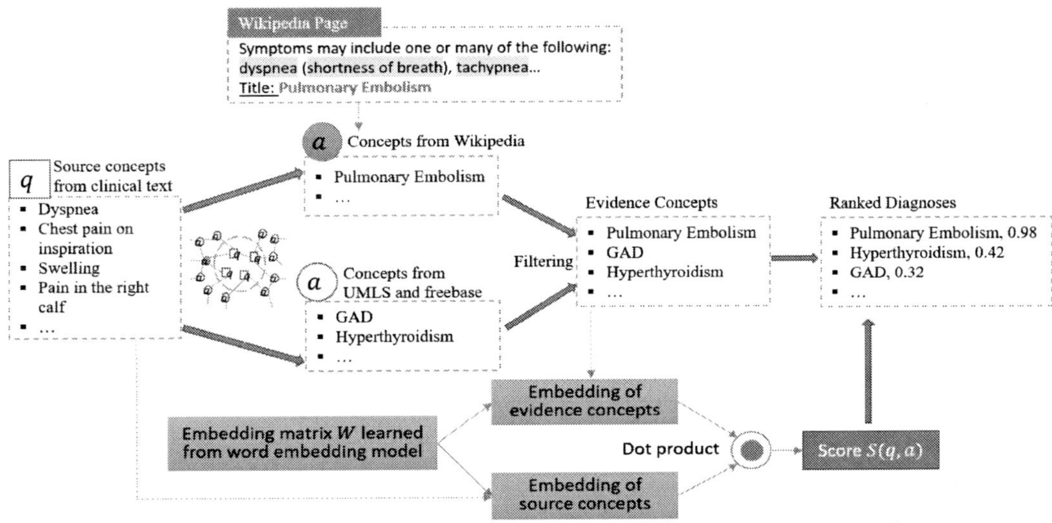

Figure 1: Overview of our system.

r refers to a relation, an edge is used to connect node q_i and node a_j. w_{ij} represents the weight for that edge, and let $w_{ij} = 1$, if the corresponding triple occurs at least once. Due to the incompleteness of the KBs, there may exist multiple missing connections between a potential evidence concept a_j and a source concept q_i. Unstructured knowledge from Wikipedia and MayoClinic can replenish these missing connections. For each page p, the page title represents an evidence concept a_j. We use each source concept q_i as a query, and page p as a document, and then calculate a query-document similarity to measure the edge weight w_{ij} between node a_j and node q_i. We only take evidence concepts as all nodes connected to source concepts in a distance of at most 2 (step 4-6).

4.2 Representing Clinical Case

We combine the source concepts q and get a single vector v_q to represent the clinical case narrative. The source concepts from narratives for clinical diagnosis inference should be differentiated. Some source concepts are major symptoms for a diagnosis, while others are less critical. These major source concepts should be identified and given higher weight values. We develop two kinds of weighting schema for the differential expression of the source concepts. The source concept is represented as $v_q = \frac{1}{N} \sum_{q_i \in q} \gamma_i v_{q_i}$. N is the total number of source concepts. v_{q_i} is the vector representation for one source concept q_i.

(1) A longer concept usually convey more information (e.g. *malar rash* vs. *rash*), so it should be given more weights. We define this weight value as $\gamma_1 = \#Words\,in\,Concept$.

(2) For some commonly seen concepts (e.g. *fever*), usually, there are more edges connected to them. Sometimes, a common concept is less important for diagnosis inference, while some unique concepts are critical to infer a specific diagnosis. We define this weight value for each concept as $\gamma_2 = \frac{1}{\#Connected\,Edges}$. A higher weight value means the source concept is more unique.

4.3 Inferring Concepts for Diagnosis

Extracting Potential Evidence Concepts: From source concept nodes q, we find their connected concepts in the graph as evidence concepts. Traversing all edges in a graph is computationally expensive and often unnecessary for finding potential diagnoses. The solution is to use a subgraph. We follow the idea proposed in Bordes et al. (2014). The evidence concepts are defined as all nodes connected to source concepts in a distance of at most 2.

Ranking Evidence Concepts: We rank each evidence concept a' according to its matching score $S(q, a')$ to the source concepts. The matching score $S(q, a')$ is a dot product of embedding representation of the evidence concept a' and the source concept q by taking the edge weights w_{ij} into consideration. $S(q, a') = w_{ij}v_{a'} \cdot v_q$. $v_{a'}$ and

v_q are embedding representations for a' and q. The embedding $E \in R^{k \times N}$ for concepts are trained using embedding models (Section 4.4). N is the total number of concepts and k is the predefined dimensions for the embedding vector. Each concept in the graph can find a k dimensional vector representation in E. For a set of source concepts and evidence concepts $A(q)$, the top-ranked evidence concept can be computed as:

$$a = argmax_{(a' \in A(q))} S(q, a') \qquad (1)$$

4.4 Word Embedding Models

We use the skip-gram model as the basic model. The skip-gram model predicts surrounding words $w_{t-c}, \ldots, w_{t-1}, w_{t+1}, \ldots, w_{t+c}$ given the current center word w_t. We further enhance the skip-gram model by adding a graph regularizer. Given a sequence of training words $w_1, w_2, \ldots, w_T$, the objective function is:

$$J = \max \frac{1}{T} \sum_{t=1}^{T} (1-\lambda) \sum_{-c \le j \le c, j \ne 0} \log p(w_{t+j}|w_t) - \lambda \sum_{r=1}^{R} D(v_t, v_r),$$

$$(2)$$

where v_t and v_r are the representation vectors for word w_t and word w_r. λ is a parameter to leverage the graph regularizer and original objective. Suppose, word w_t is mentioned having relations with a set of other words $w_r, r \in \{1, \ldots, R\}$ in KBs. The graph regularizer $\lambda \sum_{r=1}^{R} D(v_t, v_r)$ integrates extra knowledge about semantic relationships among words within the graph structure. $D(v_t, v_r)$ represents the distance between v_t and v_r. In our experiments, the distance between two concepts is measured using KL-Divergence. $D(v_t, v_r)$ can be calculated using any other types of distance metrics. By minimizing $D(v_t, v_r)$, we expect if two concepts have a close relation in KBs, their vector representations will also be close to each other.

5 Experiments

5.1 Datasets for Clinical Diagnosis Inference

Our first dataset is from the 2015 TREC CDS track (Roberts et al., 2015). It contains 30 topics, where each topic is a medical case narrative that describes a patient scenario. Each case is associated with the ground truth diagnosis. We use MetaMap[3] to extract the source concepts from a narrative and then manually refine them to remove redundancy.

Our second dataset is curated from HumanDx[4], a project to foster integrating efforts to map health problems to their possible diagnoses. We curate diagnosis-findings relationships from HumanDx and create a dataset with 459 diagnosis-findings entries. Note that, the findings from this dataset are used as the given source concepts for a clinical scenario.

5.2 Training Data for Word Embeddings

We curate a biomedical corpus of around 5M sentences from two data sources: PubMed Central[5] from the 2015 TREC CDS snapshot[6] and Wikipedia articles under the "Clinical Medicine" category[7]. After sentence splitting, word tokenization, and stop words removal, we train our word embedding models on this corpus. UMLS Metathesaurus and Freebase are used as KBs to train the graph regularizer. We use stochastic gradient descent (SGD) to maximize the objective function and set the parameters empirically.

5.3 Results

We use Mean Reciprocal Rank (MRR) and Average Precision at 5 (P@5) to evaluate our models. MRR is a statistical measure to evaluate a process that generates a list of possible responses to a sample of queries, ordered by probability of correctness. Average P@5 is calculated as precision at top 5 predicted results divided by the total number of topics. Since our dataset only has one correct diagnosis for each topic, all results have poor Average P@5 scores.

Table 1 presents the results for our experiments. We report two baselines: *Skip-gram* refers to the basic word embedding model, and *Skip-gram** refers to the graph-regularized model using KBs. We also show the results for using different unstructured knowledge sources and different weighting schema. We can see that the best scores are obtained by the graph-regularized models with both the unstructured knowledge sources with variable weighting schema (Section 4.2).

5.4 Discussion

Unstructured text is a critical supplement: We analyze the source concepts and the corresponding evidence concepts for CDS topics, and investigate

---

[3]https://metamap.nlm.nih.gov/

[4]https://www.humandx.org/
[5]https://www.ncbi.nlm.nih.gov/pmc/
[6]http://www.trec-cds.org/2015.html#documents
[7]https://en.wikipedia.org/wiki/Category:Clinical_medicine

	TREC CDS		HumanDx	
Method	**MRR**	**Average P@5**	**MRR**	**Average P@5**
Baselines				
Skip-gram	21.66	8.88	18.56	5.08
Skip-gram*	22.60	8.88	18.63	5.15
Skip-gram* + Different Unstructured Text Datasets				
Wikipedia	26.01	8.96	19.42	5.76
MayoClinic	32.64	9.52	19.46	5.80
Both	32.29	9.60	19.12	5.76
Skip-gram* + Both Text Datasets + Different Weights				
γ_1	32.22	10.40	**21.09**	5.88
γ_2	**32.77**	**12.00**	20.86	**5.93**

Table 1: Evaluation results.

the origin of the correct diagnoses. 70% of the correct diagnoses can be inferred from Wikipedia, 60% of the correct diagnoses from MayoClinic, 56% of the correct diagnoses from Freebase, and only 7% are from UMLS. Hence, Wikipedia and MayoClinic are very important sources for finding the correct diagnoses.

Source concepts should be differentiated: In clinical narratives, some concepts are more critical than others for the clinical diagnosis inference. We developed two weighting schema to assign higher weight values to more important concepts. The results in Table 1 show that differentiating the source concepts with different weight values has a large impact on the model performance.

Enhanced skip-gram is better: We propose the enhanced skip-gram model by using a graph regularizer to integrate the semantic relationships among concepts from KBs. Experimental results show that diagnosis inference is improved by using word embedding representations from the enhanced skip-gram model.

6 Conclusion

We proposed a novel approach to the task of clinical diagnosis inference from clinical narratives. Our method overcomes the limitations of structured KBs by making use of the integrated structured and unstructured knowledge. Experimental results showed that the enhanced skip-gram model with differential expression of source concepts improved the performance on two benchmark datasets.

References

Sören Auer, Christian Bizer, Georgi Kobilarov, Jens Lehmann, Richard Cyganiak, and Zachary Ives. 2007. Dbpedia: A nucleus for a web of open data. In *The semantic web*, pages 722–735. Springer.

Saeid Balaneshin-kordan and Alexander Kotov. 2016. Optimization method for weighting explicit and latent concepts in clinical decision support queries. In *Proceedings of the 2016 ACM on International Conference on the Theory of Information Retrieval*, pages 241–250. ACM.

Junwei Bao, Nan Duan, Ming Zhou, and Tiejun Zhao. 2014. Knowledge-based question answering as machine translation. *Cell*, 2(6).

Olivier Bodenreider. 2004. The unified medical language system (umls): integrating biomedical terminology. *Nucleic acids research*, 32(suppl 1):D267–D270.

Kurt Bollacker, Colin Evans, Praveen Paritosh, Tim Sturge, and Jamie Taylor. 2008. Freebase: a collaboratively created graph database for structuring human knowledge. In *Proceedings of the 2008 ACM SIGMOD international conference on Management of data*, pages 1247–1250. ACM.

Antoine Bordes, Jason Weston, Ronan Collobert, and Yoshua Bengio. 2011. Learning structured embeddings of knowledge bases. In *Conference on artificial intelligence*.

Antoine Bordes, Sumit Chopra, and Jason Weston. 2014. Question answering with subgraph embeddings. *arXiv preprint arXiv:1406.3676*.

Andrew Carlson, Justin Betteridge, Bryan Kisiel, Burr Settles, Estevam R Hruschka Jr, and Tom M Mitchell. 2010. Toward an architecture for never-ending language learning. In *AAAI*, volume 5, page 3.

Li Dong, Furu Wei, Ming Zhou, and Ke Xu. 2015. Question answering over freebase with multi-column convolutional neural networks. In *Proceedings of Association for Computational Linguistics*, pages 260–269.

David Ferrucci, Anthony Levas, Sugato Bagchi, David Gondek, and Erik T Mueller. 2013. Watson: beyond jeopardy! *Artificial Intelligence*, 199:93–105.

Travis R. Goodwin and Sanda M. Harabagiu. 2016. Medical question answering for clinical decision support. In *Proceedings of the 25th ACM International on Conference on Information and Knowledge Management*, pages 297–306. ACM.

Sadid A. Hasan, Yuan Ling, Joey Liu, and Oladimeji Farri. 2015. Using neural embeddings for diagnostic inferencing in clinical question answering. In *TREC*.

Sadid A. Hasan, Siyuan Zhao, Vivek Datla, Joey Liu, Kathy Lee, Ashequl Qadir, Aaditya Prakash, and Oladimeji Farri. 2016. Clinical question answering using key-value memory networks and knowledge graph. In *TREC*.

Adam Lally, Sugato Bachi, Michael A. Barborak, David W. Buchanan, Jennifer Chu-Carroll, David A. Ferrucci, Michael R. Glass, Aditya Kalyanpur, Erik T. Mueller, J. William Murdock, et al. 2014. Watsonpaths: scenario-based question answering and inference over unstructured information. *Yorktown Heights: IBM Research*.

Quan Liu, Hui Jiang, Si Wei, Zhen-Hua Ling, and Yu Hu. 2015. Learning semantic word embeddings based on ordinal knowledge constraints. In *Proceedings of the 53rd Annual Meeting of the Association for Computational Linguistics and the 7th International Joint Conference on Natural Language Processing (ACL-IJCNLP)*, pages 1501–1511.

Tomas Mikolov, Kai Chen, Greg Corrado, and Jeffrey Dean. 2013a. Efficient estimation of word representations in vector space. *arXiv preprint arXiv:1301.3781*.

Tomas Mikolov, Ilya Sutskever, Kai Chen, Greg S. Corrado, and Jeff Dean. 2013b. Distributed representations of words and phrases and their compositionality. In *Advances in neural information processing systems*, pages 3111–3119.

Alexander Miller, Adam Fisch, Jesse Dodge, Amir-Hossein Karimi, Antoine Bordes, and Jason Weston. 2016. Key-value memory networks for directly reading documents. *CoRR*, abs/1606.03126.

George A. Miller. 1995. Wordnet: a lexical database for english. *Communications of the ACM*, 38(11):39–41.

Aaditya Prakash, Siyuan Zhao, Sadid A. Hasan, Vivek Datla, Kathy Lee, Ashequl Qadir, Joey Liu, and Oladimeji Farri. 2016. Condensed memory networks for clinical diagnostic inferencing. *arXiv preprint arXiv:1612.01848*.

Kirk Roberts, Matthew S. Simpson, Ellen Voorhees, and William R. Hersh. 2015. Overview of the trec 2015 clinical decision support track. In *TREC*.

Richard Socher, Danqi Chen, Christopher D. Manning, and Andrew Ng. 2013. Reasoning with neural tensor networks for knowledge base completion. In *Advances in Neural Information Processing Systems*, pages 926–934.

Fabian M. Suchanek, Gjergji Kasneci, and Gerhard Weikum. 2007. Yago: a core of semantic knowledge. In *Proceedings of the 16th international conference on World Wide Web*, pages 697–706. ACM.

Zhen Wang, Jianwen Zhang, Jianlin Feng, and Zheng Chen. 2014. Knowledge graph and text jointly embedding. In *EMNLP*, pages 1591–1601. Citeseer.

Robert West, Evgeniy Gabrilovich, Kevin Murphy, Shaohua Sun, Rahul Gupta, and Dekang Lin. 2014. Knowledge base completion via search-based question answering. In *Proceedings of the 23rd international conference on World wide web*, pages 515–526. ACM.

Jason Weston, Antoine Bordes, Oksana Yakhnenko, and Nicolas Usunier. 2013. Connecting language and knowledge bases with embedding models for relation extraction. *arXiv preprint arXiv:1307.7973*.

Xuchen Yao and Benjamin Van Durme. 2014. Information extraction over structured data: Question answering with freebase. In *ACL (1)*, pages 956–966. Citeseer.

Ziwei Zheng and Xiaojun Wan. 2016. Graph-based multi-modality learning for clinical decision support. In *Proceedings of the 25th ACM International on Conference on Information and Knowledge Management*, pages 1945–1948. ACM.

Guangyou Zhou, Tingting He, Jun Zhao, and Po Hu. 2015. Learning continuous word embedding with metadata for question retrieval in community question answering. In *Proceedings of ACL*, pages 250–259.

Classifying Lexical-semantic Relationships by Exploiting Sense/Concept Representations

Kentaro Kanada, Tetsunori Kobayashi and **Yoshihiko Hayashi**
Waseda University, Japan
kanada@pcl.cs.waseda.ac.jp
koba@waseda.jp
yshk.hayashi@aoni.waseda.jp

Abstract

This paper proposes a method for classifying the type of lexical-semantic relation between a given pair of words. Given an inventory of target relationships, this task can be seen as a multi-class classification problem. We train a supervised classifier by assuming that a specific type of lexical-semantic relation between a pair of words would be signaled by a carefully designed set of relation-specific similarities between the words. These similarities are computed by exploiting "sense representations" (sense/concept embeddings). The experimental results show that the proposed method clearly outperforms an existing state-of-the-art method that does not utilize sense/concept embeddings, thereby demonstrating the effectiveness of the sense representations.

1 Introduction

Given a pair of words, classifying the type of lexical-semantic relation that could hold between them may have a range of applications. In particular, discovering typed lexical-semantic relation instances is vital in building a new lexical-semantic resource, as well as for populating an existing lexical-semantic resource. As argued in (Boyd-Graber et al., 2006), even Princeton WordNet (henceforth PWN) (Miller, 1995) is noted for its sparsity of useful internal lexical-semantic relations. A distributional thesaurus (Weeds et al., 2014), usually built with an automatic method such as that described in (Rychlý and Kilgarriff, 2007), often comprises a disorganized semantic network internally, where a variety of lexical-semantic relations are incorporated without having proper relation labels attached. These issues could

be addressed if an accurate method for classifying the type of lexical-semantic relation is available.

A number of research studies on the classification of lexical-semantic relationships have been conducted. Among them, Necsuleşcu et al. (2015) recently presented two classification methods that utilize word-level feature representations including word embedding vectors. Although the reported results are superior to the compared systems, neither of the proposed methods exploited "sense representations," which are described as *the fine-grained representations of word senses, concepts, and entities* in the description of this workshop[1].

Motivated by the above-described issues and previous work, this paper proposes a supervised classification method that exploits sense representations, and discusses their utilities in the lexical relation classification task. The major rationales behind the proposed method are: (1) a specific type of lexical-semantic relation between a pair of words would be indicated by a carefully designed set of relation-specific similarities associated with the words; and (2) the similarities could be effectively computed by exploiting sense representations.

More specifically, for each word in the pair, we first collect relevant sets of sense/concept nodes (*node sets*) from an existing lexical-semantic resource (PWN), and then compute similarities for some designated pairs of node sets, where each node is represented by an embedding vector depending on its type (sense/concept). In terms of its design, each node set pair is constructed such that it is associated with a specific type of lexical-semantic relation. The resulting array of similarities, along with the underlying word/sense/concept embedding vectors is finally

---

[1] https://sites.google.com/site/
senseworkshop2017/background

Proceedings of the 1st Workshop on Sense, Concept and Entity Representations and their Applications, pages 37–46,
Valencia, Spain, April 4 2017. ©2017 Association for Computational Linguistics

fed into the classifier as features.

The empirical results that use the BLESS dataset (Baroni and Lenci, 2011) demonstrate that our method clearly outperformed existing state-of-the-art methods (Necsuleşcu et al., 2015) that did not employ sense/concept embeddings, confirming that properly combining the similarity features also with the underlying semantic/conceptual-level embeddings is indeed effective. These results in turn highlight the utility of "the sense representations" (the sense/concept embeddings) created by the existing system referred to as AutoExtend (Rothe and Schütze, 2015).

The remainder of the paper first reviews related work (section 2), and then presents our approach (section 3). As our experiments (section 4) utilize the BLESS dataset, the experimental results are directly compared with that of (Necsuleşcu et al., 2015) (section 5). Although our methods were proved to be superior through the experiments, our operational requirement (sense/concept embeddings should be created from the underlying lexical-semantic resource) could be problematic especially when having to process *unknown* words. We conclude the present paper by discussing future work to address this issue (section 6).

2 Related work

A lexical-semantic relationship is a fundamental relationship that plays an important role in many NLP applications. A number of research efforts have been devoted to developing an automated and accurate method to type the relationship between an arbitrary pair of words. Most of these studies (Fu et al., 2014; Kiela et al., 2015; Shwartz et al., 2016), however, concentrated on the *hypernymy* relation, since it is the most fundamental relationship that forms the core taxonomic structure in a lexical-semantic resource. In comparison, fewer studies considered a broader range of lexical-semantic relations, e.g., (Necsuleşcu et al., 2015) and our present work.

Lenci and Benotto (2012), among the hypernymy-centered researches, compared existing directional similarity measures (Kotlerman et al., 2010) to identify hypernyms, and proposed a new measure that slightly modified an existing measure. The rationale behind their work is: as hypernymy is a prominent asymmetric semantic relation, it might be detected by the higher similarity score yielded by an asymmetric similarity measure. Their idea of exploiting a specific type of similarity to detect a specific type of lexical-semantic relationship is highly feasible.

Recently, distributional and distributed word representations (word embeddings) have been widely utilized, partly because the offset vector simply brought about by vector subtraction over word embeddings can capture some relational aspects including a lexical-semantic relationship. Given these useful resources, Weeds et al. (2014) presented a supervised classification approach that employs a pair of distributional vectors for a given word pair as the feature, arguing that concatenation and subtraction were almost equally effective vector operations. Similar lines of work were presented by (Necsuleşcu et al., 2015) and (Vylomova et al., 2016): the former suggested concatenation might be slightly superior to subtraction, whereas the latter especially highlighted the subtraction. Here it should be noted that Necsuleşcu et al. (2015) employed two kinds of vectors: one is a CBOW-based vector (Mikolov et al., 2013b), and the other involves word embeddings with a dependency-based skip-gram model (Levy and Goldberg, 2014).

The present work exploits semantic/conceptual-level embeddings, which were actually derived by applying the AutoExtend (Rothe and Schütze, 2015) system. Among the recent proposals for deriving semantic/conceptual-level embeddings (Huang et al., 2012; Pennington et al., 2014; Neelakantan et al., 2014; Iacobacci et al., 2015), we adopt the AutoExtend system, since it elegantly exploits the network structure provided by an underlying semantic resource, and naturally consumes existing word embeddings. More importantly, the underlying word embeddings are directly comparable with the derived sense representations. In the present work, we applied the AutoExtend system to the Word2Vec CBOW embeddings (Mikolov et al., 2013b) by referring to PWN version 3.0 as the underlying lexical-semantic resource. As far as the authors know, AutoExtend-derived embeddings have been evaluated in the tasks of similarity measurements and word sense disambiguation: they are yet to be applied to a semantic relation classification task.

There are a few datasets (Baroni and Lenci, 2011; Santus et al., 2015) available that were prepared for the evaluation of lexical-semantic rela-

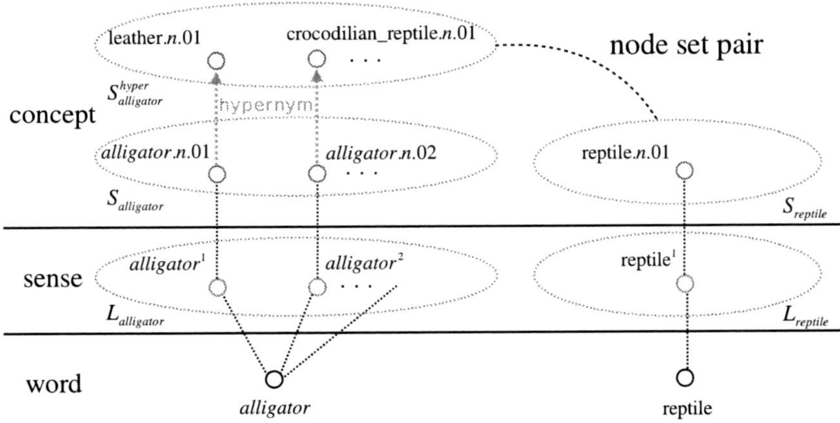

Figure 1: Creating node sets and node set pairs (in *hypernymy* relation).

tion classification tasks. We utilized the BLESS dataset (Baroni and Lenci, 2011) in order to directly compare our proposed method with the related methods given in (Necsuleşcu et al., 2015).

3 Proposed method

We adopt a supervised learning approach for classifying the type of semantic relationship between a pair of words (w_1, w_2), expecting that the plausibility of a specific semantic lexical-relationship can be measured by the similarity between the senses/concepts associated with each of the words.

Figure 1 exemplifies the fundamental rationale behind the proposed method. We assume that the plausibility of the *hypernymy* relation between "alligator" (w_1) and "reptile" (w_2) can be mainly measured by the similarity between the set of hypernym concepts of "alligator" $(S_{w_1}^{hyper})$ and the set of concepts of "reptile" (S_{w_2}). Based on this assumption, we calculate the similarities by the following steps. Recall that these similarities are assumed to measure the plausibilities of relationships that could hold between a given word pair.

1. Collect pre-defined types of node sets for each word (five types; detailed in section 3.1).

2. Build some useful pairs of node sets by considering the possible relationships assumed to be held between the words (7 pair types; detailed in section 3.2).

3. Calculate the similarities for each node set pair by three types of calculation methods (detailed in section 3.3).

In total we calculate 21 (7 pairs $\times$ 3 methods) similarities per word pair along with the cosine similarity between word embeddings. We use these similarities and vector pairs that yielded the similarities as feature.

3.1 Collecting node sets for each word

By consulting PWN, we collect the following five types of node sets for each word. These node set types are selected so as to characterize relevant lexical-semantic relationships in the target inventory detailed in section 4.1.

- L_w: a set of senses that a word w has

- S_w: a set of concepts each denoted by a member of L_w

- S_w^{hyper}: a set of concepts whose member is directly linked from a member of S_w by the PWN `hypernymy` relation

- S_w^{attri}: a set of concepts whose member is directly linked from a member of S_w by the PWN `attribute` relation

- S_w^{mero}: a set of concepts whose member is directly linked from a member of S_w by the PWN `meronymy` relation

3.2 Building node set pairs

Given a pair of words (w_1, w_2), we build seven types of node set pairs as shown in Table 1. Each row in the table defines the combination of node sets and presents the associated mnemonic.

Table 1: Node set pairs built for (w_1, w_2).

Node set pair		Mnemonic
L_{w_1}	L_{w_2}	sense
S_{w_1}	S_{w_2}	concept
$S_{w_1}^{hyper}$	S_{w_2}	hyper
$S_{w_1}^{hyper}$	$S_{w_2}^{hyper}$	coord
$S_{w_1}^{attri}$	S_{w_2}	attri_1
S_{w_1}	$S_{w_2}^{attri}$	attri_2
$S_{w_1}^{mero}$	S_{w_2}	mero

These types of node set pairs are defined in expecting that:

- sense, concept: captures semantic similarity/relatedness between the words;

- hyper: captures *hypernymy* relation between the words;

- coord: dictates if the words share a common hypernym;

- attri_1, attri_2: dictates if w_1 describes some aspect of w_2 (attri_1) or vice versa (attri_2);

- mero: captures the *meronymy* relation between the words.

Note that the italicized words indicate lexical relationships often used in linguistic literature.

3.3 Similarity calculation

In a pair of node sets, each node set could have a different number of elements, meaning that we cannot apply element-wise computation (e.g., cosine) for measuring the similarity between the node sets. We thus propose the following three similarity calculation methods and compare them in the experiments.

In the following formulations: c indicates a certain node set pair type defined in Table 1; (X_{w_1}, X_{w_2}) is the node set pair for (w_1, w_2) specified by c; and $sim(\vec{x_1}, \vec{x_2})$ is the cosine similarity between $\vec{x_1}$ and $\vec{x_2}$.

sim_{max}^{c} **method:**

$$sim_{max}^{c}(w_1, w_2) = \max_{x_1 \in X_{w_1}, x_2 \in X_{w_2}} sim(\vec{x_1}, \vec{x_2}) \tag{1}$$

As the formula defines, this method selects a combination of the node sets that yield the maximum similarity, implying that it achieves a disambiguation functionality.

The vector pair from the most similar node sets $(\vec{x_1}, \vec{x_2})$ is also used as feature. The actual usage of this pair in the experiments is detailed in section 4.2.

sim_{sum}^{c} **method:**

$$sim_{sum}^{c}(w_1, w_2) = sim\left(\sum_{x_1 \in X_{w_1}} \vec{x_1}, \sum_{x_2 \in X_{w_2}} \vec{x_2} \right) \tag{2}$$

As defined by the formula, this method firstly makes a holistic meaning representation by summing all embeddings of the nodes contained in each node set. We devised this method with the expectation that it could dictate *semantic relatedness* rather than *semantic similarity* (Budanitsky and Hirst, 2006). The pair of the summed embeddings $(\sum_{x_1 \in X_{w_1}} \vec{x_1}, \sum_{x_2 \in X_{w_2}} \vec{x_2})$ is also used as feature.

sim_{med}^{c} **method:**

$$sim_{med}^{c}(w_1, w_2) = \underset{x_1 \in X_{w_1}, x_2 \in X_{w_2}}{\text{median}} sim(\vec{x_1}, \vec{x_2}) \tag{3}$$

The method is expected to express the similarity between mediated representations of each node set. Instead of the arithmetic average, we employ the median to select a representative node in each node set, allowing us to use the associated vector pair as feature.

4 Experiments

We evaluated the effectiveness of the proposed supervised approach by conducting a series of classification experiments using the BLESS dataset (Baroni and Lenci, 2011). Among the possible learning algorithms, we adopted the Random Forest™ algorithm as it maintains a balance between performance and efficiency. The results are assessed by using standard measures such as Precision (P), Recall (R), and $F1$. We employed the pre-trained Word2Vec embeddings[2].

---

[2]300-dimensional vectors by CBoW, available at https://code.google.com/archive/p/word2vec/

We trained sense/concept embeddings by applying the AutoExtend system[3] (Rothe and Schütze, 2015) while using the Word2Vec embeddings as the input and consulting PWN 3.0 as the underlying lexical-semantic resource.

4.1 Dataset

We utilized the BLESS dataset, which was developed for the evaluation of distributional semantic models. It provides 14,400 tetrads of $(w_1, w_2,$ lexical-semantic relation type, topical domain type): where the topical domain type designates a semantic class from the coarse semantic classification system consisting of 17 English concrete noun categories (e.g., tools, clothing, vehicles, and animals). The lexical-semantic relation types defined in BLESS and their counts are described as follows:

- COORD (3565 word pairs): they are co-hyponyms (e.g., alligator-lizard).

- HYPER (1337 word pairs): w_2 is a hypernym of w_1 (e.g., alligator-animal).

- MERO (2943 word pairs): w_2 is a component/organ/member of w_1 (e.g., alligator-mouth).

- ATTRI (2731 word pairs): w_2 is an adjective expressing an attribute of w_1 (e.g., alligator-aquatic).

- EVENT (3824 word pairs): w_2 is a verb referring to an action/activity/happening/event associated with w_1 (e.g., alligator-swim).

Note here that these lexical-semantic relation types are not completely concord with the PWN relations described in section 3.1.

Data division: In order to compare the performance for the present task we divided the data in three ways: *In domain*, *Out-of-domain* (as employed in (Necsuleşcu et al., 2015)), and *Collapsed-domain*. For the *In-domain* setting, the data in the same domain were used both for training and testing. We thus conducted a five-fold cross validation for each domain. For the *Out-of-domain* setting, one domain is used for testing and the remaining data is used for training. In addition, we prepared the *Collapsed-domain* setting, where we conducted a 10-fold cross validation for the entire dataset irrespective of the domain.

---

[3]The default hyperparameters were used.

4.2 Comparing methods

A supervised relation classification system referred to as **WECE** (**W**ord **E**mbeddings **C**lassification syst**E**m) in (Necsuleşcu et al., 2015) was especially chosen for comparisons, since this method combines and uses the word embeddings of a given word pair (w_1, w_2) as feature. They compare two types of approaches described as $WECE_{offset}$ and $WECE_{concat}$: $WECE_{offset}$ uses the offset of the word embeddings $(\vec{w_2} - \vec{w_1})$ as the feature vector, whereas $WECE_{concat}$ uses the concatenation of the word embeddings. Moreover, they use two types of word embeddings: a bag-of-words model (BoW) (Mikolov et al., 2013a) and a dependency-based skip-gram model (Dep) (Levy and Goldberg, 2014). In summary, the WECE system has the following variations: $WECE_{BoW}^{offset}, WECE_{Dep}^{offset}, WECE_{BoW}^{concat}$ and $WECE_{Dep}^{concat}$.

As described in Section 3, we utilize 22 kinds of similarity and the underlying vector as features. In order to make reasonable comparisons, we compare two vector composition methods. In addition to the already described array of similarities, the $Proposal_{concat}$ method uses the concatenated vector of the underlying vectors, whereas the $Proposal_{concat}$ method employs the difference vector. As a result, the dimensionalities of the resulting vectors employed in these methods are 13,222 (22 similarities + 22 × 600 dimensions for concatenated vectors) and 6,622 (22 similarities + 22 × 300 dimensions for difference vectors), respectively.

Baseline: As detailed in section 3, our methods utilize PWN neighboring concepts linked by particular lexical-semantic relationships, such as (hypernymy, attribute, and meronymy). We thus set the baseline as follows while respecting the direct relational links defined in PWN.

- Given a word pair (w_1, w_2), if any concept in S_{w_1} and that in S_{w_2} are directly linked by a certain relationship in PWN, let w_1 and w_2 be in the relation.

Note that the baseline method cannot find any word pair that is annotated to have the EVENT relation in the BLESS dataset, because there are no links in PWN that share the same or a similar definition. Likewise it is not capable for the method to find any word pair with the ATTRI

	In-domain			Out-of-domain			Collapsed-domain		
	P	R	$F1$	P	R	$F1$	P	R	$F1$
$WECE_{BoW}^{offset}$	0.900	0.909	0.904	0.680	0.669	0.675	-	-	-
$WECE_{Dep}^{offset}$	0.853	0.865	0.859	0.687	0.623	0.654	-	-	-
$Proposal_{offset}$	0.913	0.907	0.906	0.766	0.762	0.753	0.867	0.867	0.865
$WECE_{BoW}^{concat}$	0.899	0.910	0.904	0.838	0.570	0.678	-	-	-
$WECE_{Dep}^{concat}$	0.859	0.870	0.865	0.782	0.638	0.703	-	-	-
$Proposal_{concat}$	**0.973**	**0.971**	**0.971**	**0.839**	**0.819**	**0.812**	0.970	0.970	0.970

Table 2: Comparison of the overall classification results.

relation in BLESS, because the definition of the `attribute` relationship in PWN differs from the definition of the ATTRI relation in the BLESS dataset. Thus, we can only compare the results for the relationships COORD, HYPER, and MERO with the common measures, P, R, and $F1$.

5 Results

5.1 Major results

Table 2 compares our results with that of the WECE systems in the three data set divisions (In/Out/Collapsed domains). The results show that $Proposal_{concat}$ performed best in all measures of each division (shown in bold font). We observe two common trends across the approaches including WECE: (1) Every score in the Out-of-domain setting was lower than that in the In-domain setting; and (2) The methods using vector concatenation achieved higher scores than those using vector offsets. The former trend is reasonable, since information that is also more relevant to the test data is contained in the training data in the In-domain settings. The latter trend suggests that concatenated vectors may be more informative than offset vectors, supporting the conclusion presented in (Necsulescu et al., 2015).

Nevertheless, the results in the table clearly show that $Proposal_{offset}$ outperformed both $WECE_{BoW}^{concat}$ and $WECE_{Dep}^{concat}$ not only in Precision but also in Recall in the Out-of-domain setting. This may confirm that sense representations, acquired by exploiting a richer structure encoded in PWN, are richer in semantic content than word embeddings learned from textual corpora, and hence, even the offset vectors are capable of abstracting some characteristics of potential lexical-semantic relations between a word pair effectively.

Table 3 breaks down the results obtained

Relationship	P	R	F1
COORD	0.761	0.559	0.645
by *Baseline*	*0.550*	*0.108*	*0.180*
HYPER	0.767	0.654	0.706
by *Baseline*	*0.746*	*0.199*	*0.314*
MERO	0.625	0.809	0.705
by *Baseline*	*0.934*	*0.034*	*0.065*
ATTRI	0.913	0.995	0.952
EVENT	0.974	0.983	0.979

Table 3: Breakdown of the results obtained by $Proposal_{concat}^{OoD}$. The *Baseline* results are shown in *italics*.

by $Proposal_{concat}$ in the Out-of-domain setting ($Proposal_{concat}^{OoD}$), and compares them with the *Baseline* results, showing that $Proposal_{concat}$ clearly outperformed the *Baseline* in Recall and F1. This clearly confirms that the direct relational links defined in PWN are insufficient for classifying the BLESS relationships. With respect to the internal comparison of the $Proposal_{concat}^{OoD}$ results, a prominent fact is the high-performance classification of the ATTRI and EVENT relationships. By definition, these relationships link a noun to an adjective (ATTRI) or to a verb (EVENT), whereas the COORD, HYPER, and MERO relationships connect a noun to another noun. This may suggest that the information carried by part-of-speech plays a role in this classification task.

Table 4 further details the results obtained by $Proposal_{concat}^{OoD}$ by showing the confusion matrix, also endorsing that the fine-grained classification of inter-noun relationships (COORD, HYPER, and MERO) is far more difficult than distinguishing cross-POS relationships (ATTRI and EVENT). In particular, as suggested in (Shwartz et al., 2016), *synonymy* is difficult to distinguish from *hypernymy* even by humans.

	HYPER	COORD	ATTRI	MERO	EVENT
HYPER	875	157	10	282	13
COORD	189	1994	220	1118	44
ATTRI	1	13	2716	1	0
MERO	74	423	24	2380	42
EVENT	2	32	5	27	3758

Table 4: Confusion matrix for the results by $Proposal^{OoD}_{concat}$ in the Out-of-domain setting.

5.2 Ablation tests

This section more closely considers the results in the Out-of-domain setting. Table 5 shows the results of the ablation tests for the $Proposal^{OoD}_{concat}$ setting, comparing the effectiveness of the source of the similarities. Each row other than $Proposal^{OoD}_{concat}$ displays the results when the designated feature is ablated. The $-word$ row shows the result when ablating the 601-dimensional features created from the pair of word embeddings, and the other rows show the results when ablating the corresponding 1803-dimensional features (three similarities and the three vector pairs that yielded the similarities) generated from each node set pair.

	P	R	$F1$	$F1$ diff
$Proposal^{OoD}_{concat}$	0.839	0.819	0.812	-
$-word$	0.845	0.827	0.819	0.008
$-sense$	0.833	0.815	0.806	-0.006
$-concept$	0.826	0.809	0.802	-0.010
$-coord$	0.834	0.811	0.803	-0.009
$-hyper$	0.826	0.803	0.800	-0.012
$-attri_1$	0.826	0.806	0.798	-0.014
$-attri_2$	0.842	0.820	0.814	0.002
$-mero$	0.835	0.813	0.806	-0.006

Table 5: Ablation tests comparing the effectiveness of each node set.

This table suggests that the *concept*, *hyper*, and $attri_1$ node set pairs are effective, as indicated by the relatively large decreases in $F1$. Surprisingly, however, the features generated from the word embeddings affected the performance. This implies that abstract-level semantics encoded in sense/concept embeddings are more robust in the classification of the target lexical-semantic relationships. However, the utility of sense embeddings was modest. This may result from the learning method in AutoExtend: it tries to split a word embedding into the senses' embeddings without considering the virtual distribution of senses in the

Word2Vec training corpus. It is a potential future work to address this issue.

Table 6 compares the effectiveness of the *types* of features. The *only similarities* row shows the results when ablating the vectoral features and only using the 22-dimensional similarity features (21 semantic/conceptual-level similarities along with a word-level similarity). On the other hand, the *only vector pairs* row shows the results from the adverse setting, using the 22 vector pairs (using 13,200-dimensional features).

	P	R	F1	F1 diff
$Proposal^{OoD}_{concat}$	0.839	0.819	0.812	-
only similarities	0.704	0.687	0.683	-0.129
only vector pairs	0.834	0.812	0.804	-0.007

Table 6: Effectiveness comparison of the *types* of features.

It is shown that using vectorial features would produce more accurate results than simply using the similarity features, confirming the general assumption: more features yield more accurate results. However, we would have to emphasize that, even only with the similarity features, our approach outperformed the comparable method in *Recall* (shown in the Out-of domain columns of Table 2).

Table 7 shows the results of the other ablation tests, comparing the effectiveness of the similarity calculation methods. Each row in the table displays the result when ablating the 4207-dimensional features (seven similarities plus seven vector pairs that yielded these similarities).

As the results in the table show, the $F1$ scores did not change significantly in each ablated condition, showing that the effect provided by the ablated method is completed by the remaining methods. There exists some redundancy in preparing these three calculation methods.

	P	R	$F1$	$F1$ diff
$Proposal^{OoD}_{concat}$	0.839	0.819	0.812	-
$-sim_{max}$	0.835	0.812	0.805	-0.007
$-sim_{sum}$	0.843	0.822	0.816	0.004
$-sim_{med}$	0.838	0.811	0.805	-0.007

Table 7: Additional ablation tests comparing the similarity calculation methods.

6 Discussion

This section discusses two issues: the first is associated with the usage of PWN in the experiments using BLESS, and the other is concerned with the "lexical memorization" problem.

Usage of PWN: As detailed in Section 3, our methods utilize neighboring concepts linked by the particular lexical-semantic relations hypernymy, attribute, and meronymy defined in PWN. Some may consider that the HYPER, ATTRI, and MERO relationships can be estimated simply by consulting the above-mentioned PWN relationships. However, this is definitely NOT the case, since almost all of the semantic relation instances in the BLESS dataset are not immediately defined in PWN: Among the 14,400 BLESS instances, only 951 are defined in PWN. For an obvious example, there are no links in PWN that are labeled event, which is a type of semantic relation defined in BLESS. The low Recall results presented in Table 3 endorsed this fact, and clearly show the sparsity of useful semantic links in PWN. However, for some of the lexical-semantic relation types that exhibit transitivity, such as *hypernymy*, consulting the PWN indirect links could be effectively utilized to improve the results.

Lexical memorization: Levy et al. (2015) recently argued that the results achieved by many supervised methods are inflated because of the "lexical memorization" effect, which only learns "prototypical hypernymy" relations. For example, if a classifier encounters many positive examples such as (X, animals), where X is a hyponym of animal (e.g., dog, cat, ...), it only learns to classify any word pair as a *hypernym* as far as the second word is "animal." We argue that our method can be expected to be relatively free from this issue. The similarity features are not affected by this effect, since any similarity calculation is a symmetric operation, and independent of word order. More-over, the sim^{c}_{max} or sim^{c}_{med} method selects a pair of sense/concept embeddings, where the combination usually differs depending on the combination of node sets. On one hand, the sim^{c}_{sum} method could be affected by the memorization effect, since the vectorial feature for the *prototypical hypernym* is invariable.

7 Conclusion

This paper proposed a method for classifying the type of lexical-semantic relation that could hold between a given pair of words. The empirical results clearly outperformed those previously obtained with the state-of-the-art results, demonstrating that our rationales behind the proposal are valid. In particular, it would be reasonable to assume that the plausibility of a specific type of lexical-semantic relation between the words could be chiefly recovered by a carefully designed set of relation-specific similarities. These results also highlight the utility of "the sense representations," since our similarity calculation methods rely on the sense/concept embeddings created by the AutoExtend system.

Future work could follow two directions. First, we need to improve the classification of inter-noun semantic relations. We may particularly need to distinguish the *hypernym* relationship, which is asymmetric, from the symmetric *coordinate* relationship. In this regard, we would need to improve the creation of node sets and the combinations to capture the innate difference of the relationships.

Second, we need to address the potential drawback of our proposal, which comes from our operational requirement: a lack of sense/concept embeddings is crucial, as we cannot collect relevant node sets in this case. Therefore, we need to develop a method to assign some of the existing concepts to an *unknown* word, which is not contained in PWN, by seeking the nearest concept in the resource. A possible method would first seek the nearest concept in the underlying lexical-semantic resource for an *unknown* word, and then induce a revised set of sense/concept embeddings by iteratively applying the AutoExtend system.

Acknowledgments

The present research was supported by JSPS KAKENHI Grant Number JP26540144 and JP25280117.

References

Marco Baroni and Alessandro Lenci. 2011. How we blessed distributional semantic evaluation. In *Proceedings of the GEMS 2011 Workshop on GEometrical Models of Natural Language Semantics*, pages 1–10. Association for Computational Linguistics.

Jordan Boyd-Graber, Christiane Fellbaum, Daniel Osherson, and Robert Schapire. 2006. Adding dense, weighted connections to wordnet. In *Proceedings of the third international WordNet conference*, pages 29–36.

Alexander Budanitsky and Graeme Hirst. 2006. Evaluating wordnet-based measures of lexical semantic relatedness. *Computational Linguistics*, 32(1):13–47.

Ruiji Fu, Jiang Guo, Bing Qin, Wanxiang Che, Haifeng Wang, and Ting Liu. 2014. Learning semantic hierarchies via word embeddings. In *Proceedings of the 52nd Annual Meeting of the Association for Computational Linguistics (Volume 1: Long Papers)*, pages 1199–1209, Baltimore, Maryland, June. Association for Computational Linguistics.

Eric Huang, Richard Socher, Christopher Manning, and Andrew Ng. 2012. Improving word representations via global context and multiple word prototypes. In *Proceedings of the 50th Annual Meeting of the Association for Computational Linguistics (Volume 1: Long Papers)*, pages 873–882, Jeju Island, Korea, July. Association for Computational Linguistics.

Ignacio Iacobacci, Mohammad Taher Pilehvar, and Roberto Navigli. 2015. Sensembed: Learning sense embeddings for word and relational similarity. In *Proceedings of the 53rd Annual Meeting of the Association for Computational Linguistics and the 7th International Joint Conference on Natural Language Processing (Volume 1: Long Papers)*, pages 95–105, Beijing, China, July. Association for Computational Linguistics.

Douwe Kiela, Felix Hill, and Stephen Clark. 2015. Specializing word embeddings for similarity or relatedness. In *Proceedings of the 2015 Conference on Empirical Methods in Natural Language Processing*, pages 2044–2048, Lisbon, Portugal, September. Association for Computational Linguistics.

Lili Kotlerman, Ido Dagan, Idan Szpektor, and Maayan Zhitomirsky-Geffet. 2010. Directional distributional similarity for lexical inference. *Natural Language Engineering*, 16(04):359–389.

Alessandro Lenci and Giulia Benotto. 2012. Identifying hypernyms in distributional semantic spaces. In **SEM 2012: The First Joint Conference on Lexical and Computational Semantics – Volume 1: Proceedings of the main conference and the shared task, and Volume 2: Proceedings of the Sixth International Workshop on Semantic Evaluation (SemEval 2012)*, pages 75–79, Montréal, Canada, 7-8 June. Association for Computational Linguistics.

Omer Levy and Yoav Goldberg. 2014. Dependency-based word embeddings. In *Proceedings of the 52nd Annual Meeting of the Association for Computational Linguistics (Volume 2: Short Papers)*, pages 302–308, Baltimore, Maryland, June. Association for Computational Linguistics.

Omer Levy, Steffen Remus, Chris Biemann, and Ido Dagan. 2015. Do supervised distributional methods really learn lexical inference relations? In *Proceedings of the 2015 Conference of the North American Chapter of the Association for Computational Linguistics: Human Language Technologies*, pages 970–976, Denver, Colorado, May–June. Association for Computational Linguistics.

Tomas Mikolov, Kai Chen, Greg Corrado, and Jeffrey Dean. 2013a. Efficient estimation of word representations in vector space. *arXiv preprint arXiv:1301.3781*.

Tomas Mikolov, Ilya Sutskever, Kai Chen, Greg S Corrado, and Jeff Dean. 2013b. Distributed representations of words and phrases and their compositionality. In *Advances in neural information processing systems*, pages 3111–3119.

George A. Miller. 1995. Wordnet: a lexical database for english. *Communications of the ACM*, 38(11):39–41.

Silvia Necsulescu, Sara Mendes, David Jurgens, Núria Bel, and Roberto Navigli. 2015. Reading between the lines: Overcoming data sparsity for accurate classification of lexical relationships. In *Proceedings of the Fourth Joint Conference on Lexical and Computational Semantics*, pages 182–192, Denver, Colorado, June. Association for Computational Linguistics.

Arvind Neelakantan, Jeevan Shankar, Alexandre Passos, and Andrew McCallum. 2014. Efficient non-parametric estimation of multiple embeddings per word in vector space. In *Proceedings of the 2014 Conference on Empirical Methods in Natural Language Processing (EMNLP)*, pages 1059–1069, Doha, Qatar, October. Association for Computational Linguistics.

Jeffrey Pennington, Richard Socher, and Christopher Manning. 2014. Glove: Global vectors for word representation. In *Proceedings of the 2014 Conference on Empirical Methods in Natural Language Processing (EMNLP)*, pages 1532–1543, Doha, Qatar, October. Association for Computational Linguistics.

Sascha Rothe and Hinrich Schütze. 2015. Autoextend: Extending word embeddings to embeddings for synsets and lexemes. In *Proceedings of the 53rd Annual Meeting of the Association for Computational Linguistics and the 7th International Joint*

Conference on Natural Language Processing (Volume 1: Long Papers), pages 1793–1803, Beijing, China, July. Association for Computational Linguistics.

Pavel Rychlý and Adam Kilgarriff. 2007. An efficient algorithm for building a distributional thesaurus (and other sketch engine developments). In *Proceedings of the 45th Annual Meeting of the Association for Computational Linguistics Companion Volume Proceedings of the Demo and Poster Sessions*, pages 41–44, Prague, Czech Republic, June. Association for Computational Linguistics.

Enrico Santus, Frances Yung, Alessandro Lenci, and Chu-Ren Huang. 2015. Evalution 1.0: an evolving semantic dataset for training and evaluation of distributional semantic models. In *Proceedings of the 4th Workshop on Linked Data in Linguistics (LDL-2015)*, pages 64–69.

Vered Shwartz, Yoav Goldberg, and Ido Dagan. 2016. Improving hypernymy detection with an integrated path-based and distributional method. In *Proceedings of the 54th Annual Meeting of the Association for Computational Linguistics (Volume 1: Long Papers)*, pages 2389–2398, Berlin, Germany, August. Association for Computational Linguistics.

Ekaterina Vylomova, Laura Rimell, Trevor Cohn, and Timothy Baldwin. 2016. Take and took, gaggle and goose, book and read: Evaluating the utility of vector differences for lexical relation learning. In *Proceedings of the 54th Annual Meeting of the Association for Computational Linguistics (Volume 1: Long Papers)*, pages 1671–1682, Berlin, Germany, August. Association for Computational Linguistics.

Julie Weeds, Daoud Clarke, Jeremy Reffin, David Weir, and Bill Keller. 2014. Learning to distinguish hypernyms and co-hyponyms. In *Proceedings of COLING 2014, the 25th International Conference on Computational Linguistics: Technical Papers*, pages 2249–2259, Dublin, Ireland, August. Dublin City University and Association for Computational Linguistics.

Supervised and unsupervised approaches to measuring usage similarity

Milton King and **Paul Cook**
Faculty of Computer Science, University of New Brunswick
Fredericton, NB E3B 5A3, Canada
`milton.king@unb.ca, paul.cook@unb.ca`

Abstract

Usage similarity (USim) is an approach to determining word meaning in context that does not rely on a sense inventory. Instead, pairs of usages of a target lemma are rated on a scale. In this paper we propose unsupervised approaches to USim based on embeddings for words, contexts, and sentences, and achieve state-of-the-art results over two USim datasets. We further consider supervised approaches to USim, and find that although they outperform unsupervised approaches, they are unable to generalize to lemmas that are unseen in the training data.

1 Usage similarity

Word senses are not discrete. In many cases, for a given instance of a word, multiple senses from a sense inventory are applicable, and to varying degrees (Erk et al., 2009). For example, consider the usage of *wait* in the following sentence taken from Jurgens and Klapaftis (2013):

1. *And is now the time to say I can hardly **wait** for your impending new novel about the Alamo?*

Annotators judged the WordNet (Fellbaum, 1998) senses glossed as 'stay in one place and anticipate or expect something' and 'look forward to the probable occurrence of', to have applicability ratings of 4 out of 5, and 2 out of 5, respectively, for this usage of *wait*. Moreover, Erk et al. (2009) also showed that this issue cannot be addressed simply by choosing a coarser-grained sense inventory. That a clear line cannot be drawn between the various senses of a word has been observed as far back as Johnson (1755). Some have gone so far as

to doubt the existence of word senses (Kilgarriff, 1997).

Sense inventories also suffer from a lack of coverage. New words regularly come into usage, as do new senses for established words. Furthermore, domain-specific senses are often not included in general-purpose sense inventories. This issue of coverage is particularly relevant for social media text, which contains a higher rate of out-of-vocabulary words than more-conventional text types (Baldwin et al., 2013).

These issues pose problems for natural language processing tasks such as word sense disambiguation and induction, which rely on, and seek to induce, respectively, sense inventories, and have traditionally assumed that each instance of a word can be assigned one sense.[1] In response to this, alternative approaches to word meaning have been proposed that do not rely on sense inventories. Erk et al. (2009) carried out an annotation task on "usage similarity" (USim), in which the similarity of the meanings of two usages of a given word are rated on a five-point scale.

Lui et al. (2012) proposed the first computational approach to USim. They considered approaches based on topic modelling (Blei et al., 2003), under a wide range of parameter settings, and found that a single topic model for all target lemmas (as opposed to one topic model per target lemma) performed best on the dataset of Erk et al. (2009). Gella et al. (2013) considered USim on Twitter text, noting that this model of word meaning seems particularly well-suited to this text type because of the prevalence of out-of-vocabulary words. Gella et al. (2013) also considered topic modelling-based approaches, achieving their best results using one topic model per

---

[1] Recent word sense induction systems and evaluations have, however, considered graded senses and multi-sense applicability (Jurgens and Klapaftis, 2013).

Proceedings of the 1st Workshop on Sense, Concept and Entity Representations and their Applications, pages 47–52,
Valencia, Spain, April 4 2017. ©2017 Association for Computational Linguistics

target word, and a document expansion strategy based on medium frequency hashtags to combat the data sparsity of tweets due to their relatively short length. The methods of Lui et al. (2012) and Gella et al. (2013) are unsupervised; they do not rely on any gold standard USim annotations.

In this paper we propose unsupervised approaches to USim based on embeddings for words (Mikolov et al., 2013; Pennington et al., 2014), contexts (Melamud et al., 2016), and sentences (Kiros et al., 2015), and achieve state-of-the-art results over the USim datasets of both Erk et al. (2009) and Gella et al. (2013). We then consider supervised approaches to USim based on these same methods for forming embeddings, which outperform the unsupervised approaches, but perform poorly on lemmas that are unseen in the training data.

2 USim models

In this section we describe how we represent a target word usage in context, and then how we use these representations in unsupervised and supervised approaches to USim.

2.1 Usage representation

We consider four ways of representing an instance of a target word based on embeddings for words, contexts, and sentences. For word embeddings, we consider word2vec (Mikolov et al., 2013) and GloVe (Pennington et al., 2014). In each case we represent a token instance of the target word in a sentence as the average of the word embeddings for the other words occurring in the sentence, excluding stopwords.

Context2vec (Melamud et al., 2016) can be viewed as an extension of word2vec's continuous bag-of-words (CBOW) model. In CBOW, the context of a target word token is represented as the average of the embeddings for words within a fixed window. In contrast, context2vec uses a richer representation based on a bidirectional LSTM capturing the full sentential context of a target word token. During training, context2vec embeds the context of word token instances in the same vector space as word types. As this model explicitly embeds word contexts it seems particularly well-suited to USim.

Kiros et al. (2015) proposed skip-thoughts, a sentence encoder that can be viewed as a sentence-level version of word2vec's skipgram model, i.e.,

during training, the encoding of a sentence is used to predict surrounding sentences. Kiros et al. (2015) showed that skip-thoughts out-performs previous approaches to measuring sentence-level relatedness. Although our goal is to determine the meaning of a word in context, the meaning of a sentence could be a useful proxy for this.[2]

2.2 Unsupervised approach

In the unsupervised setup, we measure the similarity between two usages of a target word as the cosine similarity between their vector representations, obtained by one of the methods described in Section 2.1. This method does not require gold standard training data.

2.3 Supervised approach

We also consider a supervised approach. For a given pair of token instances of a target word, t_1 and t_2, we first form vectors v_1 and v_2 representing each of the two instances of the target, using one of the approaches in Section 2.1. To represent each pair of instances, we follow the approach of Kiros et al. (2015). We compute the componen-twise product, and absolute difference, of v_1 and v_2, and concatenate them. This gives a vector of length $2d$ — where d is the dimensionality of the embeddings used — representing each pair of instances. We then train ridge regression to learn a model to predict the similarity of unseen usage pairs.

3 Materials and methods

3.1 USim Datasets

We evaluate our methods on two USim datasets representing two different text types: ORIGINAL, the USim dataset of Erk et al. (2009), and TWITTER from Gella et al. (2013). Both USim datasets contain pairs of sentences; each sentence in each pair includes a usage of a particular target lemma. Each sentence pair is rated on a scale of 1–5 for how similar in meaning the usages of the target words are in the two sentences.

ORIGINAL consists of sentences from McCarthy and Navigli (2007), which were drawn from a web corpus (Sharoff, 2006). This dataset contains 34 lemmas, including nouns, verbs, adjectives, and adverbs. Each lemma is the target

---

[2]Inference requires only a single sentence, so the model can infer skip-thought vectors for sentences taken out-of-context, as in the USim datasets.

word in 10 sentences. For each lemma, sentence pairs (SPairs) are formed based on all pairwise comparisons, giving 45 SPairs per lemma. Annotations were provided by three native English speakers, with the average taken as the final gold standard similarity. In a small number of cases the annotators were unable to judge similarity. Erk et al. (2009) removed these SPairs from the dataset, resulting in a total of 1512 SPairs.

TWITTER contains SPairs for ten nouns from ORIGINAL. In this case the "sentences" are in fact tweets. 55 SPairs are provided for each noun. Unlike ORIGINAL, the SPairs are not formed on the basis of all pairwise comparisons amongst a smaller set of sentences. This dataset was annotated via crowd sourcing and carefully cleaned to remove outlier annotations.

3.2 Evaluation

Following Lui et al. (2012) and Gella et al. (2013) we evaluate our systems by calculating Spearman's rank correlation coefficient between the gold standard similarities and the predicted similarities. This enables direct comparison of our results with those reported in these previous studies.

We evaluate our supervised approaches using two cross-validation methodologies. In the first case we apply 10-fold cross-validation, randomly partitioning all SPairs for all lemmas in a given dataset. Using this approach, the test data for a given fold consists of SPairs for target lemmas that were seen in the training data. To determine how well our methods generalize to unseen lemmas, we consider a second cross-validation setup in which we partition the SPairs in a given dataset by lemma. Here the test data for a given fold consists of SPairs for one lemma, and the training data consists of SPairs for all other lemmas.

3.3 Embeddings

We train word2vec's skipgram model on two corpora:[3] (1) a corpus of English tweets collected from the Twitter Streaming APIs[4] from November 2014 to March 2015 containing 1.3 billion tokens; and (2) an English Wikipedia dump from 1 September 2015 containing 2.6 billion tokens. Because of the relatively-low cost of training word2vec, we consider several settings of

D	W	ORIGINAL	TWITTER
50	2	0.251	0.246
50	5	0.262	0.272
50	8	**0.286**	0.282
100	2	0.267	0.248
100	5	0.273	0.253
100	8	0.273	0.298
300	2	0.275	0.266
300	5	0.279	0.295
300	8	0.281	**0.300**

Table 1: Spearman's ρ on each dataset using the unsupervised approach with word2vec embeddings trained using several settings for the number of dimensions (D) and window size (W). The best ρ for each dataset is shown in boldface.

window size (W=2,5,8) and number of dimensions (D=50,100,300). Embeddings trained on Wikipedia and Twitter are used for experiments on ORIGINAL and TWITTER, respectively.

For the other embeddings we use pre-trained models. We use GloVe vectors from Wikipedia and Twitter, with 300 and 200 dimensions, for experiments on ORIGINAL and TWITTER, respectively.[5] For context2vec we use a 600 dimensional model trained on the ukWaC (Ferraresi et al., 2008), a web corpus of approximately 2 billion tokens.[6] We use a skip-thoughts model with 4800 dimensions, trained on a corpus of books.[7] We use these context2vec and skip-thoughts models for experiments on both ORIGINAL and TWITTER.

4 Experimental results

We first consider the unsupervised approach using word2vec for a variety of window sizes and number of dimensions. Results are shown in Table 1. All correlations are significant ($p < 0.05$). On both ORIGINAL and TWITTER, for a given number of dimensions, as the window size is increased, ρ increases. Embeddings for larger window sizes tend to better capture semantics, whereas embeddings for smaller window sizes tend to better reflect syntax (Levy and Goldberg, 2014); the

---

[3]In preliminary experiments the alternative word2vec CBOW model achieved substantially lower correlations than skipgram, and so CBOW was not considered further.

[4]https://dev.twitter.com/

[5]http://nlp.stanford.edu/projects/glove/

[6]https://github.com/orenmel/context2vec

[7]https://github.com/ryankiros/skip-thoughts

| Dataset | Embeddings | Unsupervised | Supervised | |
			All	Lemma
ORIGINAL	Word2vec	0.281*	0.435*	0.220*
	GloVe	0.218*	0.410*	**0.230***
	Skip-thoughts	0.177*	**0.436***	0.099*
	Context2vec	**0.302***	0.417*	0.172*
TWITTER	Word2vec	**0.300***	**0.384***	**0.196***
	GloVe	0.122*	0.314*	0.134*
	Skip-thoughts	0.095*	0.360*	0.058
	Context2vec	0.122*	0.193*	0.067

Table 2: Spearman's ρ on each dataset using the unsupervised method, and supervised methods with cross-validation folds based on random sampling across all lemmas (All) and holding out individual lemmas (Lemma), for each embedding approach. The best ρ for each experimental setup, on each dataset, is shown in boldface. Significant correlations ($p < 0.05$) are indicated with *.

more-semantic embeddings given by larger window sizes appear to be better-suited to the task of predicting USim. For a given window size, a higher number of dimensions also tends to achieve higher ρ. For example, for a given window size, $D = 300$ gives a higher ρ than $D = 50$ in each case, except for $W = 8$ on ORIGINAL.

The best correlations reported by Lui et al. (2012) on ORIGINAL, and Gella et al. (2013) on TWITTER, were 0.202 and 0.29, respectively. The best parameter settings for our unsupervised approach using word2vec embeddings achieve higher correlations, 0.286 and 0.300, on ORIGINAL and TWITTER, respectively. Lui et al. (2012) and Gella et al. (2013) both report drastic variation in performance for different settings of the number of topics in their models. We also observe some variation with respect to parameter settings; however, any of the parameter settings considered achieves a higher correlation than Lui et al. (2012) on ORIGINAL. For TWITTER, parameter settings with $W \geq 5$ and $D \geq 100$ achieve a correlation comparable to, or greater than, the best reported by Gella et al. (2013)

We now consider the unsupervised approach, using the other embeddings. Based on the previous findings for word2vec, we only consider this model with $W = 8$ and $D = 300$ here. Results are shown in Table 2 in the column labeled "Unsupervised". For ORIGINAL, context2vec performs best (and indeed outperforms word2vec for all parameter settings considered). This result demonstrates that approaches to predicting USim that explicitly embed the context of a target word can

outperform approaches based on averaging word embeddings (i.e., word2vec and GloVe) or embedding sentences (skip-thoughts). This result is particularly strong because we consider a range of parameter settings for word2vec, but only used the default settings for context2vec.[8] Word2vec does however perform best on TWITTER. The relatively poor performance of context2vec and skip-thoughts here could be due to differences between the text types these embedding models were trained on and the evaluation data. GloVe performs poorly, even though it was trained on tweets for these experiments, but that it performs less well than word2vec is consistent with the findings for ORIGINAL.

Turning to the supervised approach, we first consider results for cross-validation based on randomly partitioning all SPairs in a dataset (column "All" in Table 2). The best correlation on TWITTER (0.384) is again achieved using word2vec, while the best correlation on ORIGINAL (0.434) is obtained with skip-thoughts. The difference in performance amongst the various embedding approaches is, however, somewhat less here than in the unsupervised setting. For each embedding approach, and each dataset, the correlation in the supervised setting is better than that in the unsupervised setting, suggesting that if labeled training data is available, supervised approaches can give substantial improvements over unsupervised approaches to predicting USim.[9] However, this experimental setup does not show the extent to which the supervised approach is able to generalize to previously-unseen lemmas.

The column labeled "Lemma" in Table 2 shows results for the supervised approach for cross-validation using lemma-based partitioning. In these experiments, the test data consists of usages of a target lemma that was not seen as a target lemma during training. For each dataset, the correlations achieved here for each type of embedding are lower than those of the corresponding unsupervised method, with the exception of GloVe. In

---

[8]The context2vec model has 600 dimensions, and was trained on the ukWac, whereas our word2vec model for ORIGINAL is trained on Wikipedia. To further compare these approaches we also trained word2vec on the ukWaC with 600 dimensions and a window size of 8. These word2vec settings also did not outperform context2vec.

[9]These results on ORIGINAL must be interpreted cautiously, however. The same sentences, albeit in different SPairs, occur in both the training and testing data for a given fold. This issue does not affect TWITTER.

the case of ORIGINAL, the higher correlation for GloVe relative to the unsupervised setup appears to be largely due to improved performance on adverbs. Nevertheless, for each dataset, the correlations achieved by GloVe are still lower than those of the best unsupervised method on that dataset. These results demonstrate that the supervised approach generalizes poorly to new lemmas. This negative result indicates an important direction for future work — identifying strategies to training supervised approaches to predicting USim that generalize to unseen lemmas.

5 Conclusions

Word senses are not discrete, and multiple senses are often applicable for a given usage of a word. Moreover, for text types that have a relatively-high rate of out-of-vocabulary words, such as social media text, many words will be missing from sense inventories. USim is an approach to determining word meaning in context that does not rely on a sense inventory, addressing these concerns.

We proposed unsupervised approaches to USim based on embeddings for words, contexts, and sentences. We achieved state-of-the-art results over USim datasets based on Twitter text and more-conventional texts. We further considered supervised approaches to USim based on these same methods for forming embeddings, and found that although these methods outperformed the unsupervised approaches, they performed poorly on lemmas that were unseen in the training data.

The approaches to learning word embeddings that we considered (word2vec and GloVe) both learn a single vector representing each word type. There are, however, approaches that learn multiple embeddings for each type that have been applied to predict word similarity in context (Huang et al., 2012; Neelakantan et al., 2014, for example). In future work, we intend to also evaluate such approaches for the task of predicting usage similarity. We also intend to consider alternative strategies to training supervised approaches to USim in an effort to achieve better performance on unseen lemmas.

Acknowledgments

This research was financially supported by the Natural Sciences and Engineering Research Council of Canada, the New Brunswick Innovation Foundation, ACENET, and the University of New Brunswick.

References

Timothy Baldwin, Paul Cook, Marco Lui, Andrew MacKinlay, and Li Wang. 2013. How noisy social media text, how diffrnt social media sources? In *Proceedings of the 6th International Joint Conference on Natural Language Processing (IJCNLP 2013)*, pages 356–364, Nagoya, Japan.

David M. Blei, Andrew Y. Ng, and Michael I. Jordan. 2003. Latent dirichlet allocation. *Journal of Machine Learning Research*, 3:993–1022.

Katrin Erk, Diana McCarthy, and Nicholas Gaylord. 2009. Investigations on word senses and word usages. In *Proceedings of the Joint Conference of the 47th Annual Meeting of the ACL and the 4th International Joint Conference on Natural Language Processing of the AFNLP*, pages 10–18, Singapore.

Christiane Fellbaum, editor. 1998. *WordNet: An Electronic Lexical Database*. MIT Press, Cambridge, MA.

Adriano Ferraresi, Eros Zanchetta, Marco Baroni, and Silvia Bernardini. 2008. Introducing and evaluating ukWaC, a very large web-derived corpus of English. In *Proceedings of the 4th Web as Corpus Workshop: Can we beat Google*, pages 47–54, Marrakech, Morocco.

Spandana Gella, Paul Cook, and Bo Han. 2013. Unsupervised word usage similarity in social media texts. In *Second Joint Conference on Lexical and Computational Semantics (*SEM) Volume 1: Proceedings of the Main Conference and the Shared Task: Semantic Textual Similarity*, pages 248–253, Atlanta, USA.

Eric Huang, Richard Socher, Christopher Manning, and Andrew Ng. 2012. Improving word representations via global context and multiple word prototypes. In *Proceedings of the 50th Annual Meeting of the Association for Computational Linguistics (Volume 1: Long Papers)*, pages 873–882, Jeju Island, Korea.

Samuel Johnson. 1755. *A Dictionary of the English Language*. London.

David Jurgens and Ioannis Klapaftis. 2013. Semeval-2013 task 13: Word sense induction for graded and non-graded senses. In *Proceedings of the 7th International Workshop on Semantic Evaluation (SemEval 2013)*, pages 290–299, Atlanta, USA.

Adam Kilgarriff. 1997. "I Don't Believe in Word Senses". *Computers and the Humanities*, 31(2):91–113.

Ryan Kiros, Yukun Zhu, Ruslan Salakhutdinov, Richard S. Zemel, Antonio Torralba, Raquel Urtasun, and Sanja Fidler. 2015. Skip-thought vectors. In C. Cortes, N. D. Lawrence, D. D. Lee,

M. Sugiyama, and R. Garnett, editors, *Advances in Neural Information Processing Systems 28*, pages 3276–3284. Curran Associates, Inc.

Omer Levy and Yoav Goldberg. 2014. Dependency-based word embeddings. In *Proceedings of the 52nd Annual Meeting of the Association for Comouational Linguistics*, pages 302–308, Maryland, USA.

Marco Lui, Timothy Baldwin, and Diana McCarthy. 2012. Unsupervised estimation of word usage similarity. In *Proceedings of the Australasian Language Technology Association Workshop 2012*, pages 33–41, Dunedin, New Zealand.

Diana McCarthy and Roberto Navigli. 2007. Semeval-2007 task 10: English lexical substitution task. In *Proceedings of the Fourth International Workshop on Semantic Evaluations (SemEval-2007)*, pages 48–53, Prague, Czech Republic.

Oren Melamud, Jacob Goldberger, and Ido Dagan. 2016. context2vec: Learning generic context embedding with bidirectional lstm. In *Proceedings of The 20th SIGNLL Conference on Computational Natural Language Learning*, pages 51–61.

Tomas Mikolov, Kai Chen, Greg Corrado, and Jeffrey Dean. 2013. Efficient estimation of word representations in vector space. In *Proceedings of Workshop at the International Conference on Learning Representations, 2013*, Scottsdale, USA.

Arvind Neelakantan, Jeevan Shankar, Alexandre Passos, and Andrew McCallum. 2014. Efficient non-parametric estimation of multiple embeddings per word in vector space. In *Proceedings of the 2014 Conference on Empirical Methods in Natural Language Processing (EMNLP)*, pages 1059–1069, Doha, Qatar.

Jeffrey Pennington, Richard Socher, and Christopher D. Manning. 2014. Glove: Global vectors for word representation. In *Empirical Methods in Natural Language Processing (EMNLP)*, pages 1532–1543.

Serge Sharoff. 2006. Open-source corpora: Using the net to fish for linguistic data. *Corpus Linguistics*, 11(4):435–462.

Lexical Disambiguation of Igbo through Diacritic Restoration

Ignatius Ezeani   **Mark Hepple**   **Ikechukwu Onyenwe**
NLP Research Group,
Department of Computer Science,
University of Sheffield, UK.
{ignatius.ezeani,m.r.hepple,i.onyenwe}@sheffield.ac.uk

Abstract

Properly written texts in Igbo, a low resource African language, are rich in both orthographic and tonal diacritics. Diacritics are essential in capturing the distinctions in pronunciation and meaning of words, as well as in lexical disambiguation. Unfortunately, most electronic texts in diacritic languages are written without diacritics. This makes diacritic restoration a necessary step in corpus building and language processing tasks for languages with diacritics. In our previous work, we built some $n-$gram models with simple smoothing techniques based on a closed-world assumption. However, as a classification task, diacritic restoration is well suited for and will be more generalisable with machine learning. This paper, therefore, presents a more standard approach to dealing with the task which involves the application of machine learning algorithms.

1   Introduction

Diacritics are marks placed over, under, or through a letter in some languages to indicate a different sound value from the same letter. English does not have diacritics (apart from a few borrowed words) but many of the world's languages use a wide range of diacritized letters in their orthography. Automatic Diacritic Restoration Systems (ADRS) enable the restoration of missing diacritics in texts. Many forms of such tools have been proposed, designed and developed but work on Igbo is still in its early stages.

1.1   Diacritics and Igbo language

Igbo, a major Nigerian language and the native language of the people of the south-eastern Nige-

ria, is spoken by over 30 million people worldwide. It uses the Latin scripts and has many dialects. Most written works, however, use the official orthography produced by the *Ọnwụ Committee*[1].

The orthography has 8 vowels (*a, e, i, o, u, ị, ọ, ụ*) and 28 consonants (*b, gb, ch, d, f, g, gw, gh, h, j, k, kw, kp, l, m, n, nw, ny, ṅ, p, r, s, sh, t, v, w, y, z*).

Table 1, shows Igbo characters with their orthographic or tonal (or both) diacritics and possible changes in meanings of the words they appear in[2].

Char	Ortho	Tonal
a	–	à,á, ā
e	–	è,é, ē
i	ị	ì, í, ī, ị̀, ị́, ị̄
o	ọ	ò, ó, ō, ọ̀, ọ́, ọ̄
u	ụ	ù, ú, ū, ụ̀, ụ́, ụ̄
m	–	m̀,ḿ, m̄
n	ṅ	ǹ,ń, n̄

Table 1: Igbo diacritic complexity

Most Igbo electronic texts collected from social media platforms are riddled with flaws ranging from dialectal variations and spelling errors to lack of diacritics. For instance, consider this raw excerpt from a chat on a popular Nigerian online chat forum *www.nairaland.com*[3]:

> *otu ubochi ka'm no na amaghi ihe mu*
> *na uwa ga-eje. kam noo n'eche ihe*
> *a,otu mmadu wee kpoturum,m lee anya*
> *o buru nwoke mara mma puru iche,mma*
> *ya turu m n'obi.o gwam si nne kedu*

---

[1] http://www.columbia.edu/itc/mealac/pritchett/00fwp/igbo/txt_onwu_1961.pdf

[2] *m* and *n*, nasal consonants, are sometimes treated as tone marked vowels.

[3] Source: *http://www.nairaland.com/189374/igbo-love-messages*

Proceedings of the 1st Workshop on Sense, Concept and Entity Representations and their Applications, pages 53–60,
Valencia, Spain, April 4 2017. ©2017 Association for Computational Linguistics

*k'idi.onu ya dika onu ndi m'ozi, ihu ya
dika anyanwu ututu,ahu ya n'achakwa
bara bara ka mmiri si n'okwute. ka ihe
niile no n'agbam n'obi,o sim na ohuru
m n'anya.na ochoro k'anyi buru enyi,a
hukwuru m ya n'anya.anyi wee kweko-
rita wee buru enyi onye'a m n'ekwu
maka ya bu odinobi m,onye ihe ya
n'amasi m*

In the above example, you can observe that there is zero presence of diacritics - tonal or orthographic - in the entire text. As pointed out above, although there are other issues with regards to standard in the text, lack of diacritics seems to be harder to control or avoid than the others. This is partly because diacritics or lack of it does affect human understanding a great deal; and also the rigours a writer will go through to insert them may not worth the effort. The challenge, however, is that NLP systems built and trained with such poor quality non standard data will most likely be unreliable.

1.2 Diacritic restoration and other NLP systems

Diacritic restoration is important for other NLP systems such as speech recognition, text generation and machine translations systems. For example, although most translation systems are now very impressive, not a lot of them support Igbo language. However, for the few that do (e.g. *Google Translate*), diacritic restoration still plays a huge role in how well they perform. The example below shows the effect of diacritic marks on the output of *Google Translate*'s Igbo-to-English translation.

Statement	Google Translate	Comment
O ji *egbe* ya gbuo *egbe*	He used his **gun** to kill *gun*	wrong
O ji **égbè** ya gbuo **égbé**	He used his **gun** to kill **kite**	correct
Akwa ya di n'elu *akwa* ya	It was on the **bed** in his room	fair
Ákwà ya di n'elu **àkwà** ya	his **clothes** on his **bed**	correct
Oke riri *oke* ya	Her addiction	confused
Òké riri **òkè** ya	**Mouse** ate his **share**	correct
O jiri *ugbo* ya bia	He came with his *farm*	wrong
O jiri **ụgbọ** ya bia	He came with his **car**	correct

Table 2: Diacritic disambiguation for *Google Translate*

1.3 Diacritic restoration and WSD

Yarowsky (1994a) observed that, although diacritic restoration is not a hugely popular task in NLP research, it shares similar properties with such tasks as word sense disambiguation with regards to resolving both syntactic and semantic ambiguities. Indeed it was referred to as an instance of a closely related class of problems which includes word choice selection in machine translation, homograph and homophone disambiguation and capitalisation restoration (Yarowsky, 1994b).

Diacritic restoration, like sense disambiguation, is not an end in itself but an *"intermediate task"* (Wilks and Stevenson, 1996) which supports better understanding and representation of meanings in human-machine interactions. In most non-diacritic languages, sense disambiguation systems can directly support such tasks as machine translation, information retrieval, text processing, speech processing etc. (Ide and Véronis, 1998). But it takes more for diacritic languages, where possible, to produce standard texts. So for those languages, to achieve good results with such systems as listed above, diacritic restoration is required as a boost for the sense disambiguation task.

We note however, that although diacritic restoration is related to word sense disambiguation (WSD), it does not eliminate the need for sense disambiguation. For example, if the word-key *akwa* is successfully restored to *àkwà*, it could still be referring to either *bed* or *bridge*. Another good example is the behaviour of *Google Translate* as the context around the word *àkwà* changes.

Statement	Google Translate	Comment
Akwa ya di n'elu *akwa*	It was on the high	confused
Akwa ya di n'elu *akwa* ya	It was on the bed in his room	fair
Ákwà ya di n'elu **àkwà**	His clothing was on the bridge	okay
Ákwà ya di n'elu **àkwà** ya	His clothing on his bed	good

Table 3: Disambiguation challenge for *Google Translate*

The last two statements, with proper diacritics on the ambiguous wordkey *akwa* seem both correct. Some disambiguation system in Google Translate must have been used to select the right form. However, it highlights the fact that such a disambiguation system may perform better when diacritics are restored.

2 Problem Definition

As explained above, lack of diacritics can often lead to some lexical ambiguities in written Igbo sentences. Although a human reader can, in most cases, infer the intended meaning from context, the machine may not. Consider the sentences in sections 2.1 and 2.2 and their literal translations:

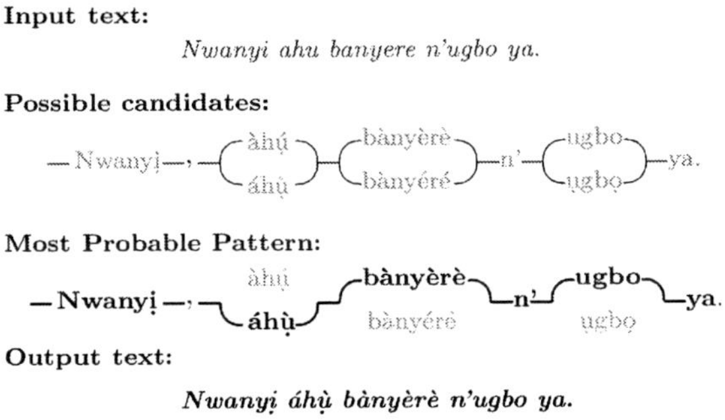

Input text:

Nwanyi ahu banyere n'ugbo ya.

Possible candidates:

— Nwanyị —, (àhú / áhụ) (bànyèrè / bànyéré) —n'— (ugbo / ụgbọ) —ya.

Most Probable Pattern:

— Nwanyị —, (áhụ̀ / áhụ) (bànyèrè / bànyére) —n'— (ugbo / ụgbọ) —ya.

Output text:

Nwanyị áhụ̀ bànyèrè n'ugbo ya.

Figure 1: Illustrative View of the Diacritic Restoration Process (Ezeani et al., 2016)

2.1 Missing orthographic diacritics

1. *Nwanyi ahu banyere n'ugbo ya.* (The woman entered her **[farm|boat/craft]**)

2. *O kwuru banyere olu ya.* (He/she talked about his/her **[neck/voice|work/job]**)

2.2 Missing tonal diacritics

1. *Nwoke ahu nwere egbe n'ulo ya.* (That man has a **[gun|kite]** in his house)

2. *O dina n'elu akwa.* (He/she is lying on the **[cloth|bed,bridge|egg|cry]**)

3. *Egwu ji ya aka.* (He/she is held/gripped by **[fear|song/dance/music]**)

Ambiguities arise when diacritics – orthographic or tonal – are omitted in Igbo texts. In the first examples, we could see that **ugbo**(*farm*) and **ụgbọ**(*boat/craft*) as well as **olu**(*neck/voice*) and **ọlụ**(*work/job*) were candidates in their sentences.

Also the second examples show that **égbé**(*kite*) and **égbè**(*gun*); **ákwà**(*cloth*), **àkwà**(*bed or bridge*), **àkwá**(*egg*), or even **ákwá**(*cry*) in a philosophical or artistic sense; as well as **égwù**(*fear*) and **égwú**(*music*) are all qualified to replace the ambiguous word in their respective sentences.

3 Related Literature

Diacritic restoration techniques for low resource languages adopt two main approaches: *word based* and *character based*.

3.1 Word level diacritic restoration

Different schemes of the word-based approach have been described. They generally involve *pre-processing*, *candidate generation* and *disambiguation*. Simard (1998) applied POS-tags and HMM language models for French. On the Croatian language, Šantić et al. (2009) used substitution schemes, a dictionary and language models in implementing a similar architecture. For Spanish, Yarowsky (1999) used dictionaries with decision lists, Bayesian classification and Viterbi decoding the surrounding context.

Crandall (2005), using Bayesian approach, HMM and a hybrid of both, as well as different evaluation method, attempted to improve on Yarowsky's work. Cocks and Keegan (2011) worked on Māori using naïve Bayes and word-based *n*-grams relating to the target word as instance features. Tufiş and Chiţu (1999) used POS tagging to restore Romanian texts but backed off to character-based approach to deal with "unknown words". Generally, there seems to be a consensus on the superiority of the word-based approach for well resourced languages.

3.2 Grapheme or letter level diacritic restoration

For low-resource languages, there is often lack of adequate data and resources (large corpora, dictionaries, POS-taggers etc.). Mihalcea (2002) as well as Mihalcea and Nastase (2002) argued that letter-based approach will help to resolve the issue of lack of resources. They implemented instance based and decision tree classifiers which gave a high letter-level accuracy. However, their evaluation method implied a possibly much lower word-level accuracy.

Versions of Mihalcea's approach with improved evaluation methods have been implemented on other low resourced languages (Wagacha et al., 2006; De Pauw et al., 2011; Scannell, 2011). Wagacha et al. (2006), for example, reviewed the evaluation method in Mihalcea's work and introduced a word-level method for Gĩkũyũ. De Pauw et al. (2011) extended Wagacha's work by applying the method to multiple languages.

Our earlier work on Igbo diacritic restoration (Ezeani et al., 2016) was more of a proof of concept aimed at extending the initial work done by Scannell (2011). We built a number of *n*–gram models – basically unigrams, bigrams and trigrams – along with simple smoothing techniques. Although we got relatively high results, our evaluation method was based on a closed-world assumption where we trained and tested on the same set of data. Obviously, that assumption does not model the real world and so it is being addressed in this paper.

3.3 Igbo Diacritic Restoration

Igbo is low-resourced and is generally neglected in NLP research. However, an attempt at restoring Igbo diacritics was reported by Scannell (2011) in which a combination of word- and character-level models were applied. Two lexicon lookup methods were used: *LL* which replaces ambiguous words with the most frequent word and *LL2* that uses a bigram model to determine the right replacement.

They reported word-level accuracies of 88.6% and 89.5% for the models respectively. But the size of training corpus (31k tokens with 4.3k word types) was too little to be representative and there was no language speaker in the team to validate the data used and the results produced. Therefore, we implemented a range of more complex n-gram models, using similar evaluation techniques, on a comparatively larger sized corpus (1.07m with 14.4k unique tokens) and had improved on their results (Ezeani et al., 2016).

In this work, we introduce machine learning approaches to further generalise the process and to better learn the intricate patterns in the data that will help better restoration.

4 Experimental Setup

4.1 Experimental Data

The corpus used in these experiments were collected from the Igbo version of the bible available from the Jehova Witness website[4]. The basic corpus statistics are presented in Table 4.

In Table 4, we refer to the "latinized" form of a word as its *wordkey*[5]. Less than 10% (529/15696) of the wordkeys are ambiguous. However, these ambiguous wordkeys represent 529 ambiguous sets that yield 348,509 of the corpus words (i.e. words that share the same *wordkey* with at least one other word). These ambiguous words constitutes approximately 38.22% (348,509/911892) of the entire corpus. Some of the top most occurring, as well as the bottom least occurring ambiguous sets are shown in Table 5.

---

[4]jw.org

[5]Expectedly, many Igbo words are the same with their wordkeys

Item	Number
Total tokens	1070429
Total words	902150
Numbers/punctuations	168279
Unique words	563383
Ambiguous words	348509
Wordkeys	15696
Unique wordkeys	15167
Ambiguous wordkeys	529
2 variants	502
3 variants	15
4 variants	10
5 variants	2
>5 variants	0
Approx. ambiguity	38.22%

Table 4: Corpus statistics

Top	Variants(count)
na(29272)	ná(1332), na(27940)
o(22418)	o(4757), ò(64), ó(5), ọ(17592)
Bottom	**Variants(count)**
Giteyịm(2)	Giteyịm(1), Giteyim(1)
Galim(2)	Galim(1), Galịm(1)

Table 5: Most and least frequent wordkeys

4.2 Preprocessing

The preprocessing task relied substantially on the approaches used by Onyenwe et al. (2014). Observed language based patterns were preserved. For example, *ga–*, *na–* and *n'* are retained as they are due to the specific lexical functions the special characters "–" or " ' " confer on them. For instance, while *na* implies conjunction (e.g. **ji na ede**: yam and cocoa-yam), *na–* is a verb auxiliary (e.g. **Obi na–agba ọsọ**: Obi is running) and *n'* is shortened form of the preposition *na* (e.g. **Ọ dị n'elu àkwà**: It is on the bed.).

Also for consistency, diacritic formats are normalized using the unicode's *Normalization Form Canonical* NFC composition. For example, the character *é* from the combined unicode characters *e* (u0065) and ´ (u0301) will be decomposed and recombined as a single canonically equivalent character *é* (u00e9). Also the character *ṅ*, which is often wrongly replaced with *ñ* and *n̄* in some text, is generally restored back to its standard form.

The diacritic marking of the corpus used in this research is sufficient but not full or perfect. The orthographic diacritics (mostly dot-belows) have been included throughout. However, the tonal diacritics are fairly sparse, having been included only where they were for disambiguation (i.e. where the reader might not be able to decide the correct form from context.

Therefore, through manual inspection, some observed errors and anomalies were corrected by language speakers. For example, 3153 out of 3154 occurrences of the key *mmadu* were of the class *mmadu*. The only one that was *mmadu* was corrected to *mmadu* after inspection. By repeating this process, a lot of the generated ambiguous sets were resolved and removed from the list to reduce the noise. Examples are as shown in the table below:

wordkey	Freq	var1Freq	var2Freq
akpu	106	ákpụ–1	akpụ–105
agbu	112	agbụ–111	ágbụ–1
aka	3690	aka–3689	ákà–1
iri	2036	iri–2035	ịrị–1

Table 6: Some examples of corrected and removed ambiguous set

4.3 Feature extraction for training instances

The feature sets for the classification models were based on the works of Scannell (2011) on character-based restoration which was extended by Cocks and Keegan (2011) to deal with word-based restoration for Māori. These features consist of a combination of n-grams – represented in the form (x,y), where x is the relative position to the target key and y is the token length – at different positions within the left and right context of the target word. The datasets are built as described below for each of the ambiguous keys:

- **FS1[(-1,1), (1,1)]:** Unigrams on each side of the target key

- **FS2[(-2,2), (2,2)]:** Bigrams on each side

- **FS3[(-3,3), (3,3)]:** Trigrams on each side

- **FS4[(-4,4), (4,4)]:** 4-grams on each side

- **FS5[(-5,5), (5,5)]:** 5-grams on each side

- **FS6[(-2,1), (-1,1), (1,1), (2,1)]:** 2 unigrams on both sides

- **FS7[(-3,1), (-2,1), (-1,1), (1,1), (2,1), (3,1)]:** 3 unigrams on each side

- **FS8[(-4,1), (-3,1), (-2,1), (-1,1), (1,1), (2,1), (3,1), (4,1)]:** 4 unigrams on each side

- **FS9[(-5,1), (-4,1), (-3,1), (-2,1), (-1,1), (1,1), (2,1), (3,1), (4,1), (5,1)]:** 5 unigrams on each side

- **FS10[(-2,2), (-1,1), (1,1), (2,2)]:** 1 unigram and 1 bigram on each side

- **FS11[(-3,3), (-2,2), (2,2), (3,3)]:** 1 bigram and 1 trigram on each side

- **FS12[(-3,3), (-2,2), (-1,1), (1,1), (2,2), (3,3)]:** 1 unigram, 1 bigram and 1 trigram on each side

- **FS13[(-4,4), (-3,3), (-2,2), (-1,1), (1,1), (2,2), (3,3), (4,4)]:** 1 unigram, 1 bigram, 1 trigram and a 4-gram on each side

4.3.1 Appearance threshold and stratification

We removed low-frequency wordkeys in our data by defining an *appearance threshold* as a percentage of the total tokens in our data. This is given by the

$$appThreshold = \frac{C(wordkeys)}{C(tokens)} * 100$$

and wordkeys with *appThreshold* below the stated value[6] were removed from the experiment.

As part of our data preparation for a standard cross-validation, we also passed each of our datasets through a simple stratification process. Instances of each label[7], where possible, are evenly distributed to appear at least once in each fold or removed from the dataset.

Our stratification algorithm basically picks only labels from each dataset that have a population p such that $p >= nfolds$. $nfolds$ is the number of folds which in our case has a default value of 10. In order to make the task a little more challenging, this process was augmented by the removal of some high frequency, but low *entropy* datasets where using the most common class (MCC) produces very high accuracies[8]. Entropy is loosely used here to refer to the degree of dominance of a particular class across the dataset and it is simply defined as:

$$entropy = 1 - \frac{max[Count(label_i)]}{len(dataset)}$$

---

[6]In this work, we used an *appThreshold* of 0.005%

[7]*labels* are basically diacritic variants.

[8]Datasets with more than 95% accuracy on the most common class (i.e. with entropy lower than 0.05) were removed.

where $i = 1..n$ and n =number of distinct labels in the dataset. Table 7 shows 10 of the 30 lowest entropy datasets that were removed by this process.

wordkey	Counts	MCCscore	Label(count)
e(2)	5476	99.78%	è(12); e(5464)
anyi(2)	5390	99.63%	anyi(5370); ànyị(20)
ma(2)	6713	99.61%	ma(6687); mà(26)
ike(2)	3244	99.54%	ikè(15); ike(3229)
unu(2)	8662	99.53%	ùnu(41); unu(8621)
Ha(2)	2266	99.29%	Hà(16); Ha(2250)
a(2)	12275	99.10%	a(12165); à(110)
onye(2)	8937	98.87%	onye(8836); ònye(101)
ohu(2)	790	98.73%	ohu(780); ọhụ(10)
eze(2)	2633	98.14%	eze(2584); ezé(49)

Table 7: Low entropy datasets

At end of these pruning processes, our remaining datasets came to 110 with the distribution as follows:

- *datasets with only 2 variants: = 93*

- *datasets with 3 variants: = 7*

- *datasets with 4 variants: = 8*

- *datasets with 5 variants: = 2*

Some datasets that originally had multiple variants lost some of their variants. For example, the dataset from *akwa* which originally had five variants and 1067 instances comprising of *ákwá* (355), *ákwà*(485), *akwa*(216), *àkwà*(1) and *àkwá*(10) retained only four variants (after dropping *àkwà*) and 1066 instances.

4.4 Classification algorithms

This work applied versions of five of the commonly used machine learning algorithms in NLP classification tasks namely:

- Linear Discriminant Analysis(LDA)

- K Nearest Neighbors(KNN)

- Decision Trees(DTC)

- Support Vector Machines(SVC)

- Naïve Bayes(MNB)

Their default parameters on Scikit-learn toolkit were used with 10-fold cross-validation and the evaluation metrics used is mainly the accuracy of prediction of the correct diacritic form in the test data. The effect of the accuracy obtained for a

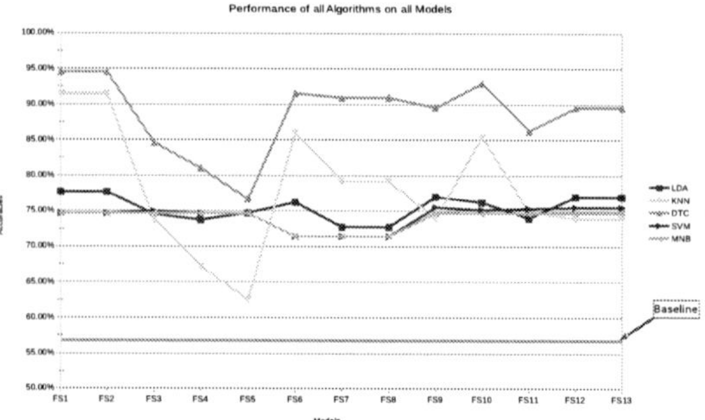

Figure 2: Evaluation of algorithm performance on each feature set model

dataset on the overall performance depends on the weight of the dataset. Each dataset is assigned a weight corresponding to the number of instances it generates from the corpus which is determined by its frequency of occurrence.

So the actual performance of each learning algorithm, on a particular feature set model, is the overall weighted average of the its performances across all the 110 datasets. The *bottom line* accuracy is the result of replacing each word with its *wordkey* which gave an accuracy of 30.46%. However, the actual baseline to beat is **52.79%** which is achieved by always predicting the most common class.

4.5 Results and Discussions

The results of our experiments are as shown in Table 8 and Figure 2.

Models	LDA	KNN	DTC	SVM	MNB
Baseline:	**52.79%**				
FS1	**77.65%**	**91.47%**	**94.49%**	74.64%	74.64%
FS2	**77.65%**	**91.47%**	**94.49%**	74.64%	74.64%
FS3	74.48%	73.70%	84.60%	74.92%	74.64%
FS4	73.71%	67.18%	81.00%	74.64%	74.64%
FS5	74.68%	62.48%	76.70%	74.64%	74.64%
FS6	76.21%	85.98%	91.54%	71.39%	71.39%
FS7	72.74%	79.20%	90.94%	71.39%	71.39%
FS8	72.74%	79.20%	90.94%	71.39%	71.39%
FS9	76.99%	73.88%	89.50%	**75.46%**	**74.67%**
FS10	76.18%	85.41%	92.89%	75.11%	74.64%
FS11	73.94%	74.83%	86.23%	75.29%	74.64%
FS12	76.99%	73.88%	89.50%	**75.46%**	**74.67%**
FS13	76.99%	73.88%	89.50%	**75.46%**	**74.67%**

Table 8: Summary of results

The experiments indicate that on the average all the algorithms were able to beat the baseline on all models. The decision tree algorithm (DTC) performed best across all models with an average accuracy of 88.64% (Figure 3), and the highest accuracy of 94.49% (Table 8) on both the **FS1** and **FS2** models. However, with an average standard deviation of 0.076 (Figure 4) for its results, it appears to be the least reliable.

As the next best performing algorithm, KNN falls below DTC in average accuracy (91.47%) but seems slightly more reliable. It did, however, struggle more than others as the dimension of feature n-grams increased (see its performance on **FS3**, **FS4** and **FS5**). This may be due to the increase in sparsity of features and the difficulty to find similar *neighbours*. The other algorithms – **LDA**, **SVM** and **MNB** – just trailed behind and although their results are a lot more reliable especially **SVM** and **MNB** (Figure 4). But this may be an indication that their strategies are not explorative enough. However, it could be observed that they traced a similar path in the graph and also had their highest results with the same set of models (i.e. **FS9**, **FS12** and **FS13**) with wider context.

On the models, we observed that the unigrams and bigrams have better predictive capacity than the other n-grams. Most of the algorithms got comparatively good results with **FS1**, **FS2**, **FS6** and **FS10** (Figure 5) each of which has the unigram closest to the target word (i.e. in the ±1 position) in the feature set. Also, models that excluded the closest unigrams on both sides (e.g. **FS11**) and those with fairly wider context did not perform comparatively well across algorithms.

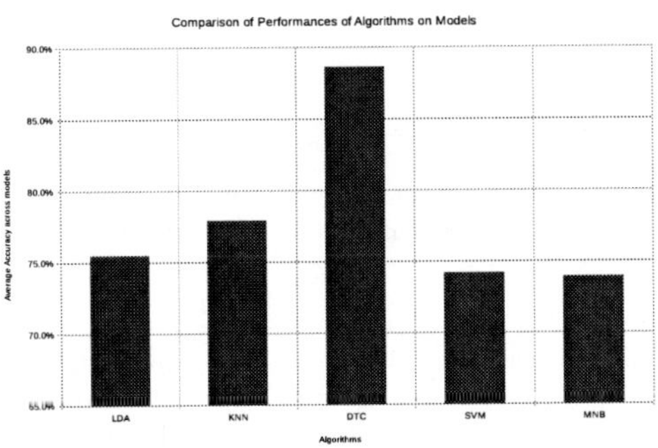

Figure 3: Average performance of algorithms

Again, it appears that beyond the three closest unigrams (i.e. those in the -3 through $+3$ positions), the classifiers tend to be confused by additional context information. Generally, **FS1** and **FS2** stood out across all algorithms as the best models while **FS6** and **FS7** also did well especially with **DTC**, **KNN** and **LDA**.

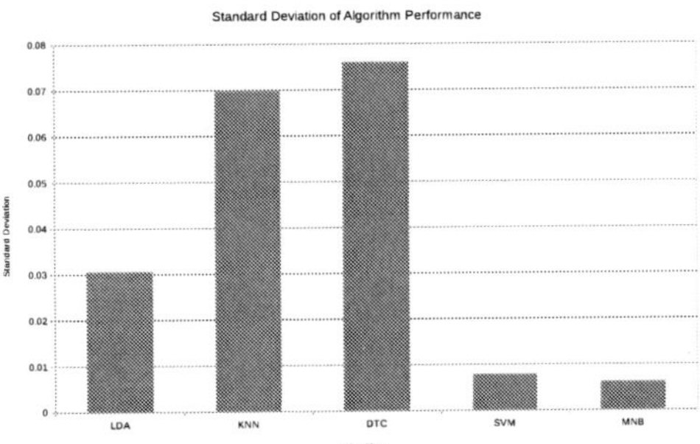

Figure 4: Average standard deviation for algorithms

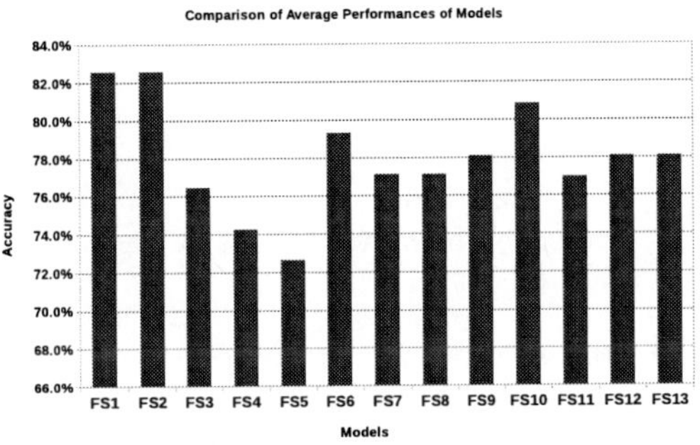

Figure 5: Average performance of models

4.6 Future Research Direction

Although our results show a substantial improvement from the baseline accuracy by all the algorithms on all the models, there is still a lot of room for improvement. Our next experiments will involve attempts to improve the results by focusing on the following key aspects:

- *Reviewing the feature set models:*
  So far we have used instances with similar features on both sides of the target words. In our next experiments, we may consider varying these features.

- *Exploiting the algorithms:*
  We were more explorative with the algorithms and so only the default parameters of the algorithms on Scikit-learn were tested. Subsequent experiments will involve tuning the parameters of the algorithms and possibly using more evaluation metrics.

- *Expanding data size and genre:*
  A major challenge for this research work is lack of substantially marked corpora. So although, we achieved a lot with the bible data,

it is inadequate and not very representative of the contemporary use of the language. Future research efforts will apply more resources to increasing the data size across other genres.

- *Predicting unknown words:*
  Our work is yet to properly address the problem of unknown words. We are considering a closer inspection of the structural patterns in the target word to see if they contain elements with predictive capacity.

- *Broad based standardization:*
  Beside lack of diacritics online Igbo texts are riddled with spelling errors, lack of standard orthographic and dialectal forms, poor writing styles, foreign words and so on. It may therefore be good to consider a broader based process that includes, not just diacritic restoration but other aspects of standardization.

- *Interfacing with other NLP systems:*
  Although it seems obvious, it will be interesting to investigate, in empirical terms, the relationship between diacritic restoration and others NLP tasks and systems such as POS-tagging, morphological analysis and even the broader field of word sense disambiguation.

Acknowledgements

The IgboNLP Project @ The University of Sheffield, UK is funded by TETFund & Nnamdi Azikiwe University, Nigeria.

References

John Cocks and Te-Taka Keegan. 2011. A Word-based Approach for Diacritic Restoration in Māori. In *Proceedings of the Australasian Language Technology Association Workshop 2011*, pages 126–130, Canberra, Australia, December.

David Crandall. 2005. Automatic Accent Restoration in Spanish text. http://www.cs.indiana.edu/~djcran/projects/674_final.pdf. [Online: accessed 7-January-2016].

Guy De Pauw, Gilles maurice De Schryver, Laurette Pretorius, and Lori Levin. 2011. Introduction to the Special Issue on African Language Technology. *Language Resources and Evaluation*, 45:263–269.

Ignatius Ezeani, Mark Hepple, and Ikechukwu Onyenwe, 2016. *Automatic Restoration of Diacritics for Igbo Language*, pages 198–205. Springer International Publishing, Cham.

Nancy Ide and Jean Véronis. 1998. Introduction to the special issue on word sense disambiguation: The state of the art. *Comput. Linguist.*, 24(1):2–40, March.

Rada F. Mihalcea and Vivi Nastase. 2002. Letter level learning for language independent diacritics restoration. *In: Proceedings of CoNLL-2002, Taipei, Taiwan*, pages 105–111.

Rada F. Mihalcea. 2002. Diacritics Restoration: Learning from Letters versus Learning from Words. *In: Gelbukh, A. (ed.) CICLing LNCS*, pages 339–348.

Ikechukwu Onyenwe, Chinedu Uchechukwu, and Mark Hepple. 2014. Part-of-speech Tagset and Corpus Development for igbo, an African Language. *LAW VIII - The 8th Linguistic Annotation Workshop.*, pages 93–98.

Kevin P. Scannell. 2011. Statistical unicodification of african languages. *Language Resource Evaluation*, 45(3):375–386, September.

Michel Simard. 1998. Automatic Insertion of Accents in French texts. *Proceedings of the Third Conference on Empirical Methods in Natural Language Processing*, pages 27–35.

Dan Tufiş and Adrian Chiţu. 1999. Automatic Diacritics Insertion in Romanian texts. In *Proceedings of COMPLEX99 International Conference on Computational Lexicography*, pages 185–194, Pecs, Hungary.

Nikola Šantić, Jan Šnajder, and Bojana Dalbelo Bašić, 2009. *Automatic Diacritics Restoration in Croatian Texts*, pages 126–130. Dept of Info Sci, Faculty of Humanities and Social Sciences, University of Zagreb , 2009. ISBN: 978-953-175-355-5.

Peter W. Wagacha, Guy De Pauw, and Pauline W. Githinji. 2006. A Grapheme-based Approach to Accent Restoration in Gĩkũyũ. In *Proceedings of the Fifth International Conference on Language Resources and Evaluation*, pages 1937–1940, Genoa, Italy, May.

Yorick Wilks and Mark Stevenson. 1996. The grammar of sense: Is word-sense tagging much more than part-of-speech tagging? *CoRR*, cmp-lg/9607028.

David Yarowsky. 1994a. A Comparison of Corpus-based Techniques for Restoring Accents in Spanish and French Text. In *Proceedings, 2nd Annual Workshop on Very Large Corpora*, pages 19–32, Kyoto.

David Yarowsky. 1994b. Decision Lists for Lexical Ambiguity Resolution: Application to Accent Resolution in Spanish and French Text. In *Proceedings of ACL-94*, Las Cruces, New Mexico.

David Yarowsky, 1999. *Corpus-based Techniques for Restoring Accents in Spanish and French Text*, pages 99–120. Kluwer Academic Publishers.

Creating and Validating Multilingual Semantic Representations for Six Languages: Expert versus Non-Expert Crowds

Mahmoud El-Haj, Paul Rayson, Scott Piao and Stephen Wattam
School of Computing and Communications, Lancaster University, Lancaster, UK
`initial.surname@lancaster.ac.uk`

Abstract

Creating high-quality wide-coverage multilingual semantic lexicons to support knowledge-based approaches is a challenging time-consuming manual task. This has traditionally been performed by linguistic experts: a slow and expensive process. We present an experiment in which we adapt and evaluate crowdsourcing methods employing native speakers to generate a list of coarse-grained senses under a common multilingual semantic taxonomy for sets of words in six languages. 451 non-experts (including 427 Mechanical Turk workers) and 15 expert participants semantically annotated 250 words manually for Arabic, Chinese, English, Italian, Portuguese and Urdu lexicons. In order to avoid erroneous (spam) crowdsourced results, we used a novel task-specific two-phase filtering process where users were asked to identify synonyms in the target language, and remove erroneous senses.

1 Introduction

Machine understanding of the meaning of words, phrases, sentences and documents has challenged computational linguists since the 1950s, and much progress has been made at multiple levels. Different types of semantic annotation have been developed, such as word sense disambiguation, semantic role labelling, named entity recognition, sentiment analysis and content analysis. Common to all of these tasks, in the supervised setting, is the requirement for a wide coverage semantic lexicon acting as a knowledge base from which to select or derive potential word or phrase level sense annotations.

The creation of large-scale semantic lexical resources is a time-consuming and difficult task. For new languages, regional varieties, dialects, or domains the task will need to be repeated and then revised over time as word meanings evolve. In this paper, we report on work in which we adapt crowdsourcing techniques to speed up the creation of new semantic lexical resources. We evaluate how efficient the approach is, and how robust the semantic representation is across six languages.

The task that we focus on here is a particularly challenging one. Given a word, each annotator must decide on its meaning[s] and assign the word to single or multiple tags in a pre-existing semantic taxonomy. This task is similar to that undertaken by trained lexicographers during the process of writing or updating dictionary entries. Even for experts, this is a complex task. Kilgarriff (1997) highlighted a number of issues related to lexicographers 'lumping' or 'splitting' senses of a word and cautioned that even lexicographers do not believe in words having a "discrete, non-overlapping set of senses". Véronis (2001) showed that inter-annotator agreement is very low in sense tagging using a traditional dictionary. For our purpose, we use the USAS taxonomy.[1] If a linguist were undertaking this task, as they have done in the past with Finnish (Löfberg et al., 2005) and Russian (Mudraya et al., 2006) USAS taxonomies, they would first spend some time learning the semantic taxonomy. In this experimental scenario, we aim to investigate whether or not non-expert native speakers can succeed on the word-to-senses classification task without being trained on the taxonomy in advance, therefore mitigating a significant overhead for the work. In addition, further motivation for our experiments is to validate the applicability of the USAS taxonomy (Rayson et

---

[1]The UCREL Semantic Analysis System (USAS), see http://ucrel.lancaster.ac.uk/usas/

Proceedings of the 1st Workshop on Sense, Concept and Entity Representations and their Applications, pages 61–71,
Valencia, Spain, April 4 2017. ©2017 Association for Computational Linguistics

al., 2004), with a non-expert crowd, as a framework for multilingual sense representation. The USAS taxonomy was selected for this experiment since it offers a manageable coarse-grained set of categories that have already been applied to a number of languages. This taxonomy is distinct from other potential choices, such as WordNet. The USAS tagset is originally loosely based on the Longman Lexicon of Contemporary English (McArthur, 1981) and has a hierarchical structure with 21 major domains (see table 1) subdividing into three levels. Versions of the USAS tagger or tagset exist in 15 languages in total and for each language, native speakers have re-evaluated the applicability of the tagset with some specific extensions for Chinese (Qian and Piao, 2009) but otherwise the tagset is stable across all languages. For each language tagger, separate linguistic resources (lexicons) have been created, but they all use the same taxonomy.

Domain	Description
A	General and abstract terms
B	The body and the individual
C	Arts and crafts
E	Emotion
F	Food and farming
G	Government and public
H	Architecture, housing and the home
I	Money and commerce in industry
K	Entertainment, sports and games
L	Life and living things
M	Movement, location, travel and transport
N	Numbers and measurement
O	Substances, materials, objects and equipment
P	Education
Q	Language and communication
S	Social actions, states and processes
T	Time
W	World and environment
X	Psychological actions, states and processes
Y	Science and technology
Z	Names and grammar

Table 1: USAS top level semantic fields

In terms of main contributions, our research goes beyond the previous work on crowdsourcing word meanings which requires workers to pick a word sense from an existing list that matches provided contextual examples, such as a concordance list. In our work, we require the participants to define the list of all possible senses that a word could take in different contexts. We also see that our two-stage filtering process tailored for this task helps to improve results. We compare inter-rater scores for two groups of experts and non-experts to examine the feasibility of extracting high-quality semantic lexicons via the untrained crowd. Non-experts achieved results between 45-97% for accuracy, between 48-92% for completeness, with an average of 18% of tasks having erroneous senses being left in. Experts scored 64-96% for accuracy, 72-95% for completeness, but achieve better results in terms of only 1% of erroneous senses left behind. Our experimental results show that the non-expert crowdsourced annotation process is of a good quality and comparable to that of expert linguists in some cases, although there are variations across different languages. Crowdsourcing provides a promising approach for the speedy generation and expansion of semantic lexicons on a large scale. It also allows us to validate the semantic representations embedded in our taxonomy in the multilingual setting.

2 Related Work

The crowdsourcing approach, in particular Mechanical Turk (MTurk), has been successfully applied for a number of different Natural Language Processing (NLP) tasks. Alonso and Mizzaro (2009) adopted MTurk for five types of NLP tasks, resulting in high agreement between expert gold standard labels and non-expert annotations, where a small number of workers can emulate an expert. With the possibility of achieving good results quickly and cheaply, MTurk has been tested for a variety of tasks, such as image annotation (Sorokin and Forsyth, 2008), Wikipedia article quality assessment (Kittur et al., 2008), machine translation (Callison-Burch, 2009), extracting key phrases from documents (Yang et al., 2009), and summarization (El-Haj et al., 2010). Practical issues such as payment and task design play an important part in ensuring the quality of the resulting work. Many designers pay between $0.01 to $0.10 for a task taking a few minutes. Quality control and evaluation are usually achieved through confidence scores and gold-standards (Donmez et al., 2009; Bhardwaj et al., 2010). Past research has shown (Aker et al., 2012) that the use of radio button design seems to lead to better results compared to the free text design. Particularly important in our case is the language demographics of MTurk (Pavlick et al., 2014), since we need to find enough native speakers in a number of languages.

There is a growing body of crowdsourcing work related to semantic annotation. Snow et al. (2008) applied MTurk to the Word Sense Disambiguation (WSD) task and achieved 100% precision with simple majority voting for the correct sense of the word 'president' in 177 example sentences. Rumshisky et al. (2012) derived a sense inventory and sense-annotated corpus from MTurkers comparison of senses in pairs of example sentences. They used clustering methods to identify the strength of coders' tags, something that is poorly suited to rejecting work from spammers (participants who try to cheat the system with scripts or random answers) and would likely not transfer well to our experiment.

Akkaya et al. (2010) also performed WSD using MTurk workers. They discuss a number of methods for ensuring quality, accountability, and consistency using 9 tasks per word and simple majority voting. Kapelner et al. (2012) increased the scale to 1,000 words for the WSD task and found that workers repeating the task do not learn without feedback. A set-based agreement metric was used by Passonneau et al. (2006) to assess the validity of polysemous selections of word senses from WordNet categories. Their objective was to take into account similarity between items within a set, however, this may not be desirable in our case due to the limited depth of the USAS taxonomy.

Directly related to our research here are the experiments reported in Piao et al. (2015). A set of prototype semantic lexicons were automatically generated by transferring semantic tags from the existing USAS English semantic lexicon entries to their translation equivalents in Italian, Chinese and Portuguese via dictionaries and bilingual lexicons. While some dictionaries involved, including Chinese/English and Portuguese/English dictionaries, provided high quality lexical translations for core vocabularies of these languages, the bilingual lexicons, including FreeLang English/Italian, English/Portuguese lexicons[2] and LDC English/Chinese word list, contain erroneous and inaccurate translations. To re-

duce the error rate, some manual cleaning was carried out, particularly on the English-Italian bilingual lexicons. Because of the substantial amount of time needed for such manual work, the rest of the lexical resources were used with only minor sporadic manual checking. Due to the noise introduced from the bilingual lexicons, as well as the ambiguous nature of the translation, the automatically generated semantic lexicons for the three languages contain errors, including erroneous semantic tags caused by incorrect translations, and inaccurate semantic tags caused by ambiguous translations. When these automatically generated lexicons were integrated and applied in the USAS semantic tagger, the tagger suffered from error rates of 23.51%, 12.31% and 10.28% for Italian, Chinese and Portuguese respectively.

The improvement of the semantic lexicons is therefore an urgent and challenging task, and we hypothesise that the crowdsourcing approach can potentially provide an effective means for addressing this issue on a large scale, while at the same time allowing us to further validate the representation of word senses in the USAS sense inventory (i.e. the semantic tagset) for these languages.

3 Semantic Labeling Experiment

We test the wisdom of the crowd in building lexicons and applying the same multilingual semantic representation in six languages: Arabic, Chinese, English, Italian, Portuguese and Urdu. These languages were selected to provide a range of language families, inflectional and derivational morphology, while covering significant number of speakers worldwide. For each language, we randomly selected 250 words. All experiments presented here use the USAS taxonomy to describe semantic categories[3] (Rayson et al., 2004).

3.1 Gold Standard Semantic Tags

To prepare gold standard data we asked a group of linguists (up to two per language) to manually check 250 randomly selected words for each of the six languages, starting from the data provided by Piao et al. (2015). For additional languages (those not in Piao et al. (2015)), the Arabic and Urdu gold standards were completed manually by native speaker linguists who translated the 250 words, and we instructed the translators to opt for the most familiar Arabic or Urdu equivalents

---

[2]http://www.freelang.net/dictionary/

[3]http://ucrel.lancaster.ac.uk/usas/semtags.txt

of the English words. This was further confirmed by checking the list of words by two other Arabic and Urdu native speakers. Here the base form of verbs in Arabic is taken to be the present simple form of the verb in the interest of convenience and because there is no part of speech tag for 'present tense of a lexical verb'. Hence, the three-letter past tense verbs are tagged as 'past form of lexical verb', rather than as base forms. Also, while present and past participles (e.g., 'interesting', 'interested') are tagged as adjectives in English, these are labeled in Arabic as nouns in stand-alone positions but they can also function as adjective premodifying nouns. Linguists then used the USAS semantic tagset to semantically label each word with the most suitable senses.

3.2 Non-expert Participants

Non-expert participants are defined as those who are not familiar with the USAS taxonomy in advance of the experiment. We selected Amazon's Mechanical Turk[4] – an online marketplace for work that requires human intelligence – and published "Human Intelligence Tasks" (HITs) for English, Chinese and Portuguese only. For Arabic, Italian, and Urdu initial experiments using MTurk showed that not enough native speakers are available to complete the tasks. Therefore, we employed 12 non-expert participants directly with four native speakers for each of the three languages. All participants used the same interface (Figure 1).

On MTurk, we paid workers an average of 7 US dollars per hour. We paid Portuguese workers 50% more to try and attract more participants due to the lack of Portuguese native speakers on MTurk. We paid the other directly contacted participants an average of 8 British pounds per hour. Those payments were made using Amazon[5] and Apple iTunes[6] vouchers.

3.3 Expert Participants

Expert participants are defined as those who were already familiar with the USAS taxonomy before the experiments took place. For four languages (Arabic, English, Chinese and Urdu) we asked a total of 15 participants (3 for English and 4 for the other languages) to carry out the same task as

the non-experts. All expert and non-expert participants (whether MTurk workers or direct-contact) used the same user interface (Figure 1) as described in section 3.5.

3.4 Experimental Design

Obtaining reliable results from the crowd remains a challenging task (Kazai et al., 2009), which requires a careful experimental design and preselection of crowdsourcers. In our experiments, we worked on minimising the effort required by participants through designing a user-friendly interface.[7] Aside from copying the final output code to a text-box everything else is done using mouse clicks. Poorly designed experiments can negatively affect the quality of the results conducted by MTurk workers (Downs et al., 2010; Welinder et al., 2010; Kazai, 2011).

Feedback from a short sample run with local testers helped us update the interface and provide more information to make the task efficient. Figure 1 shows a sample task for the word 'car'. The majority of the testers were able to complete the task within five minutes. In response to feedback by some of the testers we provided the "Instructions" section in the six languages under consideration.

Figure 1: Sample Task for the word "Car"

3.5 Online Semantic Labeling

As shown in Figure 1, we asked the participants to label each word presented to them with a number

---

[4]http://www.mturk.com
[5]https://www.amazon.co.uk
[6]http://www.apple.com

[7]Our underlying code is freely available on GitHub at https://github.com/UCREL/BLC-WSD-Frontend

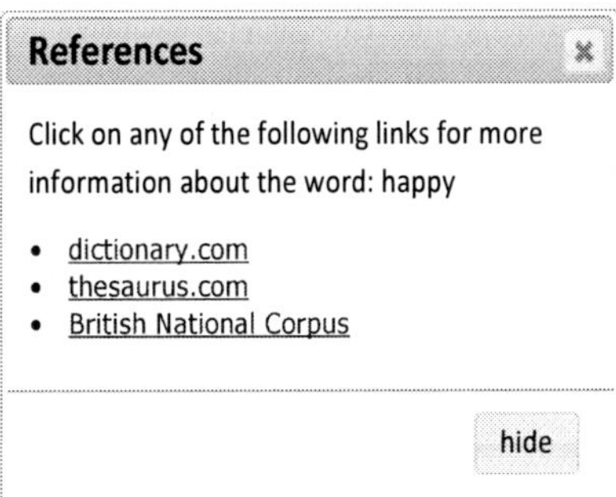

Figure 2: Dictionary and Thesauri References

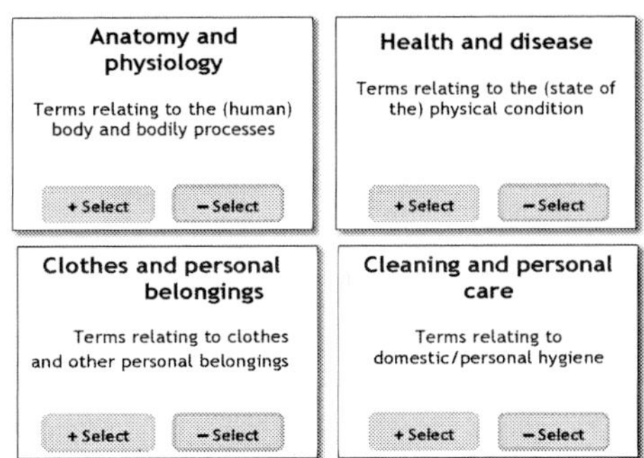

Figure 4: Subcategories

of tags that represent the word's possible meanings. The participants were asked to attach as many, or as few, as they deemed appropriate for all senses of the word, placing them in descending order of likelihood.

To assign a tag, the participants click on the `Add Tag` button, and navigate to a box from the category selection where they can select a subcategory (Figures 3 and 4). By following these steps the participants add an entry in the list, that can then be sorted by dragging and dropping the selected tags so that the most commonly used tag is at the top. We asked the users to remove any unrelated tags and make sure they do not exceed 10 tags in total.

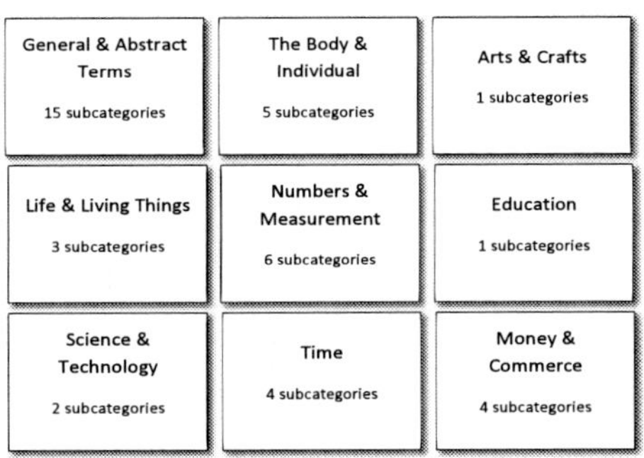

Figure 3: Categories

To help them when identifying common senses of a given word, we provided a number of links to dictionaries, thesauri, and corpora (where they can see real-world usage) for each language. The References are displayed alongside the interface, so they can still browse the tags (Figure 2). Participants are free to use other resources as they see fit. The participants then needed to submit their selections by clicking the `Submit` button at the end of the page and wait until they receive a confirmation message where they need to copy the output-code and provide it to us.

For each word we targeted a total of four non-expert participants and four expert participants to allow measurement and comparison of the agreement within each group to investigate the variability of task results and participants, rather than to take a simple weighted combination to produce an agreed list.

3.6 Filtering

Even though crowdsourcing has been shown to be effective in achieving expert quality for a variety of NLP tasks (Snow et al., 2008; Callison-Burch, 2009), we still needed to filter out workers who were not taking the task seriously or were attempting to manipulate the system for personal gain (spamming).

In order to avoid these spamming crowdsourced results, we designed a novel task-specific two stage filtering process that we considered more suitable for this type of task than previous filtering approaches. Our two stage process encompasses filters that are appropriate for experts and non-experts, and is applicable whether participants are using MTurk or not.

In stage one filtering, we asked the MTurk workers to select the correct synonym of the presented word from a list of noisy candidates in order to avoid rejection of their HITs. The list contained four words where only one word correctly fitted as a synonym. In order to set up the first filtering task for MTurk workers (on English, Chinese and Portuguese tasks), we used Multilingual WordNet to obtain the most common synonym for each word. The stage one filtering was not needed for Arabic, Italian and Urdu, since these non-expert participants were directly contacted and we knew that they were native speakers and would not submit random results. The synonyms were validated by linguists in each of the three languages and choices were randomly shuffled before being presented to the workers. Stage one filtering removed 12% of English HITS, 2% of Chinese, and 6% of the Portuguese submissions. In our results presented below, we only considered tasks by workers who chose the correct synonyms and rejected the others.

For the stage two filter, we injected random erroneous senses for each of the 250 words into the initial list of tags and the participants were expected to remove these in order to pass. We deliberately injected wrong and unrelated semantic tags in between 'potentially' correct ones before shuffling the order of the tags. For example, examining the pre-selected tags for the word 'car' in Figure 1 we can see that the semantic tag 'American Football' is unrelated to the word 'car' and in fact does not exist in the USAS semantic taxonomy. The potentially correct tag such as 'Movement/transportation: land' does exist in the semantic lexicon. Results where participants fail to pass stage two are still retained in the experiment and we report on the usefulness of this filter in section 4. All participants (MTurk workers and directly-contacted; experts and non-experts) undertook stage 2 filtering. Our experimental design did not reveal to the participants any details of the two stage filtering process.

4 Results and Discussion

To evaluate the results[8] we adopted three main metrics (inspired by those used in the SemEval procedures): Accuracy, Completeness, and Correlation.

Accuracy: measure the accuracy of the participant's selection of tags (W_{Tags}) by counting the matching tags between the worker's selection and the gold standards (G_{Tags}). To compute Accuracy we divide the number of matching tags by the number of tags selected by the participants.

$$Accuracy = \frac{W_{Tags} \cap G_{Tags}}{W_{Tags}}$$

Completeness: measure the completeness of the participant's selection of tags (W_{Tags}) by finding whether the gold standard tags (G_{Tags}) are completely or partially contained within the worker's selection. To compute Completeness we divide the number of matching tags by the number of gold standard tags.

$$Completeness = \frac{W_{Tags} \cap G_{Tags}}{G_{Tags}}$$

Correlation: To test the similarity of tag selection between workers and gold standards we used Spearman's rank correlation coefficient.

In addition to the three metrics mentioned above we used three factors that work as indicators of the quality of the tagging process:

- *Strict*: Whether worker's tags are identical to the gold standard (same tags in the same order);

- *First Tag Correct*: Whether the first tag selected by the worker matches the first tag in the gold standard;

- *Fuzzy*: Whether tags selected by a worker are contained within the gold standard tags (in any order).

For each language we asked for up to four annotators per word (1,000 HITs per language). For Portuguese, where the participants were *all* from MTurk, we only received 694 HITs even though we paid participants working on Portuguese 50% more than we paid for the English tasks.

Table 2[9] shows the aggregate averages of the non-expert HITs. In total, direct-contact participants and MTurk workers performed well and achieved comparable results to the gold standard in places. Around 50% of the English, Chinese, Urdu, and Portuguese HITs had the correct tags selected with around 15% being identical to the gold standards. In nearly all of the cases, Portuguese workers chose the correct tags although they were in a different order than the gold standard. Arabic participants achieved a high completeness score relative to the gold standard tags, but a close analysis of the results show the participants have suggested more tags than the gold standards.

The results for English suggest that the non-expert workers are consistent as can be observed

---

[9]For this and the following tables, we use: Acc: Accuracy, Com: Completeness, Corr: Spearman's, Err: Erroneous tags, Str: Strict, 1st: first tag correct, Fuz: Fuzzy.

Lang	Acc	Com	Cor	Err	Str	1st	Fuz
En	61.4	69.3	0.38	29%	16%	65%	38%
Ar	55.5	87.1	0.35	8%	8%	55%	19%
Zh	45.2	56.1	0.22	2%	15%	46%	27%
It	45.7	47.9	0.06	31%	7%	38%	22%
Pt	58.5	56.3	0.21	18%	19%	50%	94%
Ur	97.6	91.9	0.51	1%	53%	78%	95%

Table 2: Summary of performance [Non experts]

by looking at the Accuracy (Acc) and Completeness (Com) results. Spearman's correlation (Cor) suggests that the workers correlate with the expert gold standard tags, which is consistent with previous findings that MTurk is effective for a variety of NLP tasks through achieving expert quality (Snow et al., 2008; Callison-Burch, 2009). The majority of the workers matched the first tag correctly (1st) by ordering the tags so the most important (core sense) tag appeared at the top of their selection. The erroneous tags (Err) column shows that many workers did not remove some of the deliberately-wrong tags (see Section 3.5). This reflects the lack of training of the workers, but our checking of the results showed that the erroneous tags were not selected as first choice. Strict (Str) and Fuzzy (Fuz) show that many workers were consistent with the gold standard tags in terms of both tag selection and order. It is worth mentioning that languages differ in terms of ambiguity (e.g. Urdu is less ambiguous than Arabic) which can be observed in the differences between language results.

As mentioned earlier, we did not use MTurk for the Arabic lexicon, due to the lack of Arabic natives speakers on MTurk. Instead, we found four student volunteers who offered to help in semantically tagging the words, again without any training on the tagset. The results show consistent accuracy and completeness. It is worth noting that the Arabic participants obtained higher accuracy and completeness scores by having higher agreement with the gold standard tags. The Arabic language participants selected fewer erroneous tags than the English ones. The majority of the participants got the first tag correct. Arabic participants failed to match the order of tags in the gold standards as reflected by lower correlation. This is expected due to the fact that Arabic is highly inflectional and derivational, which increases ambiguity and presents a challenge to the interpretation of the words (El-Haj et al., 2014). Difficulties

in knowing the exact sense of an out of context Arabic word could result in disagreement when it comes to ordering the senses (see Section 3.1).

For the Chinese language, the result table shows that there is a slightly lower correlation between the non-expert workers' tags and the gold standards. Observing the erroneous results column we can see that the workers have made very few mistakes and deleted the random unrelated tags. The Strict and Fuzzy scores suggest the results to be of high quality. The participants managed to get the first tag correct in many cases.

For the Italian language, we sourced four non-expert undergrad student participants who are all native Italian speakers but not familiar with the tagset. The participants' results do not correlate well with the gold standards. As the tags description are all in English the annotators found it difficult to correctly select the senses and had to translate some tags into Italian which could have resulted in shifting the meaning of those tags, to communicate with them we had an Italian/English bilingual linguist as a mediator.

As with Arabic and Italian, for the Urdu language we sourced four non-expert participants who are all native Urdu speakers but not familiar with the tagset. Urdu results show that participants correlate well with the gold standards. We also notice a lower percentage of erroneous tags than other languages. The First Tag and Fuzzy scores suggest the results to be of high quality. The participants also managed to get the first tag correct in many cases. The participants all agreed it was easy to define word senses with the words being less ambiguous compared to other languages. This is shown in the high results achieved when compared to non-experts of the other languages.

We received only 694 HITs for Portuguese tasks on MTurk, which suggests there are fewer Portuguese speakers compared to English and Chinese speakers among the MTurk workers. The results for Portuguese in some cases are of very high quality. It should be noted that the gold standard tags were selected and manually checked by a Brazilian Portuguese native speaker expert. There is a difference between European and Brazilian Portuguese which could result in ambiguous words for speakers from the two regions (Frota and Vigário, 2001).

Table 3 shows the results obtained by using the second filtering mechanism to discard HITs where

Lang	Acc	Com	Cor
En	70.4	69.0	0.36
Ar	56.6	87.6	0.34
Zh	45.6	55.9	0.22
It	54.4	53.5	0.09
Pt	61.3	54.0	0.20
Ur	97.6	91.9	0.51

Table 3: Summary of performance with Second Filter [Non experts]

Lang	Acc	Com	Cor	Err	Str	1st	Fuz
En	66.1	83	0.61	1%	31%	75%	40%
Ar	78.8	72.4	0.22	1%	39%	51%	73%
Zh	50.4	60.2	0.21	1%	15%	44%	31%
Ur	96.2	94.8	0.69	1%	63%	89%	93%

Table 4: Summary of performance [Experts]

Language	Measure	OA	Fleiss	K–alpha
English	First Tag	0.82	0.46	0.46
	Fuzzy	0.64	0.27	0.27
	Strict	0.69	0.32	0.32
Arabic	First Tag	0.77	0.55	0.55
	Fuzzy	0.84	0.59	0.59
	Strict	0.21	0.55	0.55
Chinese	First Tag	0.62	0.23	0.24
	Fuzzy	0.75	0.41	0.41
	Strict	0.83	0.31	0.32
Urdu	First Tag	0.83	0.10	0.10
	Fuzzy	0.91	0.35	0.35
	Strict	0.71	0.37	0.38

Table 5: Total Inter-rater agreement [Experts].

random erroneous tags were not completely removed. This enables us to increase accuracy for English by 9.0%, Italian by 8.7% and Portuguese by 2.8% without negatively affecting completeness or correlation.

In order to allow better interpretation of the non-experts' scores, we repeated the experiments on a smaller scale with up to four experts per language (English, Arabic, Chinese and Urdu), who were already familiar with the USAS taxonomy and were researchers in the fields of corpus or computational linguistics. Experts used the same task interface to assign senses to 50 words each. The results are presented in Table 4. Most notably, experts consistently excel at removing erroneous tags, leaving only a very small number in the data.

English experts performed much better than English non-experts on completeness, correlation and strict measures while their accuracy scores are comparable. Arabic experts performed much better than Arabic non-experts on the accuracy, strict and fuzzy scores while the 1st score is comparable. Chinese experts performed slightly better than Chinese non-experts on Accuracy, completeness and Fuzzy while other scores were comparable. Urdu experts scored relatively more highly on strict and 1st measures while other scores were comparable to Urdu non-experts. Finally, Tables 5 and 6 show the Observed Agreement (OA), Fleiss' Kappa and Krippendorff's alpha scores for the inter-rater agreement between Expert and Non Expert participants. According to (Landis and Koch, 1977) our inter-rater scores show fair agreement between annotators. This serves to illustrate the task is complex even for experts.

Overall these results show that untrained crowdsourcing workers can produce results that are comparable to those of experts when performing semantic annotation tasks. Directly-contacted and MTurk workers achieved similar levels of results overall. This shows that the novel two-phase filtering method used in our experiment is effective for maintaining the quality of the results.

5 Conclusion and Future Work

In order to accelerate the task of creating multilingual semantic lexicons with coarse-grained word senses using a common multilingual semantic representation scheme, we employed non-expert native speakers via MTurk who were not trained with the semantic taxonomy. Overall, the non-expert participants semantically tagged 250 words in each of six languages: Arabic, Chinese, English, Italian, Portuguese and Urdu. We analysed the results using a number of metrics to consider the correct likelihood order of tags relative to a gold-standard, along with correct removal of random erroneous semantic tags, and completeness of tag lists. Crowdsourcing has been applied successfully for other NLP tasks in previous research, and we build on previous success in WSD tasks in three ways. Firstly, we have specific requirements for semantic tagging purposes in terms of placing coarse-grained senses into a semantic taxonomy rather than stand-alone definitions. Hence, our experimental set-up allows us to validate the sense inventory in a multilingual setting, carried out here for six languages. Secondly, we extend the usual

Language	Measure	OA	Fleiss	K–alpha
English	First Tag	0.71	0.36	0.36
	Fuzzy	0.58	0.11	0.11
	Strict	0.79	0.20	0.20
Arabic	First Tag	0.66	0.32	0.32
	Fuzzy	0.71	0.05	0.05
	Strict	0.86	0.03	0.03
Chinese	First Tag	0.73	0.45	0.45
	Fuzzy	0.74	0.38	0.38
	Strict	0.85	0.41	0.41
Italian	First Tag	0.67	0.31	0.31
	Fuzzy	0.67	0.03	0.03
	Strict	0.89	0.12	0.13
Portuguese	First Tag	0.64	0.22	0.22
	Fuzzy	0.63	0.13	0.13
	Strict	0.80	0.18	0.18
Urdu	First Tag	0.72	0.16	0.16
	Fuzzy	0.95	0.45	0.45
	Strict	0.74	0.49	0.49

Table 6: Total Inter-rater agreement [Non Experts].

classification task of putting a word into one of an existing list of senses, instead asking participants to list all possible senses that a word could take in different contexts. Thirdly, we have deployed a novel two-stage filtering approach which has been shown to improve the quality of our results by filtering out spam responses using a simple synonym recognition task as well as HITs removing random erroneous tags. Our experiment suggests that the crowdsourcing process can produce results of good quality and is comparable to the work done by expert linguists. We showed that it is possible for native speakers to apply the hierarchical semantic taxonomy without prior training by the application of a graphical browsing interface to assist selection and annotation process.

In the future, we will apply the method on a larger scale to the full semantic lexicons including multiword expressions, which are important for contextual semantic disambiguation. We will also investigate whether adaptations to our method are required to include more languages such as Czech, Malay and Spanish. In order to pursue the work beyond the existing languages in the USAS system, we will extend bootstrapping methods reported in Piao et al. (2015) with vector-based techniques and evaluate their appropriateness for multiple languages. Finally, we will test whether (a) provision of words in context through concordances, (b) prototypical examples for each semantic tag, or (c) semantic tag labels in the same language as the task word, as part of the resources available to participants would further enhance the accuracy of the crowdsourcing annotation process.

Acknowledgements

The crowdsourcing framework and interface was originally produced in an EPSRC Impact Acceleration Award at Lancaster University in 2013. This work has also been supported by the UK ESRC/AHRC-funded CorCenCC (The National Corpus of Contemporary Welsh) Project (ref. ES/M011348/1), the ESRC-funded Centre for Corpus Approaches to Social Science (ref. ES/K002155/1), and by the UCREL research centre, Lancaster University, UK via Wmatrix software licence fees. We would also like to express our thanks to the many expert and non-expert participants who were also involved in the experiments including: Dawn Archer (Manchester Metropolitan University, UK), Francesca Bianchi (Universita del Salento, Italy), Carmen Dayrell (Lancaster University, UK), Xiaopeng Hu (China Center for Information Industry Development, CCID, China), Olga Mudraya (Right Word Up, UK), Sheryl Prentice (Lancaster University, UK), Yuan Qi (China Center for Information Industry Development, CCID, China), Jawad Shafi (COMSATS Institute of Information technology, Pakistan), and May Wong (University of Hong Kong, Hong Kong, China).

References

Ahmet Aker, Mahmoud El-Haj, Udo Kruschwitz, and M-Dyaa Albakour. 2012. Assessing Crowdsourcing Quality through Objective Tasks. In *8th Language Resources and Evaluation Conference*, Istanbul, Turkey. LREC 2012.

Cem Akkaya, Alexander Conrad, Janyce Wiebe, and Rada Mihalcea. 2010. Amazon mechanical turk for subjectivity word sense disambiguation. In *Proceedings of the NAACL HLT 2010 Workshop on Creating Speech and Language Data with Amazon's Mechanical Turk*, pages 195–203, Los Angeles, USA. Association for Computational Linguistics.

Omar Alonso and Stefano Mizzaro. 2009. Can we get rid of TREC Assessors? Using Mechanical Turk for Relevance Assessment. In *SIGIR '09: Workshop on The Future of IR Evaluation*, Boston, USA.

Vikas Bhardwaj, Rebecca J. Passonneau, Ansaf Salleb-Aouissi, and Nancy Ide. 2010. Anveshan: A framework for analysis of multiple annotators' labeling behavior. In *Proceedings of the Fourth Linguistic Annotation Workshop*, LAW IV '10, pages 47–55, Stroudsburg, PA, USA. Association for Computational Linguistics.

Chris Callison-Burch. 2009. Fast, Cheap, and Creative: Evaluating Translation Quality Using Amazon's Mechanical Turk. In *Proceedings of the 2009 Conference on Empirical Methods in Natural Language Processing (EMNLP)*, pages 286–295, Singapore. Association for Computational Linguistics.

Pinar Donmez, Jaime G. Carbonell, and Jeff Schneider. 2009. Efficiently learning the accuracy of labeling sources for selective sampling. In *Proceedings of the 15th ACM SIGKDD International Conference on Knowledge Discovery and Data Mining*, KDD '09, pages 259–268, New York, NY, USA. ACM.

Julie S. Downs, Mandy B. Holbrook, Steve Sheng, and Lorrie Faith Cranor. 2010. Are your participants gaming the system?: Screening mechanical turk workers. In *Proceedings of the SIGCHI Conference on Human Factors in Computing Systems*, CHI '10, pages 2399–2402, New York, NY, USA. ACM.

Mahmoud El-Haj, Udo Kruschwitz, and Chris Fox. 2010. Using Mechanical Turk to Create a Corpus of Arabic Summaries. In *Language Resources (LRs) and Human Language Technologies (HLT) for Semitic Languages workshop held in conjunction with the 7th International Language Resources and Evaluation Conference (LREC 2010).*, pages 36–39, Valletta, Malta. LREC 2010.

Mahmoud El-Haj, Udo Kruschwitz, and Chris Fox. 2014. Creating language resources for under-resourced languages: methodologies, and experiments with Arabic. *Language Resources and Evaluation*, pages 1–32.

Sónia Frota and Marina Vigário. 2001. On the correlates of rhythmic distinctions: The European/Brazilian Portuguese case. pages 247–275.

Adam Kapelner, Krishna Kaliannan, H.Andrew Schwartz, Lyle Ungar, and Dean Foster. 2012. New insights from coarse word sense disambiguation in the crowd. In *Proceedings of COLING 2012: Posters*, pages 539–548, Mumbai, India. The COLING 2012 Organizing Committee.

Gabriella Kazai, Natasa Milic-Frayling, and Jamie Costello. 2009. Towards methods for the collective gathering and quality control of relevance assessments. In *Proceedings of the 32nd International ACM SIGIR Conference on Research and Development in Information Retrieval*, SIGIR '09, pages 452–459, New York, NY, USA. ACM.

Gabriella Kazai. 2011. In search of quality in crowdsourcing for search engine evaluation. In Paul Clough, Colum Foley, Cathal Gurrin, Gareth J.F. Jones, Wessel Kraaij, Hyowon Lee, and Vanessa Mudoch, editors, *Advances in Information Retrieval*, volume 6611 of *Lecture Notes in Computer Science*, pages 165–176. Springer Berlin Heidelberg.

Adam Kilgarriff. 1997. "I Don't Believe in Word Senses". *Computers and the Humanities*, 31(2):91–113.

Aniket Kittur, Ed H. Chi, and Bongwon Suh. 2008. Crowdsourcing user studies with mechanical turk. In *Proceedings of the SIGCHI Conference on Human Factors in Computing Systems*, CHI '08, pages 453–456, New York, NY, USA. ACM.

J.Richard Landis and Gary Koch. 1977. The measurement of observer agreement for categorical data. *Biometrics*, 33(1):159–174.

Laura Löfberg, Scott Piao, Asko Nykanen, Krista Varantola, Paul Rayson, and Jukka-Pekka Juntunen. 2005. A semantic tagger for the Finnish language. In *Proceedings of Corpus Linguistics 2005*, Birmingham, UK.

Tom McArthur. 1981. *Longman Lexicon of Contemporary English*. Longman, London, UK.

Olga Mudraya, Bogdan Babych, Scott Piao, Paul Rayson, and Andrew Wilson. 2006. Developing a Russian semantic tagger for automatic semantic annotation. In *Proceedings of Corpus Linguistics 2006*, pages 290–297, St. Petersburg, Russia.

Rebecca Passonneau, Nizar Habash, and Owen Rambow. 2006. Inter-annotator agreement on a multilingual semantic annotation task. In *Proceedings of the Fifth International Conference on Language Resources and Evaluation (LREC'06)*, Genoa, Italy. European Language Resources Association (ELRA).

Ellie Pavlick, Matt Post, Ann Irvine, Dmitry Kachaev, and Chris Callison-Burch. 2014. The language demographics of Amazon Mechanical Turk. *Transactions of the Association for Computational Linguistics*, 2:79–92.

Scott Piao, Francesca Bianchi, Carmen Dayrell, Angela D'Egidio, and Paul Rayson. 2015. Development of the multilingual semantic annotation system. In *Proceedings of North American Chapter of the Association for Computational Linguistics – Human Language Technologies Conference*, Denver, USA. (NAACL HLT 2015).

Yufang Qian and Scott Piao. 2009. The development of a semantic annotation scheme for chinese kinship. *Corpora*, 4(2):189–208.

Paul Rayson, Dawn Archer, Scott Piao, and Anthony
McEnery. 2004. The UCREL semantic analysis
system. In *Proceedings of the Beyond Named Entity Recognition Semantic Labelling for NLP tasks
workshop*, pages 7–12, Lisbon, Portugal.

Aanna Rumshisky, Nick Botchan, Sophie Kushkuley,
and James Pustejovsky. 2012. Word sense inventories by non-experts. In Nicoletta Calzolari (Conference Chair), Khalid Choukri, Thierry Declerck,
Mehmet Uur Doan, Bente Maegaard, Joseph Mariani, Jan Odijk, and Stelios Piperidis, editors, *Proceedings of the Eight International Conference on
Language Resources and Evaluation (LREC'12)*,
pages 4055–4059, Istanbul, Turkey, May. European
Language Resources Association (ELRA).

Rion Snow, Brendan O'Connor, Daniel Jurafsky, and
Andrew Y. Ng. 2008. Cheap and Fast – But is it
Good? Evaluating Non-Expert Annotations for Natural Language Tasks. In *Proceedings of the 2008
Conference on Empirical Methods in Natural Language Processing*, pages 254–263. Association for
Computational Linguistics.

Alexander. Sorokin and David Forsyth. 2008. Utility
data annotation with amazon mechanical turk. In *In
IEEE Conference on Computer Vision and Pattern
Recognition Workshops*, pages 1–8.

Jean Véronis. 2001. Sense tagging: does it make
sense? In *Proceedings of Corpus Linguistics 2001*,
Lancaster, UK. UCREL.

Peter Welinder, Steve Branson, Serge Belongie, and
Pietro Perona. 2010. The Multidimensional Wisdom of Crowds. In J. Lafferty, C. K. I. Williams,
J. Shawe-Taylor, R. S. Zemel, and A. Culotta, editors, *Advances in Neural Information Processing
Systems 23*, pages 2424–2432.

Yin Yang, Nilesh Bansal, Wisam Dakka, Panagiotis Ipeirotis, Nick Koudas, and Dimitris Papadias.
2009. Query by document. In *Proceedings of
the Second ACM International Conference on Web
Search and Data Mining*, WSDM '09, pages 34–43,
New York, NY, USA. ACM.

Using Linked Disambiguated Distributional Networks for Word Sense Disambiguation

Alexander Panchenko[‡], Stefano Faralli[†], Simone Paolo Ponzetto[†], and Chris Biemann[‡]

[‡]Language Technology Group, Computer Science Dept., University of Hamburg, Germany
[†]Web and Data Science Group, Computer Science Dept., University of Mannheim, Germany
{panchenko,biemann}@informatik.uni-hamburg.de
{faralli,simone}@informatik.uni-mannheim.de

Abstract

We introduce a new method for unsupervised knowledge-based word sense disambiguation (WSD) based on a resource that links two types of sense-aware lexical networks: one is induced from a corpus using distributional semantics, the other is manually constructed. The combination of two networks reduces the sparsity of sense representations used for WSD. We evaluate these enriched representations within two lexical sample sense disambiguation benchmarks. Our results indicate that (1) features extracted from the corpus-based resource help to significantly outperform a model based solely on the lexical resource; (2) our method achieves results comparable or better to four state-of-the-art unsupervised knowledge-based WSD systems including three hybrid systems that also rely on text corpora. In contrast to these hybrid methods, our approach does not require access to web search engines, texts mapped to a sense inventory, or machine translation systems.

1 Introduction

The representation of word senses and the disambiguation of lexical items in context is an ongoing long-established branch of research (Agirre and Edmonds, 2007; Navigli, 2009). Traditionally, word senses are defined and represented in lexical resources, such as WordNet (Fellbaum, 1998), while more recently, there is an increased interest in approaches that induce word senses from corpora using graph-based distributional approaches (Dorow and Widdows, 2003; Biemann, 2006; Hope and Keller, 2013), word sense embeddings (Neelakantan et al., 2014; Bartunov et al.,

2016) and combination of both (Pelevina et al., 2016). Finally, some hybrid approaches emerged, which aim at building sense representations using information from both corpora and lexical resources, e.g. (Rothe and Schütze, 2015; Camacho-Collados et al., 2015a; Faralli et al., 2016). In this paper, we further explore the last strain of research, investigating the utility of hybrid sense representation for the word sense disambiguation (WSD) task.

In particular, the contribution of this paper is a new unsupervised knowledge-based approach to WSD based on the *hybrid aligned resource* (HAR) introduced by Faralli et al. (2016). The key difference of our approach from prior hybrid methods based on sense embeddings, e.g. (Rothe and Schütze, 2015), is that we rely on sparse lexical representations that make the sense representation readable and allow to straightforwardly use this representation for word sense disambiguation, as will be shown below. In contrast to hybrid approaches based on sparse interpretable representations, e.g. (Camacho-Collados et al., 2015a), our method requires no mapping of texts to a sense inventory and thus can be applied to larger text collections. By linking symbolic distributional sense representations to lexical resources, we are able to improve representations of senses, leading to performance gains in word sense disambiguation.

2 Related Work

Several prior approaches combined distributional information extracted from text (Turney and Pantel, 2010) from text with information available in lexical resources, such as WordNet. Yu and Dredze (2014) proposed a model to learn word embeddings based on lexical relations of words from WordNet and PPDB (Ganitkevitch et al., 2013). The objective function of their model

Proceedings of the 1st Workshop on Sense, Concept and Entity Representations and their Applications, pages 72–78,
Valencia, Spain, April 4 2017. ©2017 Association for Computational Linguistics

combines the objective function of the skip-gram model (Mikolov et al., 2013) with a term that takes into account lexical relations of a target word. Faruqui et al. (2015) proposed a related approach that performs a post-processing of word embeddings on the basis of lexical relations from the same resources. Pham et al. (2015) introduced another model that also aim at improving word vector representations by using lexical relations from WordNet. The method makes representations of synonyms closer than representations of antonyms of the given word. While these three models improve the performance on word relatedness evaluations, they do not model word senses. Jauhar et al. (2015) proposed two models that tackle this shortcoming, learning sense embeddings using the word sense inventory of WordNet.

Iacobacci et al. (2015) proposed to learn sense embeddings on the basis of the BabelNet lexical ontology (Navigli and Ponzetto, 2012). Their approach is to train the standard skip-gram model on a pre-disambiguated corpus using the Babelfy WSD system (Moro et al., 2014). NASARI (Camacho-Collados et al., 2015a) relies on Wikipedia and WordNet to produce vector representations of senses. In this approach, a sense is represented in lexical or sense-based feature spaces. The links between WordNet and Wikipedia are retrieved from BabelNet. MUFFIN (Camacho-Collados et al., 2015b) adapts several ideas from NASARI, extending the method to the multi-lingual case by using BabelNet synsets instead of monolingual WordNet synsets.

The approach of Chen et al. (2015) to learning sense embeddings starts from initialization of sense vectors using WordNet glosses. It proceeds by performing a more conventional context clustering, similar what is found to unsupervised methods such as (Neelakantan et al., 2014; Bartunov et al., 2016).

Rothe and Schütze (2015) proposed a method that learns sense embedding using word embeddings and the sense inventory of WordNet. The approach was evaluated on the WSD tasks using features based on the learned sense embeddings.

Goikoetxea et al. (2015) proposed a method for learning word embeddings using random walks on a graph of a lexical resource. Nieto Piña and Johansson (2016) used a similar approach based on random walks on a WordNet to learn sense embeddings.

All these diverse contributions indicate the benefits of hybrid knowledge sources for learning word and sense representations.

3 Unsupervised Knowledge-based WSD using Hybrid Aligned Resource

We rely on the hybrid aligned lexical semantic resource proposed by Faralli et al. (2016) to perform WSD. We start with a short description of this resource and then discuss how it is used for WSD.

3.1 Construction of the Hybrid Aligned Resource (HAR)

The hybrid aligned resource links two lexical semantic networks using the method of Faralli et al. (2016): a corpus-based distributionally-induced network and a manually-constructed network. Sample entries of the HAR are presented in Table 1. The corpus-based part of the resource, called *proto-conceptualization* (PCZ), consists of sense-disambiguated lexical items (PCZ ID), disambiguated related terms and hypernyms, as well as context clues salient to the lexical item. The knowledge-based part of the resource, called *conceptualization*, is represented by synsets of the lexical resource and relations between them (WordNet ID). Each sense in the PCZ network is subsequently linked to a sense of the knowledge-based network based on their similarity calculated on the basis of lexical representations of senses and their neighbors. The construction of the PCZ involves the following steps (Faralli et al., 2016):

Building a Distributional Thesaurus (DT). At this stage, a similarity graph over terms is induced from a corpus, where each entry consists of the most similar 200 terms for a given term using the JoBimText method (Biemann and Riedl, 2013).

Word Sense Induction. In DTs, entries of polysemous terms are mixed, i.e. they contain related terms of several senses. The Chinese Whispers (Biemann, 2006) graph clustering is applied to the ego-network (Everett and Borgatti, 2005) of the each term, as defined by its related terms and connections between then observed in the DT to derive word sense clusters.

Labeling Word Senses with Hypernyms. Hearst (1992) patterns are used to extract hypernyms from the corpus. These hypernyms are assigned to senses by aggregating hypernym

PCZ ID	WordNet ID	Related Terms	Hypernyms	Context Clues
mouse:0	mouse:1	rat:0, rodent:0, monkey:0, ...	animal:0, species:1, ...	rat:conj_and, white-footed:amod, ...
mouse:1	mouse:4	keyboard:1, computer:0, printer:0 ...	device:1, equipment:3, ...	click:-prep_of, click:-nn, ...
keyboard:0	keyboard:1	piano:1, synthesizer:2, organ:0 ...	instrument:2, device:3, ...	play:-dobj, electric:amod, ..
keyboard:1	keyboard:1	keypad:0, mouse:1, screen:1 ...	device:1, technology:0 ...	computer, qwerty:amod ...

Table 1: Sample entries of the hybrid aligned resource (HAR) for the words "mouse" and "keyboard". Trailing numbers indicate sense identifiers. Relatedness and context clue scores are not shown for brevity.

relations over the list of related terms for the given sense into a weighted list of hypernyms.

Disambiguation of Related Terms and Hypernyms. While target words contain sense distinctions (PCZ ID), the related words and hypernyms do not carry sense information. At this step, each hypernym and related term is disambiguated with respect to the *induced* sense inventory (PCZ ID). For instance, the word "keyboard" in the list of related terms for the sense "mouse:1" is linked to its "device" sense represented ("keyboard:1") as "mouse:1" and "keyboard:1" share neighbors from the IT domain.

Retrieval of Context Clues. Salient contexts of senses are retrieved by aggregating salient dependency features of related terms. Context features that have a high weight for many related terms obtain a high weight for the sense.

3.2 HAR Datasets

We experiment with two different corpora for PCZ induction as in (Faralli et al., 2016), namely a 100 million sentence news corpus (*news*) from Gigaword (Parker et al., 2011) and LCC (Richter et al., 2006), and a 35 million sentence Wikipedia corpus (*wiki*).[1] Chinese Whispers sense clustering is performed with the default parameters, producing an average number of 2.3 (news) and 1.8 (wiki) senses per word in a vocabulary of 200 thousand words each, with the usual power-law distribution of sense cluster sizes. On average, each sense is related to about 47 senses and has assigned 5 hypernym labels. These disambiguated distributional networks were linked to WordNet 3.1 using the method of Faralli et al. (2016).

3.3 Using the Hybrid Aligned Resource in Word Sense Disambiguation

We experimented with four different ways of enriching the original WordNet-based sense repre-

sentation with contextual information from the HAR on the basis of the mappings listed below:

WordNet. This baseline model relies solely on the WordNet lexical resource. It builds sense representations by collecting synonyms and sense definitions for the given WordNet synset and synsets directly connected to it. We removed stop words and weight words with term frequency.

WordNet + Related (news). This model augments the WordNet-based representation with related terms from the PCZ items (see Table 1). This setting is designed to quantify the added value of lexical knowledge in the related terms of PCZ.

WordNet + Related (news) + Context (news). This model includes all features of the previous models and complements them with context clues obtained by aggregating features of the words from the WordNet + Related (news) (see Table 1).

WordNet + Related (news) + Context (wiki). This model is built in the same way as the previous model, but using context clues derived from Wikipedia (see Section 3.2).

In the last two models, we used up to 5000 most relevant context clues per word sense. This value was set experimentally: performance of the WSD system gradually increased with the number of context clues reaching a plateau at the value of 5000. During aggregation, we excluded stop words and numbers from context clues. Besides, we transformed syntactic context clues presented in Table 1 to terms, stripping the dependency type. so they can be added to other lexical representations. For instance, the context clue "rat:conj_and" of the entry "mouse:0" was reduced to the feature "rat".

Table 2 demonstrates features extracted from WordNet as compared to feature representations enriched with related terms of the PCZ.

Each WordNet word sense is represented with one of the four methods described above. These sense representations are subsequently used to per-

---

[1]The used PCZ and HAR resources are available at: https://madata.bib.uni-mannheim.de/171

Model	Sense Representation
WordNet	memory, device, floppy, disk, hard, disk, disk, computer, science, computing, diskette, fixed, disk, floppy, magnetic, disc, magnetic, disk, hard, disc, storage, device
WordNet + Related (news)	recorder, disk, floppy, console, diskette, handset, desktop, iPhone, iPod, HDTV, kit, RAM, Discs, Blu-ray, computer, GB, microchip, site, cartridge, printer, tv, VCR, Disc, player, LCD, software, component, camcorder, cellphone, card, monitor, display, burner, Web, stereo, internet, model, iTunes, turntable, chip, cable, camera, iphone, notebook, device, server, surface, wafer, page, drive, laptop, screen, pc, television, hardware, YouTube, dvr, DVD, product, folder, VCR, radio, phone, circuitry, partition, megabyte, peripheral, format, machine, tuner, website, merchandise, equipment, gb, discs, MP3, hard-drive, piece, video, storage device, memory device, microphone, hd, EP, content, soundtrack, webcam, system, blade, graphic, microprocessor, collection, document, programming, battery, keyboard, HD, handheld, CDs, reel, web, material, hard-disk, ep, chart, debut, configuration, recording, album, broadcast, download, fixed disk, planet, pda, microfilm, iPod, videotape, text, cylinder, cpu, canvas, label, sampler, workstation, electrode, magnetic disc, catheter, magnetic disk, Video, mobile, cd, song, modem, mouse, tube, set, ipad, signal, substrate, vinyl, music, clip, pad, audio, compilation, memory, message, reissue, ram, CD, subsystem, hdd, touchscreen, electronics, demo, shell, sensor, file, shelf, processor, cassette, extra, mainframe, motherboard, floppy disk, lp, tape, version, kilobyte, pacemaker, browser, Playstation, pager, module, cache, DVD, movie, Windows, cd-rom, e-book, valve, directory, harddrive, smartphone, audiotape, technology, hard disk, show, computing, computer science, Blu-Ray, blu-ray, HDD, HD-DVD, scanner, hard disc, gadget, booklet, copier, playback, TiVo, controller, filter, DVDs, gigabyte, paper, mp3, CPU, dvd-r, pipe, cd-r, playlist, slot, VHS, film, videocassette, interface, adapter, database, manual, book, channel, changer, storage

Table 2: Original and enriched representations of the third sense of the word "disk" in the WordNet sense inventory. Our sense representation is enriched with related words from the hybrid aligned resource.

form WSD in context. For each test instance consisting of a target word and its context, we select the sense whose corresponding sense representation has the highest cosine similarity with the target word's context.

4 Evaluation

We perform an extrinsic evaluation and show the impact of the hybrid aligned resource on word sense disambiguation performance. While there exist many datasets for WSD (Mihalcea et al., 2004; Pradhan et al., 2007; Manandhar et al., 2010, *inter alia*), we follow Navigli and Ponzetto (2012) and use the SemEval-2007 Task 16 on the "Evaluation of wide-coverage knowledge resources" (Cuadros and Rigau, 2007). This task is specifically designed for evaluating the impact of lexical resources on WSD performance. The SemEval-2007 Task 16 is, in turn, based on two "lexical sample" datasets, from the Senseval-3 (Mihalcea et al., 2004) and SemEval-2007 Task 17 (Pradhan et al., 2007) evaluation campaigns. The first dataset has coarse- and fine-grained annotations, while the second contains only fine-grained sense annotations. In all experiments, we use the official task's evaluator to compute standard metrics of recall, precision, and F-score.

5 Results

Impact of the corpus-based features. Figure 1 compares various sense representations in terms of F-score. The results show that, expanding WordNet-based sense representations with distributional information gives a clear advantage over the original representation on both Senseval-3 and SemEval-2007 datasets. Using related words specific to a given WordNet sense provides dramatic

improvements in the results. Further expansion of the sense representation with context clues (cf. Table 1) provide a modest further improvement on the SemEval-2007 dataset and yield no further improvement on the case of the Senseval-3 dataset.

Comparison to the state-of-the-art. We compare our approach to four state-of-the-art systems: KnowNet (Cuadros and Rigau, 2008), BabelNet, WN+XWN (Cuadros and Rigau, 2007), and NASARI. KnowNet builds sense representations based on snippets retrieved with a web search engine. We use the best configuration reported in the original paper (KnowNet-20), which extends each sense with 20 keywords. BabelNet in its core relies on a mapping of WordNet synsets and Wikipedia articles to obtain enriched sense representations. The WN+XWN system is the top-ranked unsupervised knowledge-based system of Senseval-3 and SemEval-2007 datasets from the original competition (Cuadros and Rigau, 2007). It alleviates sparsity by combining WordNet with the eXtended WordNet (Mihalcea and Moldovan, 2001). The latter resource relies on parsing of WordNet glosses.

For KnowNet, BabelNet, and WN+XWN we use the scores reported in the respective original publications. However, as NASARI was not evaluated on the datasets used in our study, we used the following procedure to obtain NASARI-based sense representations: Each WordNet-based sense representation was extended with all features from the lexical vectors of NASARI.[2]

Thus, we compare our method to three hybrid systems that induce sense representations on the

---

[2]We used the version of lexical vectors (July 2016) featuring 4.4 million of BabelNet synsets, yet covering only 72% of word senses of the two datasets used in our experiments.

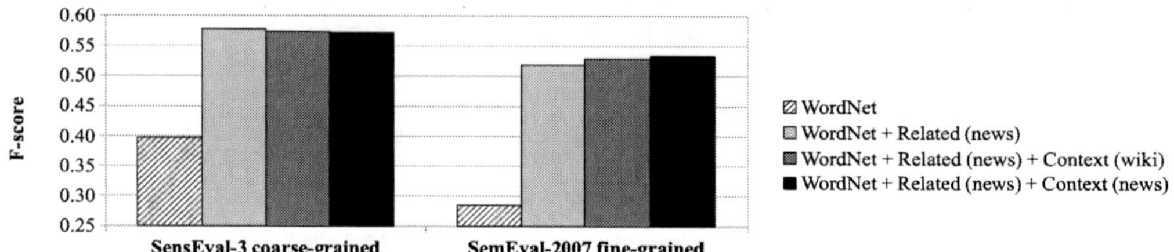

Figure 1: Performance of different word sense representation strategies.

Model	Senseval-3 fine-grained			SemEval-2007 fine-grained		
	Precision	Recall	F-score	Precision	Recall	F-score
Random	19.1	19.1	19.1	27.4	27.4	27.4
WordNet	29.7	29.7	29.7	44.3	21.0	28.5
WordNet + Related (news)	**47.5**	**47.5**	**47.5**	54.0	50.0	51.9
WordNet + Related (news) + Context (news)	47.2	47.2	47.2	54.8	51.2	52.9
WordNet + Related (news) + Context (wiki)	46.9	46.9	46.9	**55.2**	**51.6**	**53.4**
BabelNet	**44.3**	**44.3**	**44.3**	**56.9**	**53.1**	**54.9**
KnowNet	44.1	44.1	44.1	49.5	46.1	47.7
NASARI (lexical vectors)	32.3	32.2	32.2	49.3	45.8	47.5
WN+XWN	38.5	38.0	38.3	54.9	51.1	52.9

Table 3: Comparison of our approach to the state of the art unsupervised knowledge-based methods on the SemEval-2007 Task 16 (weighted setting). The best results overall are underlined.

basis of WordNet and texts (KnowNet, BabelNet, NASARI) and one purely knowledge-based system (WN+XWN). Note that we do not include the supervised TSSEM system in this comparison, as in contrast to all other considered methods, it relies on a large sense-labeled corpus.

Table 3 presents results of the evaluation. On the Senseval-3 dataset, our hybrid models show better performance than all unsupervised knowledge-based approaches considered in our experiment. On the SemEval-2007 dataset, the only resource which exceeds the performance of our hybrid model is BabelNet. The extra performance of BabelNet on the SemEval dataset can be explained by its multilingual approach: additional features are obtained using semantic relations across synsets in different languages. Besides, machine translation is used to further enrich coverage of the resource (Navigli and Ponzetto, 2012).

These results indicate on the high quality of the sense representations obtained using the hybrid aligned resource. Using related words of induced senses improves WSD performance by a large margin as compared to purely WordNet-based model on both datasets. Adding extra contextual features further improves slightly results on one dataset. Thus, we recommend enriching sense representations with related words and op-

tionally with context clues. Finally, note that, while our method shows competitive results compared to other state-of-the-art hybrid systems, it does not require access to web search engines (KnowNet), texts mapped to a sense inventory (BabelNet, NASARI), or machine translation systems (BabelNet).

6 Conclusion

The hybrid aligned resource (Faralli et al., 2016) successfully enriches sense representations of a manually-constructed lexical network with features derived from a distributional disambiguated lexical network. Our WSD experiments on two datasets show that this additional information extracted from corpora let us substantially outperform the model based solely on the lexical resource. Furthermore, a comparison of our sense representation method with existing hybrid approaches leveraging corpus-based features demonstrate its state-of-the-art performance.

Acknowledgments

We acknowledge the support of the Deutsche Forschungsgemeinschaft (DFG) under the project "JOIN-T: Joining Ontologies and Semantics Induced from Text".

References

Eneko Agirre and Philip Edmonds. 2007. *Word sense disambiguation: Algorithms and applications*, volume 33. Springer Science & Business Media.

Sergey Bartunov, Dmitry Kondrashkin, Anton Osokin, and Dmitry Vetrov. 2016. Breaking sticks and ambiguities with adaptive skip-gram. In *Proceedings of the 19th International Conference on Artificial Intelligence and Statistics (AISTATS'2016)*, pages 130–138, Cadiz, Spain. JMLR: W&CP volume 51.

Chris Biemann and Martin Riedl. 2013. Text: Now in 2D! A Framework for Lexical Expansion with Contextual Similarity. *Journal of Language Modelling*, 1(1):55–95.

Chris Biemann. 2006. Chinese whispers - an efficient graph clustering algorithm and its application to natural language processing problems. In *Proceedings of TextGraphs: the First Workshop on Graph Based Methods for Natural Language Processing*, pages 73–80, New York City. Association for Computational Linguistics.

José Camacho-Collados, Mohammad Taher Pilehvar, and Roberto Navigli. 2015a. Nasari: a novel approach to a semantically-aware representation of items. In *Proceedings of the 2015 Conference of the North American Chapter of the Association for Computational Linguistics: Human Language Technologies*, pages 567–577, Denver, Colorado. Association for Computational Linguistics.

José Camacho-Collados, Mohammad Taher Pilehvar, and Roberto Navigli. 2015b. A unified multilingual semantic representation of concepts. In *Proceedings of the 53rd Annual Meeting of the Association for Computational Linguistics and the 7th International Joint Conference on Natural Language Processing (Volume 1: Long Papers)*, pages 741–751, Beijing, China. Association for Computational Linguistics.

Tao Chen, Ruifeng Xu, Yulan He, and Xuan Wang. 2015. Improving distributed representation of word sense via wordnet gloss composition and context clustering. In *Proceedings of the 53rd Annual Meeting of the Association for Computational Linguistics and the 7th International Joint Conference on Natural Language Processing (Volume 2: Short Papers)*, pages 15–20, Beijing, China. Association for Computational Linguistics.

Montse Cuadros and German Rigau. 2007. Semeval-2007 task 16: Evaluation of wide coverage knowledge resources. In *Proceedings of the Fourth International Workshop on Semantic Evaluations (SemEval-2007)*, pages 81–86, Prague, Czech Republic. Association for Computational Linguistics.

Montse Cuadros and German Rigau. 2008. KnowNet: Building a large net of knowledge from the web. In *Proceedings of the 22nd International Conference on Computational Linguistics (Coling 2008)*, pages 161–168, Manchester, UK, August. Coling 2008 Organizing Committee.

Beate Dorow and Dominic Widdows. 2003. Discovering Corpus-Specific Word Senses. In *Proceedings of the Tenth Conference on European Chapter of the Association for Computational Linguistics - Volume 2*, EACL '03, pages 79–82, Budapest, Hungary. Association for Computational Linguistics.

Martin Everett and Stephen P. Borgatti. 2005. Ego network betweenness. *Social Networks*, 27(1):31–38.

Stefano Faralli, Alexander Panchenko, Chris Biemann, and Simone P. Ponzetto. 2016. Linked disambiguated distributional semantic networks. In *International Semantic Web Conference (ISWC'2016)*, pages 56–64, Kobe, Japan. Springer.

Manaal Faruqui, Jesse Dodge, Sujay Kumar Jauhar, Chris Dyer, Eduard Hovy, and Noah A. Smith. 2015. Retrofitting word vectors to semantic lexicons. In *Proceedings of the 2015 Conference of the North American Chapter of the Association for Computational Linguistics: Human Language Technologies*, pages 1606–1615, Denver, Colorado. Association for Computational Linguistics.

Christiane Fellbaum. 1998. *WordNet: An Electronic Database*. MIT Press, Cambridge, MA.

Juri Ganitkevitch, Benjamin Van Durme, and Chris Callison-Burch. 2013. Ppdb: The paraphrase database. In *Proceedings of the 2013 Conference of the North American Chapter of the Association for Computational Linguistics: Human Language Technologies*, pages 758–764, Atlanta, Georgia. Association for Computational Linguistics.

Josu Goikoetxea, Aitor Soroa, and Eneko Agirre. 2015. Random walks and neural network language models on knowledge bases. In *Proceedings of the 2015 Conference of the North American Chapter of the Association for Computational Linguistics: Human Language Technologies*, pages 1434–1439, Denver, Colorado. Association for Computational Linguistics.

Marti A. Hearst. 1992. Automatic acquisition of hyponyms from large text corpora. In *Proceedings of the 6th International Conference on Computational Linguistics (COLING'1992)*, pages 539–545, Nantes, France.

David Hope and Bill Keller. 2013. MaxMax: A Graph-Based Soft Clustering Algorithm Applied to Word Sense Induction. In *Computational Linguistics and Intelligent Text Processing: 14th International Conference, CICLing 2013, Samos, Greece, March 24-30, 2013, Proceedings, Part I*, pages 368–381. Springer Berlin Heidelberg, Berlin, Heidelberg.

Ignacio Iacobacci, Mohammad Taher Pilehvar, and Roberto Navigli. 2015. Sensembed: Learning sense embeddings for word and relational similarity.

In *Proceedings of the 53rd Annual Meeting of the Association for Computational Linguistics and the 7th International Joint Conference on Natural Language Processing (Volume 1: Long Papers)*, pages 95–105, Beijing, China. Association for Computational Linguistics.

Sujay Kumar Jauhar, Chris Dyer, and Eduard Hovy. 2015. Ontologically grounded multi-sense representation learning for semantic vector space models. In *Proceedings of the 2015 Conference of the North American Chapter of the Association for Computational Linguistics: Human Language Technologies*, pages 683–693, Denver, Colorado. Association for Computational Linguistics.

Suresh Manandhar, Ioannis P. Klapaftis, Dmitriy Dligach, and Sameer S. Pradhan. 2010. SemEval-2010 task 14: Word sense induction & disambiguation. In *Proceedings of the 5th International Workshop on Semantic Evaluation (ACL'2010)*, pages 63–68, Upsala, Sweden. Association for Computational Linguistics.

Rada Mihalcea and Dan Moldovan. 2001. extended wordnet: Progress report. In *In Proceedings of NAACL Workshop on WordNet and Other Lexical Resources*, pages 1–5, Pittsburgh, PA, USA. Association for Computational Linguistics.

Rada Mihalcea, Timothy Chklovski, and Adam Kilgarriff. 2004. The SENSEVAL-3 English lexical sample task. In *SENSEVAL-3: Third International Workshop on the Evaluation of Systems for the Semantic Analysis of Text*, pages 25–28, Barcelona, Spain. Association for Computational Linguistics.

Tomas Mikolov, Ilya Sutskever, Kai Chen, Gregory S. Corrado, and Jeffrey Dean. 2013. Distributed representations of words and phrases and their compositionality. In *Proceedings of Advances in Neural Information Processing Systems 26 (NIPS'2013)*, pages 3111–3119, Harrahs and Harveys, CA, USA.

Andrea Moro, Alessandro Raganato, and Roberto Navigli. 2014. Entity linking meets word sense disambiguation: a unified approach. *Transactions of the Association for Computational Linguistics*, 2:231–244.

Roberto Navigli and Simone Paolo Ponzetto. 2012. Babelnet: The automatic construction, evaluation and application of a wide-coverage multilingual semantic network. *Artificial Intelligence*, 193:217–250.

Roberto Navigli. 2009. Word sense disambiguation: A survey. *ACM CSUR*, 41(2):1–69.

Arvind Neelakantan, Jeevan Shankar, Alexandre Passos, and Andrew McCallum. 2014. Efficient non-parametric estimation of multiple embeddings per word in vector space. In *Proceedings of the 2014 Conference on Empirical Methods in Natural Language Processing (EMNLP)*, pages 1059–1069,

Doha, Qatar. Association for Computational Linguistics.

Luis Nieto Piña and Richard Johansson. 2016. Embedding senses for efficient graph-based word sense disambiguation. In *Proceedings of TextGraphs-10: the Workshop on Graph-based Methods for Natural Language Processing*, pages 1–5, San Diego, CA, USA. Association for Computational Linguistics.

Robert Parker, David Graff, Junbo Kong, Ke Chen, and Kazuaki Maeda. 2011. *English Gigaword Fifth Edition*. Linguistic Data Consortium, Philadelphia.

Maria Pelevina, Nikolay Arefiev, Chris Biemann, and Alexander Panchenko. 2016. Making sense of word embeddings. In *Proceedings of the 1st Workshop on Representation Learning for NLP*, pages 174–183, Berlin, Germany. Association for Computational Linguistics.

Nghia The Pham, Angeliki Lazaridou, and Marco Baroni. 2015. A multitask objective to inject lexical contrast into distributional semantics. In *Proceedings of the 53rd Annual Meeting of the Association for Computational Linguistics and the 7th International Joint Conference on Natural Language Processing (Volume 2: Short Papers)*, pages 21–26, Beijing, China. Association for Computational Linguistics.

Sameer Pradhan, Edward Loper, Dmitriy Dligach, and Martha Palmer. 2007. Semeval-2007 task-17: English lexical sample, srl and all words. In *Proceedings of the Fourth International Workshop on Semantic Evaluations (SemEval-2007)*, pages 87–92, Prague, Czech Republic. Association for Computational Linguistics.

Matthias Richter, Uwe Quasthoff, Erla Hallsteinsdóttir, and Chris Biemann. 2006. Exploiting the Leipzig Corpora Collection. In *Proceedings of the Fifth Slovenian and First International Language Technologies Conference (IS-LTC)*, Ljubljana, Slovenia.

Sascha Rothe and Hinrich Schütze. 2015. Autoextend: Extending word embeddings to embeddings for synsets and lexemes. In *Proceedings of the 53rd Annual Meeting of the Association for Computational Linguistics and the 7th International Joint Conference on Natural Language Processing (Volume 1: Long Papers)*, pages 1793–1803, Beijing, China, July. Association for Computational Linguistics.

Peter D. Turney and Patrick Pantel. 2010. From frequency to meaning: Vector space models of semantics. *JAIR*, 37:141–188.

Mo Yu and Mark Dredze. 2014. Improving lexical embeddings with semantic knowledge. In *Proceedings of the 52nd Annual Meeting of the Association for Computational Linguistics (Volume 2: Short Papers)*, pages 545–550, Baltimore, Maryland. Association for Computational Linguistics.

One Representation per Word — *Does it make Sense for Composition?*

Thomas Kober, Julie Weeds, John Wilkie, Jeremy Reffin and **David Weir**
TAG laboratory, Department of Informatics, University of Sussex
Brighton, BN1 9RH, UK
{t.kober, j.e.weeds, jw478, j.p.reffin, d.j.weir}@sussex.ac.uk

Abstract

In this paper, we investigate whether an *a priori* disambiguation of word senses is strictly necessary or whether the meaning of a word in context can be disambiguated through composition alone. We evaluate the performance of off-the-shelf single-vector and multi-sense vector models on a benchmark phrase similarity task and a novel task for word-sense discrimination. We find that single-sense vector models perform as well or better than multi-sense vector models despite arguably less clean elementary representations. Our findings furthermore show that simple composition functions such as pointwise addition are able to recover sense specific information from a single-sense vector model remarkably well.

1 Introduction

Distributional word representations based on counting co-occurrences have a long history in natural language processing and have successfully been applied to numerous tasks such as sentiment analysis, recognising textual entailment, word-sense disambiguation and many other important problems. More recently low-dimensional and dense neural word embeddings have received a considerable amount of attention in the research community and have become ubiquitous in numerous NLP pipelines in academia and industry. One fundamental simplifying assumption commonly made in distributional semantic models, however, is that every word can be encoded by a single representation. Combining polysemous lexemes into a single vector has the consequence of essentially creating a weighted average of all observed meanings of a lexeme in a given text corpus.

Therefore a number of proposals have been made to overcome the issue of conflating several different senses of an individual lexeme into a single representation. One approach (Reisinger and Mooney, 2010; Huang et al., 2012) is to try directly inferring a predefined number of senses from data and subsequently label any occurrences of a polysemous lexeme with the inferred inventory. Similar approaches are proposed by Reddy et al. (2011) and Kartsaklis et al. (2013) who show that appropriate sense selection or disambiguation typically improves performance for composition of noun phrases (Reddy et al., 2011) and verb phrases (Kartsaklis et al., 2013). Dinu and Lapata (2010) proposed a model that represents the meaning of a word as a probability distribution over latent senses which is modulated based on contextualisation, and report improved performance on a word similarity task and the lexical substitution task. Other approaches leverage an existing lexical resource such as BabelNet or WordNet to obtain sense labels *a priori* to creating word representations (Iacobacci et al., 2015), or as a postprocessing step after obtaining initial word representations (Chen et al., 2014; Pilehvar and Collier, 2016). While these approaches have exhibited strong performance on benchmark word similarity tasks (Huang et al., 2012; Iacobacci et al., 2015) and some downstream processing tasks such as part-of-speech tagging and relation identification (Li and Jurafsky, 2015), they have been weaker than the single-vector representations at predicting the compositionality of multi-word expressions (Salehi et al., 2015), and at tasks which require the meaning of a word to be considered in context; e.g, word sense disambiguation (Iacobacci et al., 2016) and word similarity in context (Iacobacci et al., 2015).

In this paper we consider what happens when distributional representations are composed to

Proceedings of the 1st Workshop on Sense, Concept and Entity Representations and their Applications, pages 79–90,
Valencia, Spain, April 4 2017. ©2017 Association for Computational Linguistics

form representations for larger units of meaning. In a compositional phrase, the meaning of the whole can be inferred from the meaning of its parts. Thus, assuming compositionality, the representation of a phrase such as *black mood*, should be directly inferable from the representations for *black* and for *mood*. Further, one might suppose that composing the correct senses of the individual lexemes would result in a more accurate representation of that phrase. However, our counter-hypothesis is that the act of composition contextualises or disambiguates each of the lexemes thereby making the representations of individual senses redundant. We investigate this hypothesis by evaluating the performance of single-vector representations and multi-sense representations at both a benchmark phrase similarity task and at a novel word-sense discrimination task.

Our contributions in this work are thus as follows. First, we provide quantitative and qualitative evidence that even simple composition functions have the ability to recover sense-specific information from a single-vector representation of a polysemous lexeme in context. Second, we introduce a novel word-sense discrimination task[1], which can be seen as the first stage of word-sense disambiguation. The goal is to find whether the occurrences of a lexeme in two or more sentential contexts belong to the same sense or not, without necessarily labelling the senses. While it has received relatively little attention in recent years, it is an important natural language understanding problem and can provide important insights into the process of semantic composition.

2 Evaluating Distributional Models of Composition

For evaluation we use several readily available off-the-shelf word embeddings, that have already been shown to work well for a number of different NLP applications. We compare the 300-dimensional skip-gram `word2vec` (Mikolov et al., 2013) word embeddings[2] to the dependency based version of `word2vec` — henceforth `dep2vec`[3] (Levy and Goldberg, 2014) — and the

SENSEMBED model[4] by Iacobacci et al. (2015), which creates word-sense embeddings by performing word-sense disambiguation prior to running `word2vec`.

We note that `word2vec` and `dep2vec` use a single vector per word approach and therefore conflate the different senses of a polysemous lexeme. On the other hand, SENSEMBED utilises Babelfy (Moro et al., 2014) as an external knowledge source to perform word-sense disambiguation and subsequently creates one vector representation per word sense.

For composition we use pointwise addition for all models as this has been shown to be a strong baseline in a number of studies (Hashimoto et al., 2014; Hill et al., 2016). We also experimented with pointwise multiplication as composition function but, similar to Hill et al. (2016), found its performance to be very poor (results not reported). We model any out-of-vocabulary items as a vector consisting of all zeros and determine proximity of composed meaning representations in terms of cosine similarity. We lowercase and lemmatise the data in our task but do not perform number or date normalisation, or removal of rare words.

3 Phrase Similarity

Our first evaluation task is the benchmark phrase similarity task of Mitchell and Lapata (2010). This dataset consists of 108 adjective-noun (AN), 108 noun-noun (NN) and 108 verb-object (VO) pairs. The task is to compare a compositional model's similarity estimates with human judgements by computing Spearman's ρ. An average ρ of 0.47-0.48 represents the current state-of-the-art performance on this task (Hashimoto et al., 2014; Kober et al., 2016; Wieting et al., 2015).

For single-sense representations, the strategy for carrying out this task is simple. For each phrase in each pair, we compose the constituent representations and then compute the similarity of each pair of phrases using the cosine similarity. For multi-sense representations, we adapted the strategy which has been used successfully in various word similarity experiments (Huang et al., 2012; Iacobacci et al., 2015). Typically, for each word pair, all pairs of senses are considered and the similarity of the word pair is considered to be

---

[1]Our task is available from `https://github.com/tttthomassssss/sense2017`

[2]Available from: `https://code.google.com/p/word2vec/`

[3]Available from: `https://levyomer.wordpress.com/2014/04/25/dependency-based-word-embeddings/`

[4]Available from: `http://lcl.uniroma1.it/sensembed/`

the similarity of the closest pair of senses. The fact that this strategy works well suggests that when humans are asked to judge word similarity, the pairing automatically primes them to select the closest senses. Extending this to phrase similarity requires us to compose each possible pair of senses for each phrase and then select the sense configuration which results in maximal phrase similarity. For comparison, we also give results for the configuration which results in minimal phrase similarity and the arithmetic mean[5] of all sense configurations.

3.1 Results

Model	AN	NN	VO	Average
word2vec	0.47	**0.46**	**0.45**	**0.46**
dep2vec	**0.48**	**0.46**	**0.45**	**0.46**
SENSEMBED:max	0.39	0.39	0.32	0.37
SENSEMBED:min	0.24	0.12	0.22	0.19
SENSEMBED:mean	0.46	0.35	0.37	0.39

Table 1
Results for the Mitchell and Laptata (2010) dataset.

Table 1 shows that the simple strategy of adding high quality single-vector representations is very competitive with the state-of-the-art for this task. None of the strategies for selecting a sense configuration for the multi-sense representations could compete with the single sense representations on this task. One possible explanation is that the commonly adopted closest sense strategy is not effective for composition since the composition of incorrect senses may lead to spuriously high similarities (for two "implausible" sense configurations).

Table 2 lists a number of example phrase pairs with low average human similarity scores in the Mitchell and Lapata (2010) test set. The results show the tendency of the closest sense strategy with SENSEMBED (SE) to overestimate the similarity of dissimilar phrase pairs. For a comparison we manually labelled the lexemes in the sample phrases with the appropriate BabelNet senses prior to composition (SE*). Human (H) similarity scores are normalised and averaged for an easier comparison, model estimates represent cosine similarities.

4 Word Sense Discrimination

Word-sense discrimination can be seen as the first stage of word-sense disambiguation, where the

Phrase 1	Phrase 2	SE	SE*	H
buy land	*leave house*	0.49	0.28	0.26
close eye	*stretch arm*	0.40	0.31	0.25
wave hand	*leave company*	0.42	0.08	0.20
drink water	*use test*	0.29	0.04	0.18
european state	*present position*	0.28	-0.03	0.19
high point	*particular case*	0.41	0.10	0.21

Table 2
Tendency of SENSEMBED (SE) to overestimate the similarity on phrase pairs with low average human similarity when the closest sense strategy is used.

goal is to find whether two or more occurrences of the same lexeme express identical senses, without necessarily labelling the senses yet. It has received relatively little attention despite its potential for providing important insights into semantic composition, focusing in particular on to the ability of compositional distributional semantic models to appropriately contextualise a polysemous lexeme.

Work on word-sense discrimination has suffered from the absence of a benchmark task as well as a clear evaluation methodology. For example Schütze (1998) evaluated his model on a dataset consisting of 20 polysemous words (10 naturally ambiguous lexemes and 10 artificially ambiguous "pseudo-lexemes") in terms of accuracy for coarse grained sense distinctions, and an information retrieval task. Pantel and Lin (2002), and Van de Cruys (2008) used automatically extracted words from various newswire sources and evaluated the output of their models in comparison to WordNet and EuroWordNet, respectively. Purandare and Pedersen (2004) used a subset of the words from the SENSEVAL-2 task and evaluated their models in terms of precision, recall and F1-score of how well available sense tags match with clusters discovered by their algorithms. Akkaya et al. (2012) used the concatenation of the SENSEVAL-2 and SENSEVAL-3 tasks and evaluated their models in terms of cluster purity and accuracy. Finally, Moen et al. (2013) used the semantic textual similarity (STS) 2012 task, which is based on human judgements of the similarity between two sentences.

One contribution of our work is a novel word-sense discrimination task, evaluated on a number of robust baselines in order to facilitate future research in that area. In particular, our task offers a testbed for assessing the contextualisation ability of compositional distributional semantic models. The goal is, for a given polysemous lexeme in context, to identify the sentence from a list of options

---

[5] We also tried the geometric mean and the median but these performed comparably with the arithmetic mean.

that is expressing the same sense of that lexeme as the given target sentence. These two sentences — the target and the "correct answer" — can exhibit any degree of semantic similarity as long as they convey the same sense of the target lexeme. Table 3 shows an example of the polysemous adjective *black* in our task. The goal of any model would be to determine that the expressed sense of *black* in the sentence *She was going to set him free from all of the evil and black hatred he had brought to the world* is identical to the expressed sense of *black* in the target sentence *Or should they rebut the Democrats' black smear campaign with the evidence at hand.*

Our task assesses the ability of a model to discriminate a particular sense in a sentential context from any other senses and thus provides an excellent testbed for evaluating multi-sense word vector models as well as compositional distributional semantic models. By composing the representation of a target lexeme with its surrounding context, it should be possible to determine its sense. For example, composing *black smear campaign* should lead to a compositional representation that is closer to the composed representation of *black hatred* than to *black mood*, *black sense of humour* or *black coffee*. This essentially uses the similarity of the compositional representation of a lexeme's context to determine its sense. Similar approaches to word-sense disambiguation have already been successfully used in past works (Akkaya et al., 2012; Basile et al., 2014).

4.1 Task Construction

For the construction of our dataset we made use of data from two english dictionaries (Oxford Dictionary and Collins Dictionary), accessible via their respective web APIs[6], as well as examples from the sense annotated corpus SemCor (Miller et al., 1993). Our use of dictionary data is motivated by a number of favourable properties which make it a very suitable data source for our proposed task:

- The content is of very high-quality and curated by expert lexicographers.

- All example sentences are carefully crafted in order to unambiguously illustrate the usage

of a particular sense for a given polysemous lexeme.

- The granularity of the sense inventory reflects common language use[7].

- The example sentences are typically free of any domain bias wherever possible.

- The data is easily accessible via a web API.

By using the data from curated resources we were able to avoid a setup as a sentence similarity task and any potentially noisy crowd-sourced human similarity judgements.

We were furthermore able to collect data from varying frequency bands, enabling an assessment of the impact of frequency on any model. Figure 1 shows the number of target lexemes per frequency band. While the majority of lexemes, with reference to a cleaned October 2013 Wikipedia dump[8], is in the middle band, there is a considerable amount of less frequent lexemes. The most frequent target lexeme in our task is the verb *be* with $\approx$1.8m occurrences in Wikipedia, and the least frequent lexeme is the verb *ruffle* with 57 occurrences. The average target lexeme frequency is $\approx$95k for adjectives, and $\approx$45k$-$46k for nouns and verbs[9].

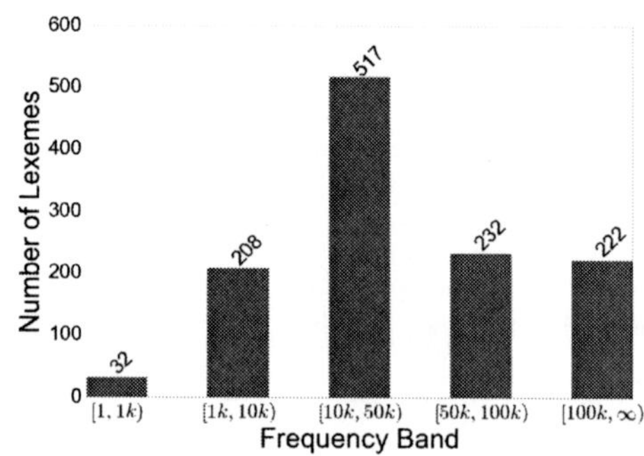

Figure 1: Binned frequency distribution of the polysemous target lexemes in our task.

---

[6] `https://developer.oxforddictionaries.com` for the Oxford Dictionary, `https://www.collinsdictionary.com/api/` for the Collins Dictionary. We use NLTK 3.2 to access SemCor.

[7] The Oxford dictionary lists 5 different senses for the noun "bank", whereas WordNet 3.0 lists 10 synsets, for example distinguishing "bank" as the concept for a financial institution and "bank" as a reference to the building where financial transactions take place.

[8] We removed any articles with fewer than 20 page views.

[9] The overall number of unique word types is smaller than the number of examples in our task as there are a number of lexemes that can occur with more than one part-of-speech.

	Sense Definition	**Sentence**
Target	full of anger or hatred	Or should they rebut the Democrats' **black** smear campaign with the evidence at hand?
Option 1	full of anger or hatred	She was going to set him free from all of the evil and **black** hatred he had brought to the world.
Option 2	(of a person's state of mind) full of gloom or misery; very depressed	I've been in a **black** mood since September 2001, it's hanging over me like a penumbra.
Option 3	(of humour) presenting tragic or harrowing situations in comic terms	Over the years I have come to believe that fate either hates me, or has one hell of a **black** sense of humour.
Option 4	(of coffee or tea) served without milk	The young man was reading a paperback novel and sipping a steaming mug of hot, **black** coffee.

Table 3: Example of the polysemous adjective *black* in our task. The goal for any model is to predict option 1 as expressing the same sense of *black* as the target sentence.

4.2 Task Setup Details

We collected data for 3 different parts-of-speech: adjectives, nouns and verbs. We furthermore created task setups with varying numbers of senses to distinguish (2-5 senses) for a given target lexeme. This is to evaluate how well a model is able to discriminate different degrees of polysemy of any lexeme. For any task setup evaluating for n senses, we included all lexemes with $> n$ senses and randomly sampled n senses from its inventory. For each lexeme, we furthermore ensured that it had at least 2 example sentences per sense. For the available senses of any given lexeme, we randomly chose a sense as the target sense, and from its list of example sentences randomly sampled 2 sentences, one as the target example and one as the "correct answer" for the list of candidate sentences. Finally we once again randomly sampled the required number of other senses and example sentences to complete the task setup. Using random sampling of word senses and targets aims to avoid a predominant sense bias.

For each part-of-speech we created a development split for parameter tuning and a test split for the final evaluation. Table 4 shows the number of examples for each setup variant of our task. The biggest category are polysemous nouns, representing roughly half of the data, followed by verbs representing another third, and the smallest category are adjectives taking up the remaining $\approx 17\%$. We measure performance in terms of accuracy of

	2 senses	**3 senses**	**4 senses**	**5 senses**
Adjective	66/209	47/170	37/137	28/115
Noun	170/618	125/499	100/412	74/345
Verb	127/438	71/354	72/295	56/256
Total	363/1265	263/1023	209/844	164/716

Table 4: Number of examples per part-of-speech and number of senses (*#dev examples/#train examples*).

correctly predicting which two sentences share the

same sense of a given target lexeme. Accuracy has the advantage of being much easier to interpret — in absolute terms as well as in the relative difference between models — in comparison to other commonly used evaluation metrics such as cluster purity measures or correlation metrics such as Spearman ρ and Pearson r.

4.3 Experimental Setup

In this paper we compare the compositional models outlined earlier with two baselines, a random baseline and a word-overlap baseline of the extracted contexts. For the single-vector representations, we composed the target lexeme with all of the words in the context window and compared it with the equivalent representation of each of the options (lexeme plus context words). The option with the highest cosine similarity was deemed to be the selected sense. For SENSEMBED, we composed all sense vectors of a target lexeme with the given context and then used the closest sense strategy (Iacobacci et al., 2015) on composed representations to choose the predicted sense[10]. The word-overlap baseline is simply the number of words in common between the context window for the target and each of the options.

We experimented with symmetric linear bag-of-words contexts of size 1, 2 and 4 around the target lexeme. We also experimented with dependency contexts, where first-order dependency contexts performed almost identical to using a 2-word bag-of-words context window (results not reported). We excluded stop words prior to extracting the context window in order to maximise the number of content words. We break ties for any of the methods — including the baselines — by randomly picking one of the options with the

---

[10]We also tried an all-by-all senses composition, however found this to be computationally not tractable.

highest similarity to the composed representation of the target lexeme with its context. Statistical significance between the best performing model and the word overlap baseline is computed by using a randomised pairwise permutation test (Efron and Tibshirani, 1994).

4.4 Results

Table 5 shows the results for all context window sizes across all parts-of-speech and number of senses. All models substantially outperform the random baseline for any number of senses. Interestingly the word overlap baseline is competitive for all context window sizes. While it is a very simple method, it has already been found to be a strong baseline for paraphrase detection and semantic textual similarity (Dinu and Thater, 2012). One possible explanation for its robust performance on our task is an occurrence of the one-sense-per-collocation hypothesis (Yarowsky, 1993). The performance of all other models is roughly in the same ballpark for all parts-of-speech and number of senses, suggesting that they form robust baselines for future models. While the results are relatively mixed for adjectives, word2vec appears to be the strongest model for polysemous nouns and verbs.

The perhaps most interesting observation in Table 5 is that word2vec and dep2vec are performing as well or better than SENSEMBED despite the fact that the former conflate the senses of a polysemous lexeme in a single vector representation. Figure 2 shows the average performance of all models across parts-of-speech per number of senses and for all context window sizes.

SENSEMBED and Babelfy

One possible explanation for SENSEMBED not outperforming the other methods despite its cleaner encoding of different word senses in the above experiments is that at train time, it had access to sense labels from Babelfy. At test time on our task however, it did not have any sense labels available. We therefore sense tagged the 5-sense noun subtask with Babelfy and re-ran SENSEMBED. As Table 6 shows, access to sense labels at test time did not give a substantive performance boost, representing further support for our hypothesis that composition in single-sense vector models might be sufficient to recover sense specific information.

Frequency Range

We chose the 2-sense noun subtask to estimate the degree sensitivity of target lexeme frequency on our task we merged the $[1, 1k)$ and $[1k, 10k)$, and $[50k, 100k)$ and $[100k, \infty)$ frequency bands from Figure 1, and sampled an equal number of target words from each band. Table 7 reports the results for this experiment. All methods outperform the random and word overlap baseline and appear to be working better for less frequent lexemes. One possible explanation for this behaviour is that less frequent lexemes have fewer senses and potentially less subtle sense differences than more frequent lexemes, which would make them easier to discriminate by distributional semantic methods.

5 Discussion

Our results suggest that pointwise addition in a single-sense vector model such as word2vec is able to discriminate the sense of a polysemous lexeme in context in a surprisingly effective way and represents a strong baseline for future work. Distributional composition can therefore be interpreted as a process of contextualising the meaning of a lexeme. This way, composition does not only act as a way to represent the meaning of a phrase as a whole, but also as a local discriminator for any lexemes in the phrase. For example the composed representation of *dry clothes* should only keep contexts that *dry* shares with *clothes* while suppressing contexts it shares with *weather* or *wine*. Hence, one would expect the same to happen with a polysemous lexeme such as *bank* in the context of *river* and *account*, respectively.

Recent work by Arora et al. (2016) has shown that the different senses of a polysemous lexeme reside in a linear substructure within a single vector and are recoverable by sparse coding. There is furthermore evidence that additive composition in low-dimensional word embeddings approximates an intersection of the contexts of two distributional word vectors (Tian et al., 2015). It therefore seems plausible that an intersective composition function should be able to recover sense specific information.

To qualitatively analyse this hypothesis we used the word2vec and SENSEMBED vectors to compose a small number of example phrases by pointwise addition and calculated their top 5 nearest neighbours in terms of cosine similarity. For SENSEMBED we manually sense tagged the

Symmetric context window of size 1

Senses	Adjective				Noun				Verb			
	2	3	4	5	2	3	4	5	2	3	4	5
Random	0.53	0.32	0.25	0.14	0.47	0.32	0.23	0.19	0.47	0.31	0.23	0.18
Word Overlap	0.63	0.46	0.47	0.40	0.55	0.40	0.37	0.34	0.54	0.44	0.38	0.29
word2vec	**0.70**	0.56	**0.61**†	0.54†	**0.66**‡	**0.52**‡	**0.50**‡	0.44‡	**0.63**‡	**0.56**‡	**0.52**‡	**0.43**‡
dep2vec	0.65	**0.64**‡	0.57	**0.57**‡	0.64‡	0.50‡	0.49‡	**0.48**‡	**0.63**‡	0.55‡	0.50‡	**0.43**‡
SENSEMBED	0.67	0.54	0.56	0.56†	0.64‡	0.49‡	**0.50**‡	0.43‡	0.62†	0.53‡	0.49‡	0.38†

Symmetric context window of size 2

Senses	Adjective				Noun				Verb			
	2	3	4	5	2	3	4	5	2	3	4	5
Random	0.53	0.32	0.25	0.14	0.47	0.32	0.23	0.19	0.47	0.31	0.23	0.18
Word Overlap	0.66	0.51	0.55	0.43	0.59	0.47	0.43	0.41	0.58	0.51	0.45	0.36
word2vec	0.70	0.64†	0.58	0.55	**0.71**‡	**0.63**‡	**0.59**‡	0.54‡	**0.68**‡	0.64‡	**0.58**‡	**0.49**‡
dep2vec	0.71	**0.65**‡	0.58	**0.57**‡	0.70‡	0.57‡	0.55‡	**0.55**‡	0.66†	0.64‡	0.54†	0.46†
SENSEMBED	**0.72**‡	0.62	**0.61**	0.52	0.69‡	0.56†	0.57‡	0.51†	0.67‡	**0.65**†	0.57	0.45

Symmetric context window of size 4

Senses	Adjective				Noun				Verb			
	2	3	4	5	2	3	4	5	2	3	4	5
Random	0.53	0.32	0.25	0.14	0.47	0.32	0.23	0.19	0.47	0.31	0.23	0.18
Word Overlap	0.67	0.55	0.58	0.51	0.62	0.50	0.49	0.45	0.59	0.55	0.50	0.40
word2vec	0.71	0.65†	**0.65**	**0.57**	**0.73**‡	**0.61**‡	**0.62**‡	**0.57**‡	**0.71**‡	**0.62**†	**0.57**	**0.53**‡
dep2vec	0.72	**0.66**†	0.60	0.54	0.71‡	0.55	0.56†	0.53†	0.67	0.62	0.54	0.50
SENSEMBED	**0.75**	0.59	0.62	0.55	0.69‡	0.57†	0.58‡	0.53†	0.68‡	0.62†	0.55	0.47

Table 5
Performance overview for all parts-of-speech and number of senses, $\ddagger$ statistically significant at the $p < 0.01$ level in comparison to the Word Overlap baseline; $\dagger$ statistically significant at the $p < 0.05$ level in comparison to the Word Overlap baseline.

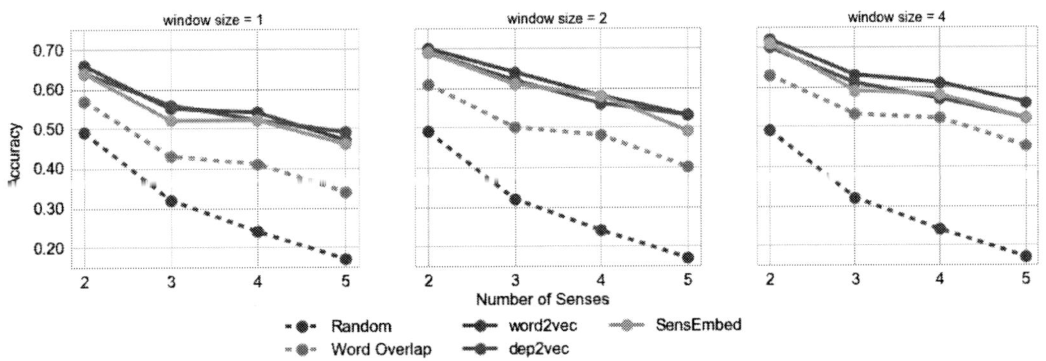

Figure 2: Average performance across parts-of-speech per number of senses and context window.

Noun - 5 Senses

Context Window Size	1	2	4
word2vec	0.44	0.54	**0.57**
dep2vec	**0.48**	**0.55**	0.53
SENSEMBED	0.43	0.51	0.53
SENSEMBED & Babelfy	0.45	0.49	0.54

Table 6
Results on the 5-sense noun subtask with SENSEMBED having access to Babelfy sense labels at test time.

Noun - 2 Senses, context window size = 2

Frequency Band	$< 10k$	$10k - 50k$	$\geq 50k$
Random	0.51	0.51	0.51
Word Overlap	0.66	0.60	0.56
word2vec	**0.81**	0.64	**0.66**
dep2vec	0.77	0.67	**0.66**
SENSEMBED	0.74	**0.68**	0.60

Table 7
Results on a subsample of the 2-sense noun subtask across frequency bands.

phrases with the appropriate BabelNet sense labels prior to composition. We omitted the BabelNet sense labels in the neighbour list for brevity, however they were consistent with the intended sense in all cases. Table 8 supports the view of composition as a way of contextualising the meaning of a lexeme. In all cases in our example the `word2vec` neighbours reflect the intended sense of the polysemous lexeme, providing evidence for the linear substructure of word senses in a single vector as discovered by Arora et al. (2016), and suggesting that distributional composition is able to recover sense specific information from a polysemous lexeme. The very fine-grained sense-level vector space of SENSEMBED is giving rise to a very focused neighbourhood, however there does not seem to be any advantage over `word2vec` from a qualitative point of view when using simple additive composition.

6 Related Work

The perhaps most popular tasks for evaluating the ability of a model to capture or encode the different senses of a polysemous lexeme in a given context are the english lexical substitution task (McCarthy and Navigli, 2007) and the Microsoft sentence completion challenge (Zweig and Burges, 2011). Both tasks require any model to fill an appropriate word into a pre-defined slot in a given sentential context. The sentence completion challenge provides a list of candidate words while the english lexical substitution task does not. However, neither task focuses on polysemy and the english lexical substitution task conflates the problems of discriminating word senses and finding meaning preserving substitutes.

Dictionary definitions have previously been used to evaluate compositional distributional semantic models where the goal is to match a dictionary entry with its corresponding definition (Kartsaklis et al., 2012; Polajnar and Clark, 2014). These datasets are commonly set up as retrieval tasks, but generally do not test the ability of a model to disambiguate a polysemous word in context, or discriminate multiple definitions of the same word.

Our task also provides a novel evaluation for compositional distributional semantic models, where the predominant strategy is to estimate the similarity of two short phrases (Bernardi et al., 2013; Grefenstette and Sadrzadeh, 2011; Kartsaklis and Sadrzadeh, 2014; Mitchell and Lapata, 2008; Mitchell and Lapata, 2010) or sentences (Agirre et al., 2016; Huang et al., 2012; Marelli et al., 2014) in comparison to human provided gold-standard judgements. One problem with these similarity tasks is that the similarity or relatedness of two sentences is very difficult to judge — especially on a fine-grained scale — even for humans. This frequently results in a relatively high variance of judgements and low inter-annotator agreement (Batchkarov et al., 2016). The short phrase datasets typically have a fixed structure that only test a very small fraction of the possible grammatical constructions in which a lexeme can occur, and furthermore provide very little context. The use of full sentences remedies the lack of context and grammatical variation, however can still contain a significant level of noise due to the automatic construction of the dataset or the variance in human ratings. In contrast, our task is not set up as a sentence similarity task and therefore avoids the use of human similarity judgements.

Our task is similar to word-sense induction (WSI), however we only focus on discriminating the sense of a polysemous lexeme in context rather than inducing a set of senses from raw data and appropriately tagging subsequent occurrences of polysemous instances with the inferred inventory. Separating the sense discrimination task from the problem of sense induction has the advantage of making our task applicable to evaluating compositional distributional semantic models in order to test their ability to appropriately contextualise a polysemous lexeme. Due to not requiring any models to perform an extra step for sense induction, our task is easier to evaluate as no matching between sense clusters identified by a model and some gold standard sense classes needs to be performed, as typically proposed in the WSI literature (Agirre and Soroa, 2007; Manandhar et al., 2010).

Most closely related to our task are the Stanford Contextual Word Similarity (SCWS) dataset by Huang et al. (2012) and the Usage Similarity (USim) task by Erk et al. (2009). The goal in both tasks is to estimate the similarity of two polysemous words in context in comparison to human provided gold standard judgements. In the SCWS dataset typically two different lexemes are considered whereas in USim and our task the same lexemes with different contexts are compared. Instead of relying on crowd-sourced human gold-standard similarity judgements, which can be prone to a considerable amount of noise[11],

---

[11]For example the average standard deviation of human ratings in the SCWS dataset is ≈ 3 on a 10-point scale, and

Phrase	word2vec neighbours	SENSEMBED neighbours
river bank	bank, river, creek, lake, rivers	bank, river, stream, creek, river basin
bank account	account, bank, accounts, banks, citibank	bank, banks, the bank, pko bank polski, handlowy
dry weather	weather, dry, wet weather, wet, unreasonably warm	dry, weather, humid, cold, cool
dry clothes	dry, clothes, clothing, rinse thoroughly, wet	dry, clothes, warm, cold, wet
capital city	capital, city, cities, downtown, town	city, capital, the capital city, town, provincial capital
capital asset	capital, asset, assets, investment, worth	capital, asset, investment, assets, investor
power plant	plant, power, plants, coalfired, megawatt	power, plant, near-limitless, pulse-power, power of the wind
garden plant	plant, garden, plants, gardens, vegetable garden	plant, garden, plants, oakville assembly, solanaceous
window bar	bar, window, windows, doorway, door	window, bar, windows, glass window, wall
sandwich bar	bar, sandwich, restaurant, burger, diner	sandwich, bar, restaurant, hot dog, cake
gasoline tank	gasoline, tank, fuel, gallon, tanks	gasoline, tank, fuel, petrol, kerosene
armored tank	armored, tank, tanks, M1A1 Abrams, armored vehicle	armored, armoured, tank, tanks, light tank
desert rock	rock, desert, rocks, desolate expanse, arid desert	desert rock, the desert, deserts, badlands
rock band	rock, band, rockers, bands, indie rock	band, rock, group, the band, rock group

Table 8

Nearest neighbours of composed phrases for word2vec and SENSEMBED. Distributional composition in word2vec is able to recover sense specific information remarkably well. Some neighbours are phrases because they have been encoded as a single token in the original vector space.

we leverage the high-quality content of available english dictionaries. Furthermore, our task is not formulated as estimating the similarity between two lexemes in context, but identifying the sentences that use the same sense of a given polysemous lexeme.

7 Conclusion

While elementary multi-sense representations of words might capture a more fine grained semantic picture of a polysemous word, that advantage does not appear to transfer to distributional composition in a straightforward way. Our experiments on a popular phrase similarity benchmark and our novel word-sense discrimination task have demonstrated that semantic composition does not appear to benefit from a fine grained sense inventory, but that the ability to contextualise a polysemous lexeme in single-sense vector models is sufficient for superior performance. We furthermore have provided qualitative and quantitative evidence that an intersective composition function such as pointwise addition for neural word embeddings is able to discriminate the meaning of a word in context, and is able to recover sense specific information remarkably well.

Lastly, our experiments have uncovered an important question for multi-sense vector models, namely how to exploit the fine-grained sense level representations for distributional composition. Our novel word-sense discrimination task provides an excellent testbed for compositional distributional semantic models, both following a single-sense or multi-sense vector modelling

can be up to 4–5 in some cases.

paradigm, due to its focus on assessing the ability of a model to appropriately contextualise the meaning of a word. Our task furthermore provides another evaluation option away from intrinsic evaluations which are based on often noisy human similarity judgements, while also not being embedded in a downstream task.

In future work we aim to extend our evaluation to more complex compositional distributional semantic models such as the lexical function model (Paperno et al., 2014) or the Anchored Packed Dependency Tree framework (Weir et al., 2016). We furthermore want to investigate how far the sense-discriminating ability of composition can be leveraged for other tasks.

Acknowledgments

We would like to thank our anonymous reviewers for their helpful comments.

References

Eneko Agirre and Aitor Soroa. 2007. Semeval-2007 task 02: Evaluating word sense induction and discrimination systems. In *Proceedings of the Fourth International Workshop on Semantic Evaluations (SemEval-2007)*, pages 7–12, Prague, Czech Republic, June. Association for Computational Linguistics.

Eneko Agirre, Carmen Banea, Daniel Cer, Mona Diab, Aitor Gonzalez-Agirre, Rada Mihalcea, German Rigau, and Janyce Wiebe. 2016. Semeval-2016 task 1: Semantic textual similarity, monolingual and cross-lingual evaluation. In *Proceedings of the 10th International Workshop on Semantic Evaluation (SemEval-2016)*, pages 497–511, San Diego, California, June. Association for Computational Linguistics.

Cem Akkaya, Janyce Wiebe, and Rada Mihalcea. 2012. Utilizing semantic composition in distributional semantic models for word sense discrimination and word sense disambiguation. In *Proceedings of ICSC*, pages 45–51.

Sanjeev Arora, Yuanzhi Li, Yingyu Liang, Tengyu Ma, and Andrej Risteski. 2016. Linear algebraic structure of word senses, with applications to polysemy. *CoRR*, abs/1601.03764.

Pierpaolo Basile, Annalina Caputo, and Giovanni Semeraro. 2014. An enhanced lesk word sense disambiguation algorithm through a distributional semantic model. In *Proceedings of COLING 2014, the 25th International Conference on Computational Linguistics: Technical Papers*, pages 1591–1600, Dublin, Ireland, August. Dublin City University and Association for Computational Linguistics.

Miroslav Batchkarov, Thomas Kober, Jeremy Reffin, Julie Weeds, and David Weir. 2016. A critique of word similarity as a method of evaluating distributional semantic models. In *Proceedings of the 1st Workshop on Evaluating Vector-Space Representations for NLP*, pages 7–12. Association for Computational Linguistics.

Raffaella Bernardi, Georgiana Dinu, Marco Marelli, and Marco Baroni. 2013. A relatedness benchmark to test the role of determiners in compositional distributional semantics. In *Proceedings of the 51st Annual Meeting of the Association for Computational Linguistics (Volume 2: Short Papers)*, pages 53–57, Sofia, Bulgaria, August. Association for Computational Linguistics.

Xinxiong Chen, Zhiyuan Liu, and Maosong Sun. 2014. A unified model for word sense representation and disambiguation. In *Proceedings of the 2014 Conference on Empirical Methods in Natural Language Processing (EMNLP)*, pages 1025–1035, Doha, Qatar, October. Association for Computational Linguistics.

Georgiana Dinu and Mirella Lapata. 2010. Measuring distributional similarity in context. In *Proceedings of the 2010 Conference on Empirical Methods in Natural Language Processing*, pages 1162–1172, Cambridge, MA, October. Association for Computational Linguistics.

Georgiana Dinu and Stefan Thater. 2012. Saarland: Vector-based models of semantic textual similarity. In **SEM 2012: The First Joint Conference on Lexical and Computational Semantics – Volume 1: Proceedings of the main conference and the shared task, and Volume 2: Proceedings of the Sixth International Workshop on Semantic Evaluation (SemEval 2012)*, pages 603–607, Montréal, Canada, 7-8 June. Association for Computational Linguistics.

Bradley Efron and Robert Tibshirani. 1994. *An Introduction to the Bootstrap*. CRC press.

Katrin Erk, Diana McCarthy, and Nicholas Gaylord. 2009. Investigations on word senses and word usages. In *Proceedings of the Joint Conference of the 47th Annual Meeting of the ACL and the 4th International Joint Conference on Natural Language Processing of the AFNLP*, pages 10–18, Suntec, Singapore, August. Association for Computational Linguistics.

Edward Grefenstette and Mehrnoosh Sadrzadeh. 2011. Experimental support for a categorical compositional distributional model of meaning. In *Proceedings of the 2011 Conference on Empirical Methods in Natural Language Processing*, pages 1394–1404, Edinburgh, Scotland, UK., July. Association for Computational Linguistics.

Kazuma Hashimoto, Pontus Stenetorp, Makoto Miwa, and Yoshimasa Tsuruoka. 2014. Jointly learning word representations and composition functions using predicate-argument structures. In *Proceedings of the 2014 Conference on Empirical Methods in Natural Language Processing (EMNLP)*, pages 1544–1555, Doha, Qatar, October. Association for Computational Linguistics.

Felix Hill, KyungHyun Cho, Anna Korhonen, and Yoshua Bengio. 2016. Learning to understand phrases by embedding the dictionary. *Transactions of the Association for Computational Linguistics*, 4:17–30.

Eric Huang, Richard Socher, Christopher Manning, and Andrew Ng. 2012. Improving word representations via global context and multiple word prototypes. In *Proceedings of the 50th Annual Meeting of the Association for Computational Linguistics (Volume 1: Long Papers)*, pages 873–882, Jeju Island, Korea, July. Association for Computational Linguistics.

Ignacio Iacobacci, Mohammad Taher Pilehvar, and Roberto Navigli. 2015. Sensembed: Learning sense embeddings for word and relational similarity. In *Proceedings of the 53rd Annual Meeting of the Association for Computational Linguistics and the 7th International Joint Conference on Natural Language Processing (Volume 1: Long Papers)*, pages 95–105, Beijing, China, July. Association for Computational Linguistics.

Ignacio Iacobacci, Mohammad Taher Pilehvar, and Roberto Navigli. 2016. Embeddings for word sense disambiguation: An evaluation study. In *Proceedings of the 54th Annual Meeting of the Association for Computational Linguistics (Volume 1: Long Papers)*, pages 897–907, Berlin, Germany, August. Association for Computational Linguistics.

Dimitri Kartsaklis and Mehrnoosh Sadrzadeh. 2014. A study of entanglement in a categorical framework of natural language. In *Proceedings of the 11th Workshop on Quantum Physics and Logic (QPL)*.

Dimitri Kartsaklis, Mehrnoosh Sadrzadeh, and Stephen Pulman. 2012. A unified sentence space for categorical distributional-compositional semantics: Theory and experiments. In *Proceedings of COLING 2012: Posters*, pages 549–558, Mumbai, India, December. The COLING 2012 Organizing Committee.

Dimitri Kartsaklis, Mehrnoosh Sadrzadeh, and Stephen Pulman. 2013. Separating disambiguation from composition in distributional semantics. In *Proceedings of the Seventeenth Conference on Computational Natural Language Learning*, pages 114–123, Sofia, Bulgaria, August. Association for Computational Linguistics.

Thomas Kober, Julie Weeds, Jeremy Reffin, and David Weir. 2016. Improving sparse word representations with distributional inference for semantic composition. In *Proceedings of the 2016 Conference on Empirical Methods in Natural Language Processing*, pages 1691–1702, Austin, Texas, November. Association for Computational Linguistics.

Omer Levy and Yoav Goldberg. 2014. Dependency-based word embeddings. In *Proceedings of the 52nd Annual Meeting of the Association for Computational Linguistics (Volume 2: Short Papers)*, pages 302–308, Baltimore, Maryland, June. Association for Computational Linguistics.

Jiwei Li and Dan Jurafsky. 2015. Do multi-sense embeddings improve natural language understanding? In *Proceedings of the 2015 Conference on Empirical Methods in Natural Language Processing*, pages 1722–1732, Lisbon, Portugal, September. Association for Computational Linguistics.

Suresh Manandhar, Ioannis Klapaftis, Dmitriy Dligach, and Sameer Pradhan. 2010. Semeval-2010 task 14: Word sense induction & disambiguation. In *Proceedings of the 5th International Workshop on Semantic Evaluation*, pages 63–68, Uppsala, Sweden, July. Association for Computational Linguistics.

Marco Marelli, Stefano Menini, Marco Baroni, Luisa Bentivogli, Raffaella bernardi, and Roberto Zamparelli. 2014. A sick cure for the evaluation of compositional distributional semantic models. In Nicoletta Calzolari, Khalid Choukri, Thierry Declerck, Hrafn Loftsson, Bente Maegaard, Joseph Mariani, Asuncion Moreno, Jan Odijk, and Stelios Piperidis, editors, *Proceedings of the Ninth International Conference on Language Resources and Evaluation (LREC'14)*, pages 216–223, Reykjavik, Iceland, May. European Language Resources Association (ELRA). ACL Anthology Identifier: L14-1314.

Diana McCarthy and Roberto Navigli. 2007. Semeval-2007 task 10: English lexical substitution task. In *Proceedings of the Fourth International Workshop on Semantic Evaluations (SemEval-2007)*, pages 48–53, Prague, Czech Republic, June. Association for Computational Linguistics.

Tomas Mikolov, Ilya Sutskever, Kai Chen, Greg S Corrado, and Jeff Dean. 2013. Distributed representations of words and phrases and their compositionality. In C.J.C. Burges, L. Bottou, M. Welling, Z. Ghahramani, and K.Q. Weinberger, editors, *Advances in Neural Information Processing Systems 26*, pages 3111–3119. Curran Associates, Inc.

George A. Miller, Claudia Leacock, Randee Tengi, and Ross T. Bunker. 1993. A semantic concordance. In *Proceedings of the Arpa Workshop on Human Language Technology*, pages 303–308.

Jeff Mitchell and Mirella Lapata. 2008. Vector-based models of semantic composition. In *Proceedings of the 46th Annual Meeting of the Association for Computational Linguistics: Human Language Technology Conference*, pages 236–244, Columbus, Ohio, June. Association for Computational Linguistics.

Jeff Mitchell and Mirella Lapata. 2010. Composition in distributional models of semantics. *Cognitive Science*, 34(8):1388–1429.

Hans Moen, Erwin Marsi, and Björn Gambäck. 2013. Towards dynamic word sense discrimination with random indexing. In *Proceedings of the Workshop on Continuous Vector Space Models and their Compositionality*, pages 83–90, Sofia, Bulgaria, August. Association for Computational Linguistics.

Andrea Moro, Alessandro Raganato, and Roberto Navigli. 2014. Entity linking meets word sense disambiguation: A unified approach. *Transactions of the Association for Computational Linguistics*, 2:231–244.

Patrick Pantel and Dekang Lin. 2002. Discovering word senses from text. In *Proceedings of the Eighth ACM SIGKDD International Conference on Knowledge Discovery and Data Mining*, KDD '02, pages 613–619, New York, NY, USA. ACM.

Denis Paperno, Nghia The Pham, and Marco Baroni. 2014. A practical and linguistically-motivated approach to compositional distributional semantics. In *Proceedings of the 52nd Annual Meeting of the Association for Computational Linguistics (Volume 1: Long Papers)*, pages 90–99, Baltimore, Maryland, June. Association for Computational Linguistics.

Mohammad Taher Pilehvar and Nigel Collier. 2016. De-conflated semantic representations. In *Proceedings of the 2016 Conference on Empirical Methods in Natural Language Processing*, pages 1680–1690, Austin, Texas, November. Association for Computational Linguistics.

Tamara Polajnar and Stephen Clark. 2014. Improving distributional semantic vectors through context selection and normalisation. In *Proceedings of the 14th Conference of the European Chapter of the Association for Computational Linguistics*, pages 230–238, Gothenburg, Sweden, April. Association for Computational Linguistics.

Amruta Purandare and Ted Pedersen. 2004. Word sense discrimination by clustering contexts in vector and similarity spaces. In Hwee Tou Ng and Ellen Riloff, editors, *HLT-NAACL 2004 Workshop: Eighth Conference on Computational Natural Language Learning (CoNLL-2004)*, pages 41–48, Boston, Massachusetts, USA, May 6 - May 7. Association for Computational Linguistics.

Siva Reddy, Ioannis Klapaftis, Diana McCarthy, and Suresh Manandhar. 2011. Dynamic and static prototype vectors for semantic composition. In *Proceedings of 5th International Joint Conference on Natural Language Processing*, pages 705–713, Chiang Mai, Thailand, November. Asian Federation of Natural Language Processing.

Joseph Reisinger and Raymond J. Mooney. 2010. Multi-prototype vector-space models of word meaning. In *Human Language Technologies: The 2010 Annual Conference of the North American Chapter of the Association for Computational Linguistics*, pages 109–117, Los Angeles, California, June. Association for Computational Linguistics.

Bahar Salehi, Paul Cook, and Timothy Baldwin. 2015. A word embedding approach to predicting the compositionality of multiword expressions. In *Proceedings of the 2015 Conference of the North American Chapter of the Association for Computational Linguistics: Human Language Technologies*, pages 977–983, Denver, Colorado, May–June. Association for Computational Linguistics.

Hinrich Schütze. 1998. Automatic word sense discrimination. *Computational Linguistics*, 24(1):97–123, mar.

Ran Tian, Naoaki Okazaki, and Kentaro Inui. 2015. The mechanism of additive composition. *CoRR*, abs/1511.08407.

Tim Van de Cruys. 2008. Using three way data for word sense discrimination. In *Proceedings of the 22nd International Conference on Computational Linguistics (Coling 2008)*, pages 929–936, Manchester, UK, August. Coling 2008 Organizing Committee.

David Weir, Julie Weeds, Jeremy Reffin, and Thomas Kober. 2016. Aligning packed dependency trees: a theory of composition for distributional semantics. *Computational Linguistics, special issue on Formal Distributional Semantics*, 42(4):727–761, December.

John Wieting, Mohit Bansal, Kevin Gimpel, and Karen Livescu. 2015. From paraphrase database to compositional paraphrase model and back. *Transactions of the Association for Computational Linguistics*, 3:345–358.

David Yarowsky. 1993. One sense per collocation. In *Proceedings of the Workshop on Human Language Technology*, HLT '93, pages 266–271, Stroudsburg, PA, USA. Association for Computational Linguistics.

Geoffrey Zweig and J.C. Chris Burges. 2011. The microsoft research sentence completion challenge. Technical report, Microsoft Research.

Elucidating Conceptual Properties from Word Embeddings

Kyoung-Rok Jang
School of Computing
KAIST
Daejeon, South Korea
kyoungrok.jang@kaist.ac.kr

Sung-Hyon Myaeng
School of Computing
KAIST
Daejeon, South Korea
myaeng@kaist.ac.kr

Abstract

In this paper, we introduce a method of identifying the components (i.e. dimensions) of word embeddings that strongly signifies *properties* of a word. By elucidating such properties hidden in word embeddings, we could make word embeddings more interpretable, and also could perform property-based meaning comparison. With the capability, we can answer questions like "To what degree a given word has the property *cuteness*?" or "In what perspective two words are similar?". We verify our method by examining how the strength of property-signifying components correlates with the degree of *prototypicality* of a target word.

1 Introduction

Modeling the meaning of words has long been studied and served as a basis for almost every kind of NLP tasks. Most recent word modeling techniques are based on neural networks, and the word representations produced by such techniques are called word embeddings, which are usually low-dimensional, dense vectors of continuous-valued components. Although word embeddings have been proved for their usefulness in many tasks, the question of what are represented in them is understudied.

Recent studies report empirical evidence that indicates word embeddings may reflect some *property* information of a target word (Erk, 2016; Levy et al., 2015). Learning the properties of a word would be helpful because many NLP tasks can be related to "finding words that possess similar properties", which include finding synonyms, named entity recognition (NER). Without a method for explicating what properties are contained in em-

beddings, however, researchers have mostly focused on improving the performance in well-known semantic benchmark tasks (e.g. SimLex-999) as a way to find better embeddings.

Performing well in such benchmark tasks is valuable but provides little help in understanding the inside of the black box. For instance, it is not possible to answer to questions like "To what degree a given word has the property *cuteness*?".

One way to solve this problem is to elucidate properties that are encoded in word embeddings and associate them with task performances. With the capability, we can not only enhance our understanding of word embeddings but also make it easier to make comparisons among heterogeneous word embedding models in more coherent ways. Our immediate goal in this paper is to show the feasibility of explicating properties contained in word embeddings.

Our research can be seen as an attempt to increase the *interpretability* of word embeddings. It is in line with an attempt to provide a human-understandable explanation for complex machine learning models, with which we can gain enough confidence to use them in decision-making processes.

There has been a line of work devoted to identifying components that are important for performing various NLP tasks such as sentiment analysis or NER (Faruqui et al., 2015; Fyshe et al., 2015; Herbelot and Vecchi, 2015; Karpathy et al., 2016; Li et al., 2016a; Li et al., 2016b; Rothe et al., 2016). Those works are analogous to ours in that they try to inspect the role of the components in word embedding. However, they just attempt to identify key features for specific tasks rather than elucidating properties. In contrast, our question is "what comprises word embeddings?" not "what components are important for performing well in a specific task?"

Proceedings of the 1st Workshop on Sense, Concept and Entity Representations and their Applications, pages 91–95,
Valencia, Spain, April 4 2017. ©2017 Association for Computational Linguistics

2 Feasibility Study

2.1 Background

Word embeddings can be seen as representing concepts of a word. As such, we attempt to design an property-related experiment around manipulation of concepts. In particular, we bring in the category theory (Murphy, 2004) where the notion of category is defined to be "grouping concepts that share similar properties". In other words, properties have a direct bearing on concepts and their categories, according to the theory.

On the other hand, researchers have argued that some concepts are more *typical* (or central) than others in a category (Rosch, 1973; Rosch, 1975). For instance, *apple* is more typical than *olive* in the fruit category. The typicality is a graded phenomenon, and may rise due to the strength of 'essential' properties that make a concept a specific category.

The key ideas from the above are 1) concepts of the same category share similar properties and 2) some concepts that have strong essential properties are considered more typical in specific category, and they guided our experiment design.

2.2 Design

The goal of this study is to show the feasibility of sifting property information from word embeddings. We assume that a concept's property information is captured and distributed over one or more components (dimensions) of embeddings during the learning process. Since the concepts that belong to the same category are likely to share similar properties, there should be some salient components that are shared among them. We call such components as SIG-PROPS (for significant properties) of a specific category.

In this feasibility study, we hypothesize that the strength of SIG-PROPS is strongly correlated with the degree of concept's typicality. This is based on the theory introduced in Section 2.1, that the typicality phenomenon rises due to the strength of essential properties a target concept possesses. So the concept that has (higher/lower) SIG-PROPS values than others should be (more typical/less typical) than other concepts.

2.3 Datasets

For our experiment dealing with typicality of concepts, we needed both (pre-trained) word embeddings and a dataset that encodes typicality scores of concepts to a set of categories. Below we describe two datasets we used in our experiment: HyperLex and Non-Negative Sparse Embedding (NNSE).

2.3.1 Dataset: Non-Negative Sparse Embedding (NNSE)

One desirable quality we wanted from the word embeddings to be used in our experiment is that there should be clear contrast between informative and non-informative components. In ordinary dense word embeddings, usually every component is filled with a non-zero value.

The Non-Negative Sparse Embedding (NNSE) (Murphy et al., 2012) fulfills the condition in the sense that insignificant components are set to zero. The NNSE component values falling between 0 and 1 (non-negative) are generated by applying the non-negative sparse coding algorithm (Hoyer, 2002) to ordinary word embeddings (e.g. word2vec).

2.3.2 Dataset: HyperLex

HyperLex is a dataset and evaluation resource that quantifies the extent of the semantic category membership (Vulić et al., 2016). A total of 2,616 concept pairs are included in the dataset, and the strength of category membership is given by native English speakers and recorded in *graded* manner. This graded category membership can be interpreted as a 'typicality score' (1–10). Some samples are shown in Table 1.

Concept	Category	Score
basketball	activity	10
spy	agent	8
handbag	bowl	0

Table 1: A HyperLex sample. The score is the answer to the question "To what degree is concept a type of category?"

3 Experiment

3.1 Preparation

We first prepared pre-trained NNSE embeddings. The authors released pre-trained model on their website[1]. We used the model trained with dependency context ('Dependency model' on the website), because as reported in (Levy and Goldberg, 2014), models trained on dependency context tend

---

[1] http://www.cs.cmu.edu/ bmurphy/NNSE/

to prefer *functional* similarity (hogwarts — sunnydale) rather than *topical* similarity (hogwarts — dumbledore)[2]. The embeddings are more sparse than ordinary embeddings and have 300 components.

Next we fetched HyperLex dataset at the author's website[3]. To make the settings suitable to our experiment goal, we selected categories with the following criteria:

1. The categories and instances must be concrete nouns (e.g. food). This is because people are more coherent in producing the properties of concrete nouns (Murphy, 2004). So the embeddings of concrete nouns should contain more clear property information than other types of words.

2. The categories must contain enough number of instances (not 1 or 2). This is to gain reliable result.

3. Some categories are sub-category of another selected category while others are not related. This is to see the discriminative and overlapping effect of identified SIG-PROPS between categories. Related categories should share a set of strong SIG-PROPS, while unrelated categories shouldn't.

As a result, we selected five categories: *food*, *fruit* (sub-category of food), *animal*, *bird* (sub-category of animal), and *instrument*. We fetched the concepts that belong to the categories and then filtered out those that aren't contained in the pre-trained NNSE embeddings. The final size of each category is shown in Table 2.

Category	# of Concepts
food	54
fruit	9
animal	46
bird	16
instrument	14

Table 2: The size of selected categories

In the next section, we explain how we identified SIG-PROPS of each category.

---

[2]We thought "sharing similar function" is more compatible with the notion of *sharing similar properties*. The topical similarity is less indicative of having properties in common.

[3]http://people.ds.cam.ac.uk/iv250/hyperlex.html

3.2 Identification of SIG-PROPS

The goal of this step is to find SIG-PROPS that might represent each category. Simply put, SIG-PROPS are the components that have on average high value compared to other components of the concepts in the same category. We identified SIG-PROPS by 1) calculating an average value of each component across the concepts with the same category, then 2) choosing those components whose average value is above h. We empirically set h to 0.2.

Category	SIG-PROPS	
	Comp. ID	**Avg.**
instrument	c88	0.806
	c258	0.769
animal	**c154**	0.587
	c265	0.221
bird	**c154**	0.550
	c265	0.213
food	c207	0.298
	c233	0.269
fruit	c229	0.492
	c27	0.369
	c156	0.349
	c44	0.264
	c233	0.206

Table 3: SIG-PROPS of each category. The strings in "Comp. ID" column are the component IDs (c1–c300). "Avg." column indicates the average value of the component across all the concepts under that category.

Table 3 shows the identified SIG-PROPS. The number of SIG-PROPS is different across categories. Interestingly, there is component overlap between taxonomically similar categories ('c154' and 'c265' between *animal–bird*, 'c233' between *food–fruit*), while there is none between unrelated categories (*instrument–animal–food*).

This initial observation is encouraging for our feasibility study in that indeed SIG-PROPS can play a role of distinguishing or associating categories. We argue that the identified SIG-PROPS strongly characterize each category, showing that we can associate vector components with properties.

3.3 Correlation between SIG-PROPS and concepts typicality scores

In this section, we check how the strength of SIG-PROPS correlates with the typicality scores. Note that the range of SIG-PROPS values differ from category to category — those for instrument are especially high, which might indicate they are highly representative.

Our assumption is that if the identified SIG-PROPS truly represent the essential quality of a category, the strength of SIG-PROPS should be proportional to concepts' typicality scores (equation 1).

$$Strength(\text{SIG-PROPS}) \propto Typicality(Concept) \tag{1}$$

We observe this phenomenon by calculating Pearson correlation between the strength of SIG-PROPS and typicality scores. For instance, suppose we calculate the correlation between 'c88' (88th component) of *instrument* concepts and their typicality score. We inspect the instrument concepts one by one, collect their 'c88' values (x) and typicality scores (y), and then measure the tendency of changes in the two variables.

The result is shown in Table 4–8 where the column 'Rank' shows the rank of the component's correlation score (compared to other components). For instance, in Table 4 'c88' has the highest correlation with the concept's typicality score.

SIG-PROPS	Correlation	Corr. rank
c88	0.926	1st
c258	0.918	2nd

Table 4: Corr(SIG-PROPS, typicality): *instrument*

SIG-PROPS	Correlation	Corr. rank
c154	0.549	1st
c265	0.265	2nd

Table 5: Corr(SIG-PROPS, typicality): *animal*

SIG-PROPS	Correlation	Corr. rank
c154	0.783	1st
c265	0.563	2nd

Table 6: Corr(SIG-PROPS, typicality): *bird*

SIG-PROPS	Correlation	Corr. rank
c233	0.255	1st
c120	0.224	2nd
c207	0.216	4th
c192	0.030	104th

Table 7: Corr(SIG-PROPS, typicality): *food*

SIG-PROPS	Correlation	Corr. rank
c229	0.743	1st
c233	0.540	4th
c27	0.516	5th
c44	0.474	7th
c156	-0.663	85th

Table 8: Corr(SIG-PROPS, typicality): *fruit*

As the results show, there is clear tendency SIG-PROPS having high correlation with the typicality scores. Most of the SIG-PROPS showed meaningful correlation (> 0.5) with the typicality score or placed at the top in the component–typicality correlation ranking. The result strongly indicates that even when we apply the simple method of identifying SIG-PROPS and regarding them as properties, they serve as strong indicators for the concept's typicality.

4 Conclusion and Future Work

Although limited in scale, our work showed the feasibility of discovering properties from word embeddings. Not only SIG-PROPS can be used to increase the interpretability of word embeddings, but also enable us more elaborate, property-based meaning comparison.

Our next step would be checking the applicability to general NLP tasks (e.g. NER, synonym identification). Also, applying our method to word embeddings that have more granular components (e.g. 2,500) might be helpful for identifying SIG-PROPS in more granular level.

Acknowledgments

This work was supported by Institute for Information & communications Technology Promotion(IITP) grant funded by the Korea government(MSIP) (No. R0126-16-1002, Development of agro-livestock cloud and application service for balanced production, transparent distribution and safe consumption based on GS1)

References

Katrin Erk. 2016. What do you know about an alligator when you know the company it keeps? *Semantics and Pragmatics Article*, 9(17):1–63.

Manaal Faruqui, Yulia Tsvetkov, Dani Yogatama, Chris Dyer, and Noah A. Smith. 2015. Sparse overcomplete word vector representations. In *Proceedings of the 53rd Annual Meeting of the Association for Computational Linguistics and the 7th International*

Joint Conference on Natural Language Processing (Volume 1: Long Papers), pages 1491–1500, Beijing, China, July.

Alona Fyshe, Leila Wehbe, Partha P. Talukdar, Brian Murphy, and Tom M. Mitchell. 2015. A compositional and interpretable semantic space. In *Proceedings of the 2015 Conference of the North American Chapter of the Association for Computational Linguistics: Human Language Technologies*, pages 32–41, Denver, Colorado, May–June.

Aurélie Herbelot and Eva Maria Vecchi. 2015. Building a shared world: Mapping distributional to model-theoretic semantic spaces. In *Proceedings of EMNLP*, number September, pages 22–32, Lisbon, Portugal.

P. O. Hoyer. 2002. Non-negative sparse coding. In *Neural Networks for Signal Processing - Proceedings of the IEEE Workshop*, volume 2002-Janua, pages 557–565.

Andrej Karpathy, Justin Johnson, and Li Fei-Fei. 2016. Visualizing and Understanding Recurrent Networks. *International Conference on Learning Representations (ICLR)*, pages 1–13.

Omer Levy and Yoav Goldberg. 2014. Dependency-based word embeddings. In *Proceedings of the 52nd Annual Meeting of the Association for Computational Linguistics (Volume 2: Short Papers)*, pages 302–308, Baltimore, Maryland, June.

Omer Levy, Steffen Remus, Chris Biemann, and Ido Dagan. 2015. Do supervised distributional methods really learn lexical inference relations? In *Proceedings of the 2015 Conference of the North American Chapter of the Association for Computational Linguistics: Human Language Technologies*, pages 970–976, Denver, Colorado, May–June.

Jiwei Li, Xinlei Chen, Eduard Hovy, and Dan Jurafsky. 2016a. Visualizing and Understanding Neural Models in NLP. In *Naacl*, pages 1–10.

Jiwei Li, Will Monroe, and Dan Jurafsky. 2016b. Understanding Neural Networks through Representation Erasure. In *Arxiv*.

Brian Murphy, Partha Pratim Talukdar, and Tom Mitchell. 2012. Learning Effective and Interpretable Semantic Models using Non-Negative Sparse Embedding. In *Proceedings of COLING 2012: Technical Papers*, number December 2012, pages 1933–1950.

Gregory Murphy. 2004. *The big book of concepts*. MIT press.

Eleanor H. Rosch. 1973. Natural categories. *Cognitive Psychology*, 4(3):328–350.

Eleanor H. Rosch. 1975. Cognitive representations of semantic categories. *Journal of experimental psychology: General*, 104(3):192.

Sascha Rothe, Sebastian Ebert, and Hinrich Schütze. 2016. Ultradense word embeddings by orthogonal transformation. In *Proceedings of the 2016 Conference of the North American Chapter of the Association for Computational Linguistics: Human Language Technologies*, pages 767–777, San Diego, California, June.

Ivan Vulić, Daniela Gerz, Douwe Kiela, Felix Hill, and Anna Korhonen. 2016. HyperLex: A Large-Scale Evaluation of Graded Lexical Entailment. *Arxiv*.

TTCS$^{\mathcal{E}}$: a Vectorial Resource
for Computing Conceptual Similarity

Enrico Mensa
University of Turin, Italy
Dipartimento di Informatica
`mensa@di.unito.it`

Daniele P. Radicioni
University of Turin, Italy
Dipartimento di Informatica
`radicion@di.unito.it`

Antonio Lieto
University of Turin, Italy
ICAR-CNR, Palermo, Italy
`lieto@di.unito.it`

Abstract

In this paper we introduce the TTCS$^{\mathcal{E}}$, a
linguistic resource that relies on BabelNet,
NASARI and ConceptNet, that has now
been used to compute the conceptual similarity between concept pairs. The conceptual representation herein provides uniform access to concepts based on Babel-
Net synset IDs, and consists of a vector-
based semantic representation which is
compliant with the Conceptual Spaces, a
geometric framework for common-sense
knowledge representation and reasoning.
The TTCS$^{\mathcal{E}}$ has been evaluated in a preliminary experimentation on a conceptual
similarity task.

1 Introduction

The development of robust and wide-coverage resources to use in different sorts of application
(such as text mining, categorization, *etc.*) has
known in the last few years a tremendous growth.
In this paper we focus on computing conceptual
similarity between pairs of concepts, based on a
resource that extends and generalizes an attempt
carried out in (Lieto et al., 2016a). In particular,
the TTCS$^{\mathcal{E}}$—so named after Text to Conceptual
Spaces-Extended— has been acquired by integrating two different sorts of linguistic resources,
such as the encyclopedic knowledge available
in BabelNet (Navigli and Ponzetto, 2012) and
NASARI (Camacho-Collados et al., 2015), and
the common-sense grasped by ConceptNet (Speer
and Havasi, 2012). The resulting representation
enjoys the interesting property of being anchored
to both resources, thereby providing a uniform
conceptual access grounded on the sense identifiers provided by BabelNet.

Conceptual Spaces (CSs) can be thought of as
a particular class of vector representations where
knowledge is represented as a set of limited though
cognitively relevant quality dimensions; in this
representation a geometrical structure is associated to each quality dimension, mostly based on
cognitive accounts. In this setting, concepts correspond to convex regions, and regions with different geometrical properties correspond to different sorts of concepts (Gärdenfors, 2014). The
geometrical features of CSs have a direct appeal
for common-sense representation and common-
sense reasoning, since prototypes (the most relevant representatives of a category from a cognitive point of view, see (Rosch, 1975)) correspond
to the geometrical centre of a convex region, the
centroid. Also exemplars-based representations
can be mapped onto points in a multidimensional
space, and their similarity can be computed as
the distance intervening between each two points,
based on some suitable metrics such as Euclidean
or Manhattan distance. *etc.*.

The CS framework has been recently used to
extend and complement the representational and
inferential power allowed by formal ontologies
—and in general symbolic representation—, that
are not suited for representing defeasible, prototypical knowledge, and for dealing with the corresponding typicality-based conceptual reasoning
(Lieto et al., 2017). Also, wide-coverage semantic resources such as DBPedia and ConceptNet, in
fact, in different cases fail to represent the sort of
common-sense information based on prototypical
and default information which is usually required
to perform forms of plausible reasoning.[1] In this

---

[1]Although DBPedia contains information on many sorts
of entities, due to its explicit encyclopedic commitment,
common-sense information is dispersed among textual de-
scriptions (e.g., in the abstracts) rather than being available in
a well-structured formal way. For instance, the *fork* entity can
be categorized as an object, whilst there is no structured information about its typical usage. On the other hand, Concept-

Proceedings of the 1st Workshop on Sense, Concept and Entity Representations and their Applications, pages 96–101,
Valencia, Spain, April 4 2017. ©2017 Association for Computational Linguistics

paper we explore whether and to what extent a linguistic resource describing concepts by means of *qualitative* and *synthetic* vectorial representation is suited to assess the conceptual similarity between pairs of concepts.

2 Vector representations with the TTCS$^{\mathcal{E}}$

The TTCS$^{\mathcal{E}}$ has been designed to build resources encoded as general conceptual representations. We presently illustrate how the resource is built, deferring to Section 3 the description of the control strategy designed to use it in the computation of conceptual similarity.

The TTCS$^{\mathcal{E}}$ takes in input a concept c referred through a BabelNet synset ID, and produces as output a vector representation $\vec{c}$ where the input concept is described along some semantic dimensions. In turn, filling each such dimension amounts to finding a set of appropriate concepts: features act like vector space dimensions, and they are based on ConceptNet relationships.[2] The dimensions are filled with BabelNet synset IDs, so that finally each concept c residing in the linguistic resource can be defined as

$$\vec{c} = \bigcup_{d \in \mathcal{D}} \{ \langle ID_d, \{c_1, \cdots, c_k\} \rangle \} \tag{1}$$

where ID_d is the identifier of the d-th dimension, and $\{c_1, \cdots, c_k\}$ is the set of values chosen for d.

The control strategy implemented by the TTCS$^{\mathcal{E}}$ includes two main steps, *semantic extraction* (composed by the *extraction* and *concept identification* phases) and the *vector injection*.

Net is more suited to structurally represent common-sense information related to typicality. However, in ConceptNet the coverage of this type of knowledge component is sometimes not satisfactory. For similar remarks on such resources, claiming for the need of new resources more suited to represent common-sense information, please also refer to (Basile et al., 2016).

[2] The full list of the employed properties, which were selected from the most salient properties in ConceptNet, includes: INSTANCEOF, RELATEDTO, ISA, ATLOCATION, DBPEDIA/GENRE, SYNONYM, DERIVED-FROM, CAUSES, USEDFOR, MOTIVATEDBYGOAL, HAS-SUBEVENT, ANTONYM, CAPABLEOF, DESIRES, CAUS-ESDESIRE, PARTOF, HASPROPERTY, HASPREREQUI-SITE, MADEOF, COMPOUNDDERIVEDFROM, HASFIRST-SUBEVENT, DBPEDIA/FIELD, DBPEDIA/KNOWNFOR, DB-PEDIA/INFLUENCEDBY, DEFINEDAS, HASA, MEMBEROF, RECEIVESACTION, SIMILARTO, DBPEDIA/INFLUENCED, SYMBOLOF, HASCONTEXT, NOTDESIRES, OBSTRUCT-EDBY, HASLASTSUBEVENT, NOTUSEDFOR, NOTCA-PABLEOF, DESIREOF, NOTHASPROPERTY, CREATEDBY, ATTRIBUTE, ENTAILS, LOCATIONOFACTION, LOCATED-NEAR.

Extraction The TTCS$^{\mathcal{E}}$ takes in input c and builds a bag-of-concepts C including the concepts associated to c through one or more ConceptNet relationships. All ConceptNet nodes related to the input concept c are collected: namely, we take the corresponding ConceptNet node for each term in the WordNet (Miller, 1995) synset of c, $s^c \in$ WN-syn$_c$. For each such term we extract all terms t linked through d, one of the aforementioned ConceptNet relationships: that is, we collect the terms $s^c \xrightarrow{d} t$ and store them in the set T. Each s^c can be considered as a different lexicalization for the same concept c, so that all t can be grouped in T, that finally contains all terms associated in any way to c.

Since ConceptNet does not provide any direct anchoring mechanism to associate its terms to meaning identifiers, it is necessary to determine which of the terms $t \in T$ are relevant for the concept c. In other words, when we access the ConceptNet page for a certain term, we find not only the association regarding that term with the sense conveyed by c, but also all the associations regarding it in any other meaning. To select only (and possibly all) the associations that concern the sense individuated through the previous phase, we introduce the notion of *relevance*. To give an intuition of this process, the terms found in ConceptNet are considered as relevant (and thus retained) either if they exhibit a heavy weight in the NASARI vector corresponding to the considered concept, or if they share at least some terms with the NASARI vector (further details on a similar approach can be found in (Lieto et al., 2016a)).

Concept identification Once the set of relevant terms has been extracted, we need to lift them to the corresponding concept(s), which will be used as value for the features. We stress, in fact, that dimension fillers are concepts rather than terms (please refer to Eq. 1). In the concept identification step, we exploit NASARI in order to provide each term $t \in T$ with a BabelNet synset ID, thus finally converting it into the bag-of-concepts C.

Given a $t_i \in T$, we distinguish two main cases. If t_i is contained in one or more synsets inside the NASARI vector of c, we obtain c_i (the concept underlying t_i) by directly assigning to t_i the identifier of the heaviest weighted synset that contains it.[3] Otherwise, if t_i is not included in any of the

---

[3] NASARI *unified* vectors are composed by a head con-

synsets in the NASARI vector associated to c, we need to choose a vector among all possible ones: we first select a list of candidate vectors (that is, those containing t_i in their vector head), and then choose the best one by retaining the vector where c's ID has highest weight.

For example, given in input the concept *bank* intended as a financial institution, we inspect the edges of the ConceptNet node 'bank' and its synonyms. Then, thanks to the relevance notion we get rid of associations such as 'bank ISA flight maneuver' since the term 'flight maneuver' is not present in the vector associated to the concept *bank*. Conversely, we accept sentences such as 'bank HASA branch' (i.e., 'branch' is added to T). Finally, 'branch' goes through the concept identification phase, resulting in a concept c_i and then it is added to C.

Vector injection The bag-of-concepts C is then scanned, and each value is injected in the template for $\vec{c}$. Each value $\{c_1, \ldots, c_n \in C\}$ is still provided with the relationship that linked it to c in ConceptNet, so this value is employed to fill the corresponding feature in $\vec{c}$. For example, if c_k is extracted from the ConceptNet relation USEDFOR (i.e., $c \xrightarrow{\text{USEDFOR}} c_k$), the value c_k will be added to the set of entities that are used for c.

2.1 Building the TTCS$^{\mathcal{E}}$ resource

In order to build the set of vectors in the TTCS$^{\mathcal{E}}$ resource, the system took in input $16,782$ concepts. Such concepts have been preliminarily computed (Lieto et al., 2016b) by starting from the $10K$ most frequent nouns present in the Corpus of Contemporary American English (COCA).[4] Then, for each input concept the TTCS$^{\mathcal{E}}$ scans some $3M$ ConceptNet nodes to retrieve the terms that appear into the WordNet synset of the input. This step allows to browse over $11M$ associations available in ConceptNet, and to extract on average 155 ConceptNet nodes for each input concept. Subsequently, the TTCS$^{\mathcal{E}}$ exploits the $2.8M$ NASARI vectors to decide whether each of the extracted nodes is relevant or not w.r.t. the input concept, and then it tries to associate a NASARI vector to each of them (concept identification step). On av-

erage, 14.90 concepts are used to fill each vector.[5]

3 Computing Conceptual Similariy

One main assumption underlying our approach is that two concepts are similar insofar as they share some values on the same dimension, such as when they are both used for the same ends, they share components, etc.. Consequently, our metrics does not employ WordNet taxonomy and distances between pairs of nodes, such as in (Wu and Palmer, 1994; Leacock et al., 1998; Schwartz and Gomez, 2008), nor it depends on information content accounts either, such as in (Resnik, 1998a; Jiang and Conrath, 1997).

The representation available to the TTCS$^{\mathcal{E}}$ is entirely filled with conceptual identifiers, so to assess the similarity between two such values we check whether both the concept vector $\vec{c}_i$ and the vector $\vec{c}_j$ share the same (concept) value for the same dimension $d \in D$, and our similarity along each dimension basically depends on this simple intuition:

$$\text{sim}(\vec{c}_i, \vec{c}_j) = \frac{1}{|D|} \cdot \sum_{d \in D} |d_i \cap d_j|.$$

The score computed by the TTCS$^{\mathcal{E}}$ system can be justified based on the dimensions actually filled: this explanation can be built automatically, since the similarity between $\vec{c}_i$ and $\vec{c}_j$ is a function of the sum of the number of shared elements in each dimension, so that one can argue that a given score x is due to the fact that along a given dimension d both concepts share some values (e.g., $\text{sim}(table, chair) = x$ because each one is a (ISA) 'furniture', both are USEDFOR 'eating', 'studying' and 'working'; both can be found AT-LOCATION 'home', 'office'; and each one HASA 'leg').

Ultimately, the TTCS$^{\mathcal{E}}$ collects information along the 44 dimensions listed in footnote 2, so that we are in principle able to assess in how far similar they are along each and every dimension. However, our approach is presently limited by the actual average filling factor, and by the noise that can be possibly collected by an automatic procedure built on top of the BabelNet knowledge base. Since we need to deal with noisy and incomplete information, some adjustments to the above formula have been necessary in order to handle

---

cept (represented by its ID in the first position) and a body, that is a list of synsets related to the head concept. Each synset ID is followed by a number that grasps the strength of its correlation with the head concept.

[4] `http://corpus.byu.edu/full-text/`.

[5] The final resource is available for download at the URL `http://ttcs.di.unito.it`.

—*intra* dimension— the possibly unbalanced number of concepts that characterize the different dimensions; and to prevent —*inter* dimensions— the computation from being biased by more richly defined concepts (i.e., those with more dimensions filled). The computation of the conceptual similarity score is thus based on the following formula:

$$\text{sim}(\vec{c}_i, \vec{c}_j) = \frac{1}{|D^*|} \cdot \sum_{d \in D} \frac{|d_i \cap d_j|}{\beta\left(\alpha a + (1 - \alpha)\, b\right) + |d_i \cap d_j|}$$

where $|d_i \cap d_j|$ counts the number of concepts that are used as fillers for the dimension d in the concept $\vec{c}_i$ and $\vec{c}_j$, respectively; and a and b are computed as $a = \min(|d_i - d_j|, |d_j - d_i|)$, $b = \max(|d_i - d_j|, |d_j - d_i|)$; and $|D^*|$ counts the dimensions filled with at least one concept in both vectors.

This formula is known as the Symmetrical Tversky's Ratio Model (Jimenez et al., 2013), which is a symmetrical reformulation for the Tversky's ratio model (Tversky, 1977). It enjoys the following properties: *i)* it allows grasping the number of common traits between the two vectors (at the numerator); *ii)* it allows tuning the balance between cardinality differences (through the parameter α), and between $|d_i \cap d_j|$ and $|d_i - d_j|, |d_j - d_i|$ (through the parameter β). Interestingly, by setting $\alpha = .5$ and $\beta = 1$ the formula equals the popular Dice's coefficient. The parameters α and β were set to .8 and .2 for the experimentation.

4 Evaluation

In the experimentation we addressed the conceptual similarity task at the *sense level*, that is the $\text{TTCS}^{\mathcal{E}}$ system has been fed with sense pairs. We considered three datasets,[6] namely the RG, MC and WS-Sim datasets, first designed in (Rubenstein and Goodenough, 1965; Miller and Charles, 1991) and (Agirre et al., 2009), respectively. Historically, while the first two (RG and MC) datasets were originally conceived for similarity measures, the WS-Sim dataset was developed as a subset of a former dataset built by (Finkelstein et al., 2001) created to test similarity by including pairs of words related through specific relationships, such as synonymy, hyponymy, and unrelated. All senses were mapped onto WordNet 3.0.

The similarity scores computed by the $\text{TTCS}^{\mathcal{E}}$ system have been assessed through Pearsons r

	ρ	r
RG	0.78	0.85
MC	0.77	0.80
WS-Sim	0.64	0.54

Table 1: Spearman (ρ) and Pearson (r) correlations obtained over the three datasets.

and Spearmans ρ correlations, that are largely adopted for the conceptual similarity task (for a recent compendium of the approaches please refer to (Pilehvar and Navigli, 2015)). The former measure captures the linear correlation of two variables as their covariance divided by the product of their standard deviations, thus basically allowing to grasp differences in their values, whilst the Spearman correlation is computed as the Pearson correlation between the *rank* values of the considered variables, so it is reputed to be best suited to assess results in a similarity ranking setting where relative scores are relevant (Schwartz and Gomez, 2011; Pilehvar and Navigli, 2015).

Table 1 shows the results obtained by the system in a preliminary experimentation.

Provided that the present task of *sense*-level similarity is slightly different from *word*-level similarity (about this distinction, please refer to (Pilehvar and Navigli, 2015)), and our results can be thus hardly compared to those in literature, the reported figures are still far from the state of the art, where the Spearman correlation ρ reaches 0.92 for the RG dataset (Pilehvar and Navigli, 2015), 0.92 for the MC dataset (Agirre et al., 2009), and 0.81 for the WS-Sim dataset (Halawi et al., 2012; Tau Yih and Qazvinian, 2012).[7]

However, we remark that the $\text{TTCS}^{\mathcal{E}}$ employs vectors of a very limited size w.r.t. the standard vector-based resources used in the current models of distributional semantics (as mentioned, each vector is defined, on average, through 14.90 concepts). Moreover, due to the explicit grounding provided by connecting the NASARI feature values to the corresponding properties in ConceptNet, the $\text{TTCS}^{\mathcal{E}}$ can be used to provide the scores returned as output with an explanation, based on the shared concepts along some given dimension. At the best of our knowledge, this is a unique feature, that cannot be easily reached by methods

---

[6]Publicly available at the URL `http://www.seas.upenn.edu/~hansens/conceptSim/`.

[7]Rich references to state-of-the-art results and works experimenting on the mentioned datasets can be found on the ACL Wiki, at the URL `https://goo.gl/NQ1b6g`.

based on Latent Semantic Analysis (such as those pioneered by (Deerwester et al., 1990)) and can be only partly approached by techniques exploiting taxonomic structures (Resnik, 1998b; Banerjee and Pedersen, 2003). Conversely, few and relevant traits are present in the final linguistic resource, which is thus *synthetic* and more *cognitively plausible* (Gärdenfors, 2014).

In some cases —27 concept pairs out of the overall 190 pairs— the system was not able to retrieve an ID for one of the concepts in the pair: such pairs were excluded from the computation of the final accuracy. Missing concepts may be lacking in (at least one of) the resources upon which the $\text{TTCS}^{\mathcal{E}}$ is built: including further resources may thus be helpful to overcome this limitation. Also, difficulties stemmed from insufficient information for the concepts at stake: this phenomenon was observed, e.g., when both concepts have been found, but no common dimension has been filled. This sort of difficulty shows that the coverage of the resource still needs to be enhanced by improving the extraction phase, so to add further concepts *per* dimension, and to fill more dimensions.

5 Conclusions

In this paper we have introduced a novel resource, the $\text{TTCS}^{\mathcal{E}}$, which is compatible with the Conceptual Spaces framework and aims at putting together encyclopedic and common-sense knowledge. The resource has been employed to compute the conceptual similarity between concept pairs. Thanks to its representational features it allows implementing a simple though effective heuristics to assess similarity: that is, concepts are similar insofar as they share some values along the same dimension. However, further heuristics will be investigated in the next future, as well.

A preliminary experimentation has been run, employing three different datasets. Provided that we consider the obtained results as encouraging, the experimentation clearly points out that there is room for improvement along two main axes: dimensions must be filled with further information, and also the quality of the extracted information should be improved. Both aspects will be the object of our future efforts.

References

Eneko Agirre, Enrique Alfonseca, Keith Hall, Jana Kravalova, Marius Paşca, and Aitor Soroa. 2009. A study on similarity and relatedness using distributional and wordnet-based approaches. In *Procs of Human Language Technologies: The 2009 Annual Conference of the North American Chapter of the Association for Computational Linguistics*, pages 19–27. ACL.

S. Banerjee and T. Pedersen. 2003. Extended gloss overlaps as a measure of semantic relatedness. In *Proceedings of the Eighteenth International Joint Conference on Artificial Intelligence*, pages 805–810.

Valerio Basile, Soufian Jebbara, Elena Cabrio, and Philipp Cimiano. 2016. Populating a knowledge base with object-location relations using distributional semantics. In Eva Blomqvist, Paolo Ciancarini, Francesco Poggi, and Fabio Vitali, editors, *EKAW*, volume 10024 of *Lecture Notes in Computer Science*, pages 34–50.

José Camacho-Collados, Mohammad Taher Pilehvar, and Roberto Navigli. 2015. NASARI: a novel approach to a semantically-aware representation of items. In *Proceedings of NAACL*, pages 567–577.

S. Deerwester, S. Dumais, G. Furnas, T. Landauer, and R. Harshman. 1990. Indexing by latent semantic analysis. *Journal of the American Society for Information Science*, 41:391–407.

Lev Finkelstein, Evgeniy Gabrilovich, Yossi Matias, Ehud Rivlin, Zach Solan, Gadi Wolfman, and Eytan Ruppin. 2001. Placing search in context: The concept revisited. In *Proceedings of the 10th international conference on World Wide Web*, pages 406–414. ACM.

Peter Gärdenfors. 2014. *The geometry of meaning: Semantics based on conceptual spaces*. MIT Press.

Guy Halawi, Gideon Dror, Evgeniy Gabrilovich, and Yehuda Koren. 2012. Large-scale learning of word relatedness with constraints. In Qiang Yang, Deepak Agarwal, and Jian Pei, editors, *KDD*, pages 1406–1414. ACM.

Jay J. Jiang and David W. Conrath. 1997. Semantic similarity based on corpus statistics and lexical taxonomy. In *Proceedings of International Conference on Research in Computational Linguisics*, Taiwan.

Sergio Jimenez, Claudia Becerra, Alexander Gelbukh, Av Juan Dios Bátiz, and Av Mendizábal. 2013. Softcardinality-core: Improving text overlap with distributional measures for semantic textual similarity. In *Second Joint Conference on Lexical and Computational Semantics*, volume 1, pages 194–201.

Claudia Leacock, George A Miller, and Martin Chodorow. 1998. Using corpus statistics and wordnet relations for sense identification. *Computational Linguistics*, 24(1):147–165.

Antonio Lieto, Enrico Mensa, and Daniele P. Radicioni. 2016a. A Resource-Driven Approach for Anchoring Linguistic Resources to Conceptual Spaces. In *Procs of the XV International Conference of the Italian Association for Artificial Intelligence*, volume 10037 of *LNAI*, pages 435–449. Springer.

Antonio Lieto, Enrico Mensa, and Daniele P. Radicioni. 2016b. Taming sense sparsity: a common-sense approach. In *Proceedings of Third Italian Conference on Computational Linguistics (CLiC-it 2016) & Fifth Evaluation Campaign of Natural Language Processing and Speech Tools for Italian*.

Antonio Lieto, Daniele P. Radicioni, and Valentina Rho. 2017. Dual PECCS: A Cognitive System for Conceptual Representation and Categorization. *Journal of Experimental & Theoretical Artificial Intelligence*, 29(2):433–452.

George A. Miller and Walter G. Charles. 1991. Contextual correlates of semantic similarity. *Language and cognitive processes*, 6(1):1–28.

George A. Miller. 1995. Wordnet: a lexical database for english. *Communications of the ACM*, 38(11):39–41.

Roberto Navigli and Simone Paolo Ponzetto. 2012. BabelNet: The automatic construction, evaluation and application of a wide-coverage multilingual semantic network. *Artificial Intelligence*, 193:217–250.

Mohammad Taher Pilehvar and Roberto Navigli. 2015. From senses to texts: An all-in-one graph-based approach for measuring semantic similarity. *Artif. Intell.*, 228:95–128.

Philip Resnik. 1998a. Semantic similarity in a taxonomy: An information-based measure and its application to problems of ambiguity in natural language. *Journal of Artificial Intelligence Research*, 11(1).

Philip Resnik. 1998b. Semantic similarity in a taxonomy: An information-based measure and its application to problems of ambiguity in natural language. *Journal of Artificial Intelligence Research*, 11(1).

Eleanor Rosch. 1975. Cognitive Representations of Semantic Categories. *Journal of experimental psychology: General*, 104(3):192–233.

Herbert Rubenstein and John B. Goodenough. 1965. Contextual correlates of synonymy. *Communications of the ACM*, 8(10):627–633.

Hansen A. Schwartz and Fernando Gomez. 2008. Acquiring knowledge from the web to be used as selectors for noun sense disambiguation. In *Procs of the Twelfth Conference on Computational Natural Language Learning*, pages 105–112. ACL.

Hansen A Schwartz and Fernando Gomez. 2011. Evaluating semantic metrics on tasks of concept similarity. In *Proc. Int. Florida Artif. Intell. Res. Soc. Conf.(FLAIRS)*, page 324.

Robert Speer and Catherine Havasi. 2012. Representing General Relational Knowledge in ConceptNet 5. In *LREC*, pages 3679–3686.

Wen Tau Yih and Vahed Qazvinian. 2012. Measuring word relatedness using heterogeneous vector space models. In *HLT-NAACL*, pages 616–620. The Association for Computational Linguistics.

Amos Tversky. 1977. Features of similarity. *Psychological review*, 84(4):327.

Zhibiao Wu and Martha Palmer. 1994. Verbs semantics and lexical selection. In *Proceedings of the 32nd annual meeting on Association for Computational Linguistics*, pages 133–138. ACL.

Measuring the Italian-English lexical gap for action verbs and its impact on translation

Lorenzo Gregori
University of Florence
lorenzo.gregori@unifi.it

Alessandro Panunzi
University of Florence
alessandro.panunzi@unifi.it

Abstract

This paper describes a method to measure the lexical gap of action verbs in Italian and English by using the IMAGACT ontology of action. The fine-grained categorization of action concepts of the data source allowed to have wide overview of the relation between concepts in the two languages. The calculated lexical gap for both English and Italian is about 30% of the action concepts, much higher than previous results. Beyond this general numbers a deeper analysis has been performed in order to evaluate the impact that lexical gaps can have on translation. In particular a distinction has been made between the cases in which the presence of a lexical gap affects translation correctness and completeness at a semantic level. The results highlight a high percentage of concepts that can be considered hard to translate (about 18% from English to Italian and 20% from Italian to English) and confirms that action verbs are a critical lexical class for translation tasks.

1 Introduction

Lexical gap is a well known phenomenon in linguistics and its identification allows to discover some relevant features related to the semantic categorization operated by languages. A lexical gap corresponds to a lack of lexicalization of a certain concept in a given language. This phenomenon traditionally emerged from the analysis of a single language by means of the detection of empty spaces in a lexical matrix (see the seminal works by Leher (1974) and Lyons (1977); see also Kjellmer (2003)). Anyway, lexical gap becomes a major issue when comparing two or more languages, as in translation tasks (Ivir, 1977). In this latter case, a lexical gap can be defined as the absence of direct lexeme in one language while comparing two languages during translation (Cvilikaitė, 2006). The presence of lexical gaps between two languages is more than a theoretical problem, having a strong impact in several related fields: lexicographers need to deal with lexical gaps in the compilation of bilingual dictionaries (Gouws, 2002); in knowledge representation the creation of multilanguage linguistic resources require a strategy to cope with the lack of concepts (Jansseen, 2004); the lexical transfer process is affected by the presence of lexical gaps in automatic translation system, reducing their accuracy (Santos, 1990).

Even if in literature it's possible to find many examples of gaps, it's hard to estimate them. This is due to the fact that most of the gaps are related to small semantic differences that are hard to identify: available linguistic resources usually represent a coarse-grained semantics, so while they are useful to discriminate the prominent senses of words, they can't capture small semantic shifts. In addition to it, a multilanguage resource is required for this purpose, but these resources are normally built up through a mapping between two or more monolingual resources and this cause an approximation in concept definitions: similar concepts tend to be grouped together in a unitary concept that represent the core-meaning and lose their semantic specificities.

2 IMAGACT

Verbs are a critical lexical class for disambiguation and translation tasks: they are much more polysemous than nouns and, moreover, their ambiguity is hard to resolve (Fellbaum et al., 2001). In particular the representation of word senses as sepa-

Proceedings of the 1st Workshop on Sense, Concept and Entity Representations and their Applications, pages 102–109,
Valencia, Spain, April 4 2017. ©2017 Association for Computational Linguistics

rate entities is tricky, since their boundaries are often vague causing the senses to be under-specified and overlapping. From this point of view the subclass of general verbs represent a crucial point, because these verbs are characterized by both high frequency in the use of language and high ambiguity.

IMAGACT[1] is a visual ontology of action that provides a video-based translation and disambiguation framework for general verbs. The resource is built on an ontology containing a fine-grained categorization of action concepts, each represented by one or more video prototypes as recorded scenes and 3D animations.

IMAGACT currently contains 1,010 scenes which encompass the action concepts most commonly referred to in everyday language usage. Data are derived from the manual annotation of verb occurrences in spontaneous spoken corpora (Moneglia et al., 2012); the dataset has been compiled by selecting action verbs with the highest frequency in the corpora and comprises 522 Italian and 554 English lemmas. Although the set of retrieved actions is necessarily incomplete, this methodology ensures to have a significant picture of the main action types performed in everyday life[2].

The links between verbs and video scenes are based on the co-referentiality of different verbs with respect to the action expressed by a scene (i.e. different verbs can describe the same action, visualized in the scene). The visual representations convey the action information in a cross-linguistic environment and IMAGACT may thus be exploited to discover how the actions are lexicalized in different languages.

In addition to it IMAGACT contains a semantic classification of each lemma, that is divided into Types: each verb Type identifies an action concept and contains one ore more scenes, that work as prototypes of that concept. Type classification is manually performed in Italian and English in parallel, through a corpus-based annotation procedure by native language annotators (Moneglia et al., 2012); this allowed to have a discrimination of verb Types based only on the annotator competence, without any attempt to fit the data into predefined semantic models. Validation results (Gagliardi, 2014) highlight a good rate of

Type discrimination agreement: a Cohen k of 0,82 for 2 expert annotators and a Fleiss k of 0.73 for 4 non-expert ones[3].

For these features IMAGACT ontology is a reliable data source to measure the lexical gap between Italian and English: in fact verb Types are defined independently, but linked together through the scenes. The comparison of Types in different language through their action prototypes allows to identify the action concepts that are shared between the two languages and the ones that don't match with any concept in the other language; in this case we have a lexical gap.

3 Type relations

In this frame we can perform a set-based comparison, considering a Type as just a set of scenes. A Type is a lexicalized concept, so a partition of the meaning, but semantic features are not represented in the ontology and, in fact, they are unknown: data are derived from the ability of competent speaker in performing a categorization of similar items with respect to a lemma, without any attempt to formalize semes. So if we look at the database we can say that Types are merely sets of scenes.

Comparing a Type (T_1) of a verb in source language (V_1) with a Type (T_2) of a verb in target language (V_2) we can have 5 possible configurations:

1. $T_1 \equiv T_2$: two Types are equivalent if they contain the same set of scenes;

2. $T_1 \cap T_2 = \emptyset$: two Types are disjoint if they don't share any scene;

3. $T_1 \subset T_2$: T_1 is a subset of T_2 if any scene of T_1 is also a scene of T_2 and the 2 Types are not equivalent;

4. $T_1 \supset T_2$: T_1 is a superset of T_2 if any scene of T_2 is also a scene of T_1 and the 2 Types are not equivalent;

5. $T_1 \cap T_2 \neq \emptyset \wedge T_1 \nsubseteq T_2 \wedge T_1 \nsupseteq T_2$: two Types are partially overlapping if they share some scenes and each Type have some scenes not belonging to the other one.

---

[1]http://www.imagact.it

[2]see Moneglia et al. (2012) and Moneglia (2014b) for details about corpora annotation numbers and methodology.

[3]Inter-annotator agreement (ITA) measured on WordNet by expert annotators on comparable verb sets (score for fine-grained sense inventories): ITA = 72% on SemEval-2007 dataset (Pradhan et al., 2007); ITA = 71% on SensEval-2 dataset (Palmer et al., 2007).

Figure 1: Two Equivalent Types belonging to the Italian verb *toccare* and to the English verb *touch*.

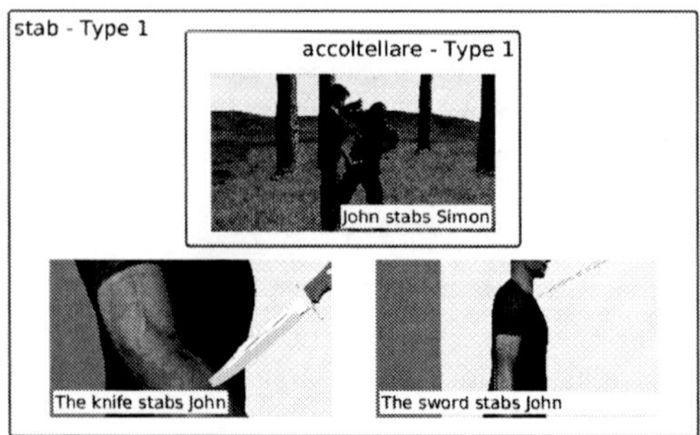

Figure 2: Two Hierarchically related Types belonging to the Italian verb *accoltellare* and to the English verb *stab*.

It's important to discuss these cases separately, because each one of them highlights a different semantic relation between verbs and has different implications for translation.

When two Types are equivalents (case 1) the 2 languages share the action concept the Types represent: we could say that there is an interlinguistic concept. This case is not problematic for translation: each occurrence of the verb V_1 that belongs to Type T_1 can be translated with V_2; moreover we can apply V_1 to translate any occurrence of V_2 belonging to T_2.

For example one Type of the English verb *to touch* and one Type of the Italian verb *toccare* are equivalent. They share 3 video scenes: *Mary touches the doll*, *Mary touches the table* and *John touches Mary* (see Fig. 1). Each scene is connected to a different set of verbs (i.e. *to brush, to graze, to caress*), representing a specific semantic concept, but they are kept together by a more general concept both in Italian and in English. So in any of these actions the verb *to touch* can be safely translated in Italian with *toccare* and vice versa.

If two Types are disjoint (case 2) the Types refer to unrelated semantic concepts and we can assume that translation between an occurrence of V_1 belonging to T_2 can not be translated with V_2.

In cases 3 and 4 the Types are hierarchically related and we can assume the existence of a semantic relation that links a general Type with a specific one. Although we can not induce the type of this relation that could be *hyponym, entailment, troponym* and so on. In this configuration we can see that translation is safe from specific to general, but not vice versa: in case 3 any occurrence of V_1 belonging to T_1 can be translated with V_2, while in case 4 V_2 can not be safely applied, because it encodes only a sub-part of the concept represented by T_1.

For example Type 1 of the English verb *to stab* and Type 1 of the Italian verb *accoltellare* categorize action where a sharp object pierces a body, but while *stab* can be applied to describe actions independently on their aim and the tool used, *accoltellare* is applicable only when the agent voluntarily injures someone and the action is accomplished with a knife. In this case the Italian Type is more specific than the English one, so translation is safe from Italian to English (*stab* can be used to translate any occurrence of *accoltellare-Type 1*), but not vice versa: *stab-Type 1* can not be always translated with *accoltellare*, because a part of its variation is covered by other Italian verbs like *trafiggere, penetrare* or *attraversare*.

Finally a partial overlap between Types (case 5) doesn't allow to induce any semantic relation between Types: in these cases we have different concepts that can refer the same action. Normally these happen when the action is interpreted from two different points of view and categorized within unrelated lexical concepts. In this case we have a translation relation between V_1 and V_2 without having any semantic relation between their Types.

For example the Italian verb *abbassare*, that is frequently translated with *lower* in English, can also be translated with *position* when applied to some (but not every) actions belonging to Type 1, categorizing actions involving the body; moreover we have the same translation relation from English to Italian where sometimes (but not always) *position-Type 2* can be translated with *abbassare*. Here there are two Types that represent semanti-

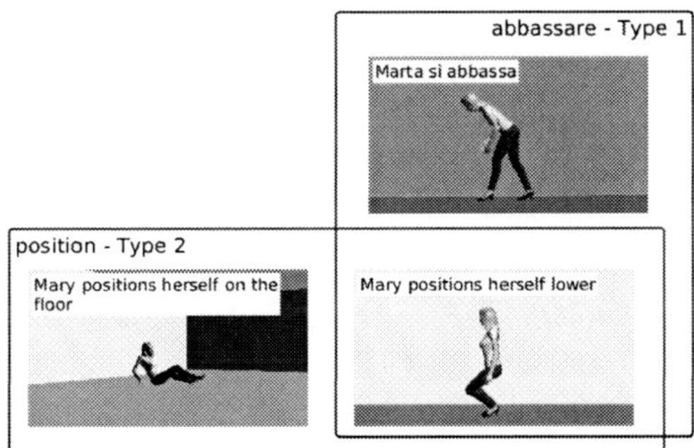

Figure 3: Two partially overlapping Types belonging to the Italian verb *abbassare* and to the English verb *position*.

cally independent concepts, but that can both be applied to describe some actions, like *Mary positions herself lower* and other similar ones.

This happens rarely in Italian - English (14 Types on our dataset) and in any of these cases there are other translation verbs as possible alternatives. Despite this, Type overlaps identification is very relevant, because it allows to discover unexpected translation candidates (i.e. target verbs that have a translation relation but not a semantic relation with the source verb) that can not be extracted from a lexico-semantic resource. In addition to it Type overlaps identification is crucial if the target verb is the only one translation possibility and this can happen, especially between two languages that are very far: some evidences for example have been discovered in Italian and Chinese (Pan, 2016) through a deep comparison of Italian Types with Chinese verbs that refer to the same scenes. This work allowed to identify some positive occurrences of this interesting phenomenon, but can not be exploited for its numeric quantification: indeed an exhaustive analysis that involves the relation between action concepts can be made only between Italian and English, since IMAGACT contains the verb Type discrimination in these two languages only.

4 Lexical gap identification

4.1 Dataset building

In order to measure the lexical gaps in Italian and English we created a working dataset by selecting the set of Types that have a full mapping in the two languages. We need to consider that IMAGACT annotation process has been carried out in

several steps: firstly verbs were annotated through a corpus-based procedure and Types were created and validated by mother tongue speakers on the basis of their linguistic competence; then for each concept a scene was produced to provide a prototypical representation of it; after that a mapping between Italian and English was performed by linking the scenes to the Types of each language; finally annotators were requested to recheck each scene and add the missing verbs that are applicable to it. This last revision enriched the scene with more verbs that don't belong to any Type.

We decided to exclude from the dataset all the scenes (and the related Types) that contain *untyped* verbs, considering that a partial typing does not ensure the coherence of verb Type discrimination: in fact it's not possible to be sure that the creation of Types for these new instances would preserve the original Type distinction.

After this pruning we obtained a set of 1,000 Italian Types and 1,027 English Types, that refer to 501 and 535 verbs respectively (see Table 1).

	IT	EN
Types	1,000	1,027
Verbs	501	535
Scenes	980	917

Table 1: Number of Types, verbs and scenes belonging to the dataset.

4.2 Methodology

According to our dataset, we can easily estimate the lexical gap by measuring the number of Types in source language that don't have an equivalent Type in target language. Namely for each concept in source language we are going to verify if there is a concept in target language that refer to the same set of actions (represented by video prototypes); if the match is not found we have a lexical gap in target language.

As we can see in table 2, the action concepts that are lexicalized in Italian and without a corresponding match in English are 33,6% (English gap); on the contrary the Italian gap for English concepts is 29,02%.

Before going ahead we need to do some considerations about these numbers. First of all we can see that these percentages are much higher than the ones calculated by Bentivogli and Pianta (2000), that found 7,4% of gaps for verbs in

	IT → EN	EN → IT
Total Types	1,000	1,027
Equiv. Types	664 (66,4%)	729 (70,98%)
Lexical gaps	**336 (33,6%)**	**298 (29,02%)**

Table 2: Types in source language that have and have not an equivalent Type in target language.

English-to-Italian comparison. This is a big shift, but it's not surprising if we consider the differences of the two experiments in terms of methodology and dataset:

- IMAGACT Type distinction is more fine-grained in respect to WordNet synsets (Bartolini et al., 2014);

- the experiment by Bentivogli and Pianta was led on MultiWordNet, in which multilanguage Wordnets are created on the basis of the Princeton Wordnet sense distinction (Pianta et al., 2002); this methodology introduce an approximation in the concepts definition;

- the 7,4% of Bentivogli and Pianta is a general value on verbs, while our experiment is focused on action verbs, which are a strongly ambiguous lexical class (Moneglia, 2014a);

- the dictionary-based methodology proposed by Bentivogli and Pianta is nearly opposite to IMAGACT reference-based approach.

Beyond these general considerations a lemma-by-lemma comparison with the experiment of Bentivogli and Pianta (whose dataset is currently not available) would better explain this numeric difference.

5 Lexical gaps and translation problems

Besides a general measure of the gaps for action concept it's important to go a step beyond to verify in which cases the presence of a lexical gap impacts the translation quality. In order to do this, we divided the Types without an equivalent in target language in three categories:

- *leaf Types*: these Types in source language represent concepts that are more specific than other ones in target language; in this case the only Type in target language that have a partial match with the Type in source language is a superset (case 3);

- *root Types*: these Types in source language represent concepts that are more general than other ones in target language: the only Type in target language that have a partial match with the Type in source language is a subset (case 4);

- *middle Types*: these Types have a partial match in target language both with a more general Type and with a more specific one (both cases 3 and 4).

As we mentioned before we did not find any case in which a partial overlapping Type (case 5) is the only one possible match in Italian and English comparison; so these cases are counted within the three categories above.

5.1 Root Types and uncertain translations

Starting from this classification we can see that *root Types* are the critical ones in terms of translation: in fact we don't have a unique lexicalized concept in target language that is able to represent the concept in source language; instead we have more than one Type (and multiple verbs) that cover different subparts of the whole general concept variation. In these cases we need to have extra information about the action in order to translate it properly. From a computational point of view we can say that a word sense disambiguation of the source verb is not enough to reach a correct translation verb.

The two sentences *The cell phone lands on the carpet* and *The pole vaulter lands on the mat*, for example, belong to the same action concept according to the semantics of the verb *to land*[4]. In Italian there is not a unique Type that collects these two actions: it's possible to use *atterrare* for the athlete, but it is not allowed for the phone, for which we need to make a semantic shift and use the verb *cadere* (that is more similar to *fall down*). Again *cadere* is not appropriate for the athlete, because it implies that the athlete stumbles and falls.

So this action concept that is lexicalized in English with *to land* does not have a unique translation verb in Italian, and extra informations are required to translate it properly (if the theme is an human being or an object, in this specific case).

Table 3 show the number of *leaf, root* and *middle Types* in Italian and English; we can see that

---

[4]unlike *The butterfly lands on the flower* or *The airplane lands* that belong to different concepts of *to land*.

	IT → EN	EN → IT
Lexical gaps	336	298
Leaf Types	217 (64.58%)	200 (67.58%)
Root Types	47 (13.99%)	43 (14.43%)
Middle Types	72 (21.43%)	55 (18.46%)

Table 3: Number of Leaf, Root and Middle Types in Italian and English (percentages on the lexical gaps).

root Types represent the 14% of the lexical gaps in both the languages, corresponding to 4-5% of the total Types.

5.2 General Types and lossy translations

Root Types are the most critical case for a translation task, because they affect the correctness; besides there are also other kinds of lexical gaps that impact on translation. In particular is useful to estimate how semantically far is the best translation candidate in the cases in which we can apply a more general Type to translate the concept in the source language. In fact in both *leaf* and *middle Types* we have a Type in target language that is more general to the source one, so it is safely applicable to any occurrence belonging to the source Type. This is not free from problems, because in translation we use a more general verb, so we miss some semes that are encoded in the source verb. In fact in this case we still have a translation problem, which is not in finding a possible target verb, but in adding more information in other lexical element of the sentence to fill the lack of semantic information. In this case the gap does not affect the correctness of the translation, but its completeness.

For example the English verb *to plonk* does not have a correspondence in Italian. In particular a sentence like *John plonks the books on the table* belongs to a Type of *plonk* that is a *leaf Type* (so there is a possible translation verb in Italian), but for which the nearest Italian Type is much wider, belonging to the very general verb *mettere*. In this case it's possible to translate in Italian with *John mette i libri sul tavolo*, but losing all the information regarding the way the books are placed on the table (*mettere* is more similar with *to put*); an addition of other lexical elements to the sentence is required to fill this gap in Italian.

Conversely we can say that a small distance between the source and the target Type does not have a negative effect on translation. Type 1 of the English verb *to throw* and Type 1 of the Italian verb *lanciare* categorize a wide set of actions in which an object is thrown by a person independently on the presence of a destination or on the action aim (*John throws the bowling bowl, John throws the rock in the field, John throws the paper in the box* etc.). However these two Types are not equivalent, because the Italian one comprise also actions performed in a limited space with a highly controlled movement, like *Marco lancia una monetina*, that require another verb in English like *to toss* (*Marco tosses a coin*). In this case the small gap between the Italian concept and English one does not affect the translation: in fact we can say that *lanciare* can be used to translate properly any action belonging to *throw - Type 1*.

Given this consideration a measure of the semantic distance with the translation verb is useful to evaluate the loss: this can be easily done from IMAGACT dataset by calculating the ratio between the cardinality (i.e. the number of scenes) of the source Type, T_1, and the one of the nearest target Type, T_2 (the Type with the minimum cardinality among the Types in target language that are supersets of the source Type). This ratio estimates the overlapping between the Types:

$$overlap = \frac{|T_1|}{|T_2|}$$

Data are represented in Figure 4, reporting the number of Types (Italian and English) for each overlap values, where this values are divided in 10 ranges.

We considered semantically distant those Types with $overlap < 0.4$ (sharing less than 2 scenes over 5). These *high distance Types* (see Table 4) are 150 for Italian (51.9% of *leaf + middle Types* and 15% of the total Types) and 145 for English (56.86% of *leaf + middle Types* and 14.12% of the total Types).

Basically we see that not only *root Types*, but also a relevant part of *leaf* and *middle Types* (more than 50% both in Italian and English) represent a critical point for translation.

	IT → EN	EN → IT
Leaf+Mid T.	289	255
Low dist. T.	139 (48.1%)	110 (43.14%)
High dist. T.	150 (51.9%)	145 (56.86%)

Table 4: Distance from the nearest general Type in target language.

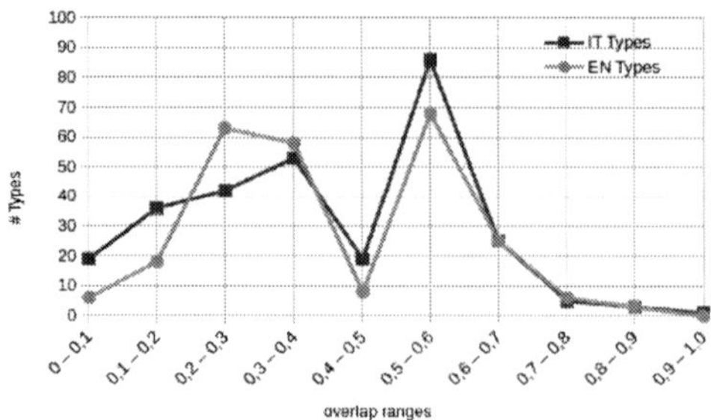

Figure 4: Number of Italian and English Types for each overlap range.

Within this numbers, that are quite homogeneous between the two languages, we can see that in the overlap range from 0 to 0.2 there are much more Italian Types than English ones (19% of *leaf + middle Types* against 9%); conversely English Types are more distributed in the range from 0.3 to 0.4 (Figure 4). This means that in this area of extreme distance between the source and the target concept, we have an higher semantic loss in the translation from Italian to English.

Finally we can have have an overall value of translation critical Types, by summing up the ones belonging to *high distance Types* class and the *root Types*. The verbs these Types belong to are the verbs for which the selection of a good translation candidate is problematic. Results are reported in Tables 5 and 6 and confirm that lexical gaps in action verbs have a strong impact on translation.

	IT	EN
Total Types	1,000	1,027
Root Types	47 (4.7%)	43 (4.2%)
High dist. T.	150 (15.0%)	145 (14.12%)
Critical Types	**197 (19.7%)**	**188 (18.3%)**

Table 5: Number of translation critical Types.

	IT	EN
Total Verbs	501	535
Verbs w/ r.T.	39 (7.78%)	38 (7.1%)
Verbs w/ h.d.T.	109 (21.76%)	125 (23.36%)
Critical Verbs	**136 (27.15%)**	**154 (28.79%)**

Table 6: Number of verbs with *root Types* and *high distance Types*.

6 Conclusions

In this paper a methodology for measuring the lexical gap of action verbs is described and applied to Italian and English, by exploiting IMAGACT ontology. We measured 33.6% of English gap and 29.02% of Italian gap. Then this result have been investigated, in order to discover when and why a lexical gap can affect a translation task. The results show that 19.7% of Italian Types and 18.3% of English ones represent action concept that are critical from a translation perspective: these concepts are lexicalized by 27.15% of the Italian verbs and 28.79% of the English verbs that we considered in our analysis. In addition to it the distinction between concepts that can not be correctly translated with a single lemma (*root Types*) and concepts that can be translated with a sensible semantic loss (*high distance Types*) is a relevant information that can lead to a different translation strategy.

Finally we feel important to note that behind these numeric values there are lists of verbs and concepts and this information could be integrated in Machine Translation and Computer Assisted Translation Systems to improve their accuracy.

Acknowledgments

This research has been supported by the MODELACT Project, funded by the Futuro in Ricerca 2012 programme (Project Code RBFR12C608); http://modelact.lablita.it .

References

Roberto Bartolini, Valeria Quochi, Irene De Felice, Irene Russo, and Monica Monachini. 2014. From synsets to videos: Enriching italwordnet multimodally. In Nicoletta Calzolari (Conference Chair), Khalid Choukri, Thierry Declerck, Hrafn Loftsson, Bente Maegaard, Joseph Mariani, Asuncion Moreno, Jan Odijk, and Stelios Piperidis, editors, *Proceedings of the Ninth International Conference on Language Resources and Evaluation (LREC'14)*, Reykjavik, Iceland, may. European Language Resources Association (ELRA).

Luisa Bentivogli and Emanuele Pianta. 2000. Looking for lexical gaps. In *Proceedings of the ninth EURALEX International Congress*, Stuttgart, Germany.

Jurgita Cvilikaitė. 2006. Lexical gaps: resolution by functionally complete units of translation. *Darbai ir dienos, 2006, nr. 45, p. 127-142.*

Christiane Fellbaum, Martha Palmer, Hoa Trang Dang, Lauren Delfs, and Susanne Wolf. 2001. Manual and automatic semantic annotation with wordnet. *Word-Net and Other Lexical Resources*, pages 3–10.

Gloria Gagliardi. 2014. *Validazione dellontologia dellazione IMAGACT per lo studio e la diagnosi del Mild Cognitive Impairment*. Ph.D. thesis, University of Florence.

Rufus Hjalmar Gouws. 2002. Equivalent relations, context and cotext in bilingual dictionaries. *Hermes*, 28(1):195–209.

Vladimir Ivir. 1977. Lexical gaps: A contrastive view. *Studia Romanica et Anglica Zagrabiensia*, (43):167–176.

M. Jansseen. 2004. Multilingual lexical databases, lexical gaps, and simullda. *International Journal of Lexicography*, 17(2):137–154.

Gran Kjellmer. 2003. Lexical gaps. In *Extending the scope of corpus-based research*, pages 149–158. Brill.

A. Lehrer. 1974. *Semantic Fields and Lexical Structure*. North-Holland linguistic series, 11. North-Holland.

John Lyons. 1977. Semantics, volume i. *Cambridge UP, Cambridge*.

Massimo Moneglia, Francesca Frontini, Gloria Gagliardi, Irene Russo, Alessandro Panunzi, and Monica Monachini. 2012. Imagact: deriving an action ontology from spoken corpora. *Proceedings of the Eighth Joint ACL-ISO Workshop on Interoperable Semantic Annotation (isa-8)*, pages 42–47.

Massimo Moneglia. 2014a. Natural Language Ontology of Action: A Gap with Huge Consequences for Natural Language Understanding and Machine Translation. In Zygmunt Vetulani and Joseph Mariani, editors, *Human Language Technology Challenges for Computer Science and Linguistics*, volume 8387 of *Lecture Notes in Computer Science*, pages 379–395. Springer International Publishing.

Massimo Moneglia. 2014b. The semantic variation of action verbs in multilingual spontaneous speech corpora. In T. Raso and H. Mello, editors, *Spoken Corpora and Linguistics Studies*, pages 152–190. John Benjamins Publishing Company.

Martha Palmer, Hoa Trang Dang, and Christiane Fellbaum. 2007. Making fine-grained and coarse-grained sense distinctions, both manually and automatically. *Natural Language Engineering*, 13(02):137–163.

Yi Pan. 2016. *Verbi dazione in Italiano e in Cinese Mandarino. Implementazione e validazione del cinese nellontologia interlinguistica dell'azione IMAGACT*. Ph.D. thesis, Università degli Studi di Firenze.

Emanuele Pianta, Luisa Bentivogli, and Christian Girardi. 2002. MultiWordNet: developing an aligned multilingual database. In *Proceedings of the First International Conference on Global WordNet*, pages 21–25.

Sameer S. Pradhan, Edward Loper, Dmitriy Dligach, and Martha Palmer. 2007. Semeval-2007 task 17: English lexical sample, srl and all words. In *Proceedings of the 4th International Workshop on Semantic Evaluations*, pages 87–92. Association for Computational Linguistics.

Diana Santos. 1990. Lexical gaps and idioms in machine translation. In *Proceedings of the 13th Conference on Computational Linguistics - Volume 2*, COLING '90, pages 330–335, Stroudsburg, PA, USA. Association for Computational Linguistics.

Word Sense Filtering Improves Embedding-Based Lexical Substitution

Anne Cocos*, **Marianna Apidianaki***† and **Chris Callison-Burch***
* Computer and Information Science Department, University of Pennsylvania
† LIMSI, CNRS, Université Paris-Saclay, 91403 Orsay
{acocos,marapi,ccb}@seas.upenn.edu

Abstract

The role of word sense disambiguation in lexical substitution has been questioned due to the high performance of vector space models which propose good substitutes without explicitly accounting for sense. We show that a filtering mechanism based on a sense inventory optimized for substitutability can improve the results of these models. Our sense inventory is constructed using a clustering method which generates paraphrase clusters that are congruent with lexical substitution annotations in a development set. The results show that lexical substitution can still benefit from senses which can improve the output of vector space paraphrase ranking models.

1 Introduction

Word sense has always been difficult to define and pin down (Kilgarriff, 1997; Erk et al., 2013). Recent successes of embedding-based, sense-agnostic models in various semantic tasks cast further doubt on the usefulness of word sense. Why bother to identify senses if even humans cannot agree upon their nature and number, and if simple word-embedding models yield good results without using any explicit sense representation?

Word-based models are successful in various semantic tasks even though they conflate multiple word meanings into a single representation. Based on the hypothesis that capturing polysemy could further improve their performance, several works have focused on creating sense-specific word embeddings. A common approach is to cluster the contexts in which the words appear in a corpus to induce senses, and relabel each word token with the clustered sense before learning embed-

dings (Reisinger and Mooney, 2010; Huang et al., 2012). Iacobacci et al. (2015) disambiguate the words in a corpus using a state-of-the-art WSD system and then produce continuous representations of word senses based on distributional information obtained from the annotated corpus. Moving from word to sense embeddings generally improves their performance in word and relational similarity tasks but is not beneficial in all settings. Li and Jurafsky (2015) show that although multi-sense embeddings give improved performance in tasks such as semantic similarity, semantic relation identification and part-of-speech tagging, they fail to help in others, like sentiment analysis and named entity extraction (Li and Jurafsky, 2015).

We show how a sense inventory optimized for *substitutability* can improve the rankings provided by two sense-agnostic, vector-based lexical substitution models. Lexical substitution requires systems to predict substitutes for target word instances that preserve their meaning in context (McCarthy and Navigli, 2007). We consider a sense inventory with high substitutability to be one which groups synonyms or paraphrases that are mutually-interchangeable in the same contexts. In contrast, sense inventories with low substitutability might group words linked by different types of relations. We carry out experiments with a syntactic vector-space model (Thater et al., 2011; Apidianaki, 2016) and a word-embedding model for lexical substitution (Melamud et al., 2015). Instead of using the senses to refine the vector representations as in (Faruqui et al., 2015), we use them to improve the lexical substitution rankings proposed by the models as a post-processing step. Our results show that senses can improve the performance of vector-space models in lexical substitution tasks.

Proceedings of the 1st Workshop on Sense, Concept and Entity Representations and their Applications, pages 110–119,
Valencia, Spain, April 4 2017. ©2017 Association for Computational Linguistics

2 A sense inventory for substitution

2.1 Paraphrase substitutability

The candidate substitutes used by our ranking models come from the Paraphrase Database (PPDB) XXL package (Ganitkevitch et al., 2013).[1] Paraphrase relations in the PPDB are defined between words and phrases which might carry different senses. Cocos and Callison-Burch (2016) used a spectral clustering algorithm to cluster PPDB XXL into senses, but the clusters contain noisy paraphrases and paraphrases linked by different types of relations (e.g. hypernyms, antonyms) which are not always substitutable. We use a slightly modified version of their method to cluster paraphrases where both the number of clusters (senses) and their contents are optimized for substitutability.

2.2 A measure of substitutability

We define a substitutability metric that quantifies the extent to which a sense inventory aligns with human-generated lexical substitution annotations. We then cluster PPDB paraphrases using the substitutability metric to optimize the sense clusters for substitutability.

Given a sense inventory C, we can define the senses of a target word t as a set of sense clusters, $C(t) = \{c_1, c_2, \ldots c_k\}$, where each cluster contains words corresponding to a single sense of t. Intuitively, if a sense inventory corresponds with substitutability, then each sense cluster c_i should have two qualities: first, words within c_i should be interchangeable with t in the same set of contexts; and second, c_i should not be missing any words that are interchangeable in those same contexts. We therefore operationalize the definition of substitutability as follows.

We begin measuring substitutability with a lexical substitution dataset, consisting of sentences where content words have been manually annotated with substitutes (see example in Table 1). We then use normalized mutual information (NMI) (Strehl and Ghosh, 2002) to quantify the level of agreement between the automatically generated sense clusters and human-suggested substitutes. NMI is an information theoretic measure of cluster quality. Given two clusterings U and V over

Sentence	Annotated Substitutes (Count)
In this world, one's **word** is a promise.	vow (1), utterance (1), tongue (1), speech (1)
Silverplate: code **word** for the historic mission that would end World War II.	phrase (3), term (2), verbiage(1), utterance (1), signal (1), name (1), dictate (1), designation (1), decree (1)
I think she only heard the last **words** of my speech.	bit (3), verbiage (2), part (2), vocabulary (1), terminology (1), syllable (1), phrasing (1), phrase (1), patter (1), expression (1), babble (1), anecdote (1)

Table 1: Example annotated sentences for the target word *word.N* from the CoInCo (Kremer et al., 2014) lexical substitution dataset. Numbers after each word indicate the number of annotators who made that suggestion.

a set of items, it measures how much each clustering reduces uncertainty about the other (Vinh et al., 2009) in terms of their mutual information $I(U,V)$ and entropies $H(U), H(V)$:

$$NMI(U,V) = \frac{I(U,V)}{\sqrt{H(U)H(V)}}$$

To calculate the NMI between a sense inventory for target word t and its set of annotated substitutes, we first define the substitutes as a clustering, $B_t = \{b_1, b_2, \ldots b_n\}$, where b_i denotes the set of suggested substitutes for each of n sentences. Table 1, for example, gives the clustered substitutes for $n = 3$ sentences for target word $t = $ word.N, where $b_1 = \{$vow, utterance, tongue, speech$\}$. We then define the substitutability of the sense inventory, C_t, with respect to the annotated substitutes, B_t, as $NMI(C_t, B_t)$.[2] Given many target words, we can further aggregate the substitutability of sense inventory C over the set of targets T in B into a single substitutability score:

$$substitutability_B(C) = \sum_{t \in T} \frac{NMI(C_t, B_t)}{|T|}$$

2.3 Optimizing for Substitutability

Having defined a substitutability score, we now automatically generate word sense clusters from the Paraphrase Database that maximize it. The idea is to use the substitutability score to choose the best number of senses for each target word which will be the number of output clusters (k) generated by our spectral clustering algorithm.

---

[1] PPDB paraphrases come into packages of different sizes (going from S to XXXL): small packages contain high-precision paraphrases while larger ones have high coverage. All are available from `paraphrase.org`

[2] In calculating NMI, we ignore words that do not appear in both C_t and B_t.

2.4 Spectral clustering method

2.4.1 Constructing the Affinity Matrix

The spectral clustering algorithm (Yu and Shi, 2003) takes as input an affinity matrix $A \in \mathbb{R}^{n \times n}$ encoding n items to be clustered, and an integer k. It generates k non-overlapping clusters of the n items. Each entry a_{ij} in the affinity matrix denotes a similarity measurement between items i and j. Entries in A must be nonnegative and symmetric. The affinity matrix can also be thought of as describing a graph, where the n rows and columns correspond to nodes, and each entry a_{ij} gives the weight of an edge between nodes i and j. Because the matrix must be symmetric, the graph is undirected.

Given a target word t, we call its set of PPDB paraphrases $PP(t)$. Note that $PP(t)$ excludes t itself. In our most basic clustering method, we cluster paraphrases for target t as follows. Given the length-n set of t's paraphrases, $PP(t)$, we construct the $n \times n$ affinity matrix A where each shared-index row and column corresponds to some word $p \in PP(t)$. We set entries equal to the cosine similarity between the applicable words' embeddings, plus one: $a_{ij} = cos(v_i, v_j) + 1$ (to enforce non-negative similarities). For our implementation we use 300-dimensional part-of-speech-specific word embeddings v_i generated using the gensim word2vec package (Mikolov et al., 2013b; Mikolov et al., 2013a; Řehůřek and Sojka, 2010).[3] In Figure 1a we show a set of paraphrases, linked by PPDB relations, and in Figure 1b we show the corresponding basic affinity matrix, encoding the paraphrases' distributional similarity.

In order to aid further discussion, we point out that the affinity matrix used for the basic clustering method encodes a fully-connected graph $G = \{PP(t), E_{PP}^{ALL}\}$ with paraphrases $PP(t)$ as nodes, and edges between every pair of words, $E_{PP}^{ALL} = PP(t) \times PP(t)$. As for all variations on the clustering method, the matrix entries correspond to distributional similarity.

2.4.2 Masking

The affinity matrix in Figure 1b ignores the graph structure inherent in PPDB, where edges connect only words that are paraphrases of one another. We experiment with enforcing the PPDB structure in the affinity matrix through a technique we call 'masking.' By masking, we mean allowing positive values in the affinity matrix only where the row and column correspond to paraphrases that appear as pairs in PPDB (Figure 1a). All entries corresponding to paraphrase pairs that are *not* connected in the PPDB graph (Figure 1a) are forced to 0.

More concretely, in the masked affinity matrix, we set each entry a_{ij} for which i and j are *not* paraphrases in PPDB to zero. The masked affinity matrix encodes the graph $G = \{PP(t), E_{PP}^{MASK}\}$ with edges connecting only pairs of words that are in PPDB, $E_{PP}^{MASK} = \{(p_i, p_j) \mid p_i \in P(p_j)\}$. Figure 1c shows the masked affinity matrix corresponding to the PPDB structure in Figure 1a.

2.4.3 Optimizing k

Because spectral clustering requires the number of output clusters, k, to be specified as input, for each target word we run the clustering algorithm for a range of k between 1 and the minimum of (n, 20). We then choose the k that maximizes the NMI of the resulting clusters with the human-annotated substitutes for that target in the development data.

2.5 Method variations

In addition to using the substitutability score to choose the best number of senses for each target word, we also experiment with two variations on the basic spectral clustering method to increase the score further: filtering by a paraphrase confidence score and co-clustering with WordNet (Fellbaum, 1998).

2.5.1 PPDB Score Thresholding

Each paraphrase pair in the PPDB is associated with a set of scores indicating the strength of the paraphrase relationship. The recently added PPDB2.0 Score (Pavlick et al., 2015) was calculated using a supervised scoring model trained on human judgments of paraphrase quality.[4] Apidianaki (2016) showed that the PPDB2.0 Score itself is a good metric for ranking substitution candidates in context, outperforming some vector space models when the number of candidates is high. With this in mind, we experimented with using a PPDB2.0 Score threshold to discard noisy PPDB

---

[3]The `word2vec` parameters we use are a context window of size 3, learning rate *alpha* from 0.025 to 0.0001, minimum word count 100, sampling parameter $1e^{-4}$, 10 negative samples per target word, and 5 training epochs.

[4]The human judgments were used to fit a regression to the features available in PPDB 1.0 plus numerous new features including cosine word embedding similarity, lexical overlap features, WordNet features and distributional similarity features.

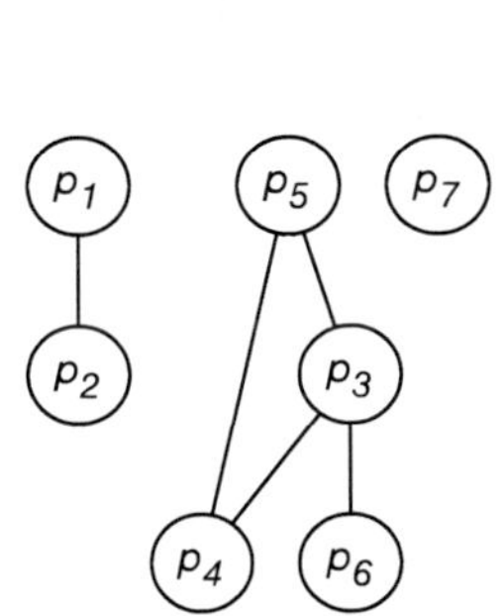 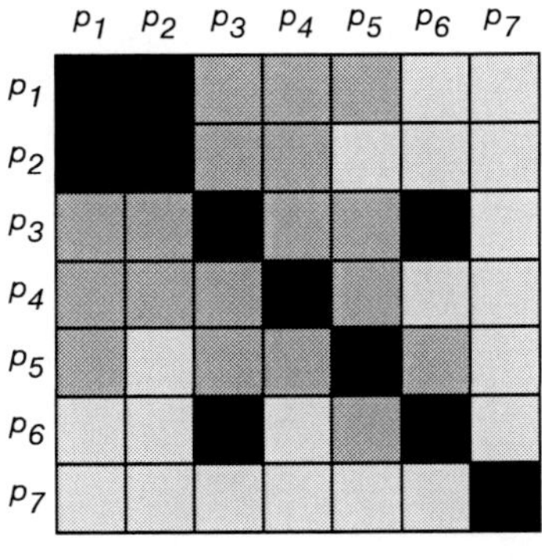 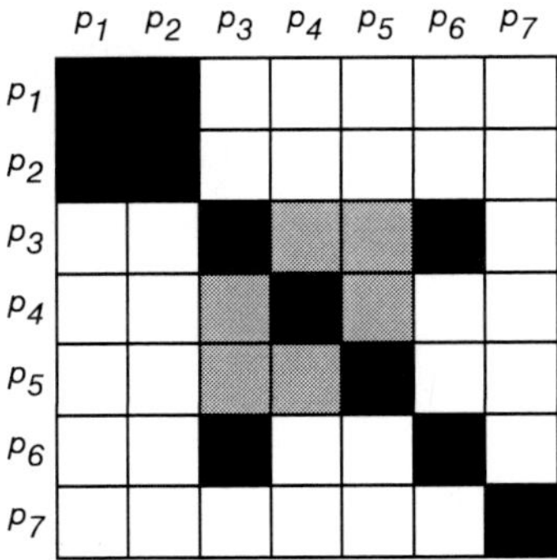

(a) PPDB graph with $n = 7$ paraphrases $PP(t)$ to be clustered.

(b) *Unmasked* affinity matrix for input to basic clustering algorithm, for paraphrases in Fig 1a. This matrix encodes a fully-connected graph $G = \{PP(t), E_{PP}^{ALL}\}$.

(c) *Masked* affinity matrix for input to clustering algorithm, enforcing the paraphrase links from the graph in Fig 1a, $G = \{PP(t), E_{PP}^{MASK}\}$.

Figure 1: Unclustered PPDB graph and its corresponding affinity matrices, encoding distributional similarity, for input to the basic (1b) and masked (1c) clustering algorithms. Masking zeros-out the values of all cells corresponding to paraphrases not connected in the PPDB graph. Cell shading corresponds to the distributional similarity score between words, with darker colors representing higher measurements.

XXL paraphrases prior to sense clustering. Our objective was to begin the clustering process with a *clean* set of paraphrases for each target word, eliminating erroneous paraphrases that might pollute the substitutable sense clusters. We implemented PPDB score thresholds in a range from 0 to 2.5.

2.5.2 Co-Clustering with WordNet

PPDB is large and inherently noisy. WordNet has smaller coverage but well-defined semantic structure in the form of synsets and relations. We sought a way to marry the high coverage of PPDB with the clean structure of WordNet by co-clustering the two resources, in hopes of creating a sense inventory that is both highly-substitutable and high-coverage.

The basic unit in WordNet is the *synset*, a set of lemmas sharing the same meaning. WordNet also connects synsets via relations, such as hypernymy, hyponymy, entailment, and 'similar-to'. We denote as $L(s)$ the set of lemmas associated with synset s. We denote as $R(s)$ the set of synsets that are related to synset s with a hypernym, hyponym, entailment, or similar-to relationship. Finally, we denote as $S(t)$ the set of synsets to which a word t belongs. We denote as $S^+(t)$ the set of t's synsets, plus all synsets to which they are related; $S^+(t) = S(t) \cup \bigcup_{s' \in S(t)} S(s')$. In other words, $S^+(t)$ includes all synsets to which t is connected by a

path of length at most 2 via one of the relations encoded in $R(s)$.

For co-clustering, we generate the affinity matrix for a graph with $m + n$ nodes corresponding to the n words in $PP(t)$ and the m synsets in $S^+(t)$, and edges between every pair of nodes. Because the edge weights are cosine similarity between vector embeddings, we need a way to construct an embedding for each synset in $S^+(t)$.[5] We therefore generate compositional embeddings for each synset s that are equal to the weighted average of the embeddings for the lemmas $l \in L(s)$, where the weights are the PPDB2.0 scores between t and l:

$$v_s = \frac{\sum_{l \in L(s)} PPDB2.0Score(t,l) \times v_l}{\sum_{l \in L(s)} PPDB2.0Score(t,l)}$$

The unmasked affinity matrix used for input to the co-clustering method, then, encodes the graph $G = \{PP(t) \cup S^+(t), E_{PP}^{ALL} \cup E_{PS}^{ALL} \cup E_{SS}^{ALL}\}$, where E_{PS}^{ALL} contains edges between every paraphrase and synset, and E_{SS}^{ALL} contains edges between every pair of synsets.

We also define masked versions of the co-clustering affinity matrix. In a masked affinity matrix, positive entries are only allowed for entries where the row and column correspond to enti-

---

[5] We don't use the NASARI embeddings (Camacho-Collados et al., 2015) because these are available only for nouns.

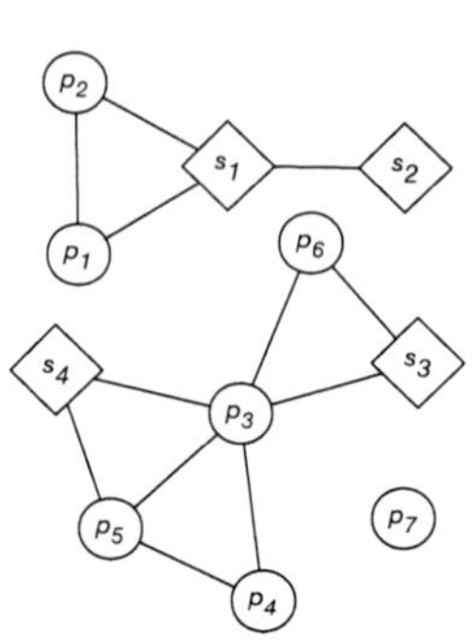 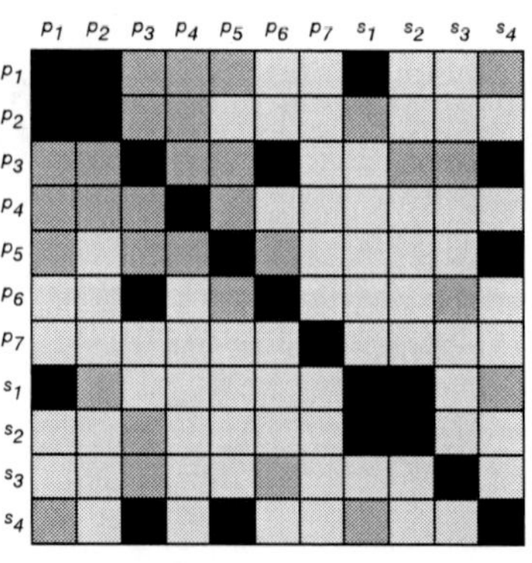 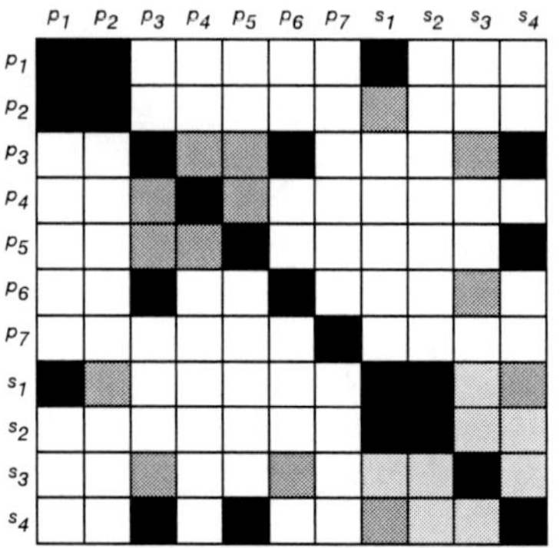

(a) Graph showing $n = 7$ PPDB paraphrases $PP(t)$ and $m = 4$ WordNet synsets $S^+(t)$ to be clustered.

(b) *Unmasked* affinity matrix for input to basic clustering algorithm, for paraphrases and synsets in Fig 2a. This matrix encodes a fully-connected graph $G = \{PP(t) \cup S^+(t), E_{PP}^{ALL} \cup E_{PS}^{ALL} \cup E_{SS}^{ALL}\}$.

(c) Affinity matrix for input to clustering algorithm, enforcing the paraphrase-paraphrase (E_{PP}^{MASK}) and paraphrase-synset (E_{PS}^{MASK}) links from the graph in 2a, but allowing all synset-synset links (E_{PP}^{ALL}).

Figure 2: Paraphrase/synset graph for input to the co-clustering model, and its corresponding affinity matrices for the basic (2b) and masked (2c) clustering algorithms. Cell shading corresponds to the distributional similarity score between words/synsets.

ties (paraphrases or synsets) that are connected by the underlying knowledge base (PPDB or Word-Net). Just as we defined masking for paraphrase-paraphrase links (E_{PP}) to allow only positive values corresponding to paraphrase pairs found in PPDB, here we separately define masking for paraphrase-synset (E_{PS}) and synset-synset (E_{SS}) based on WordNet synsets and relations. When applying the clustering algorithm, it is possible to elect to use the masked version for any or all of E_{PP}, E_{PS}, and E_{SS}. In our experiments we try all combinations.

For the synset-synset links, we define the masked version E_{SS}^{MASK} as including only nonzero edge weights where a hypernym, hyponym, entailment or similar-to relationship connects two synsets: $E_{SS}^{MASK} = \{(s_u, s_v) \mid s_u \in R(s_v) \text{ or } s_v \in R(s_u)\}$. For the paraphrase-synset links, we define the masked version E_{PS}^{MASK} to include only nonzero edge weights where the paraphrase *is* a lemma in the synset, or *is a paraphrase of* a lemma in the synset (excluding the target word): $E_{PS}^{MASK} = \{(p_i, s_u) \mid p_i \in L(s_u) \text{ or } |(P(p_i) - t) \cap L(s_u)| > 0\}$. We need to exclude the target word when calculating the overlap because otherwise all words in $PP(t)$ would connect to all synsets in $S(t)$. Figure 2 depicts the graph, unnmasked and masked affinity matrices for the co-clustering method.

2.6 Clustering Experiments

2.6.1 Datasets

We run clustering experiments using targets and human-generated substitution data drawn from two lexical substitution datasets. The first is the "Concepts in Context" (CoInCo) corpus (Kremer et al., 2014), containing over 15K sentences corresponding to nearly 4K unique target words. We divide the CoInCo dataset into development and test sets by first finding all target words that have at least 10 sentences. For each of the 327 resulting targets, we randomly divide the corresponding sentences into 60% development instances and 40% test instances. The resulting development and test sets have 4061 and 2091 sentences respectively. We cluster the 327 target words in the resulting subset of CoInCo, performing all optimization using the development portion.

In order to evaluate how well our method generalizes to other data, we also create clusters for target words drawn from the SemEval 2007 English Lexical Substitution shared task dataset (McCarthy and Navigli, 2007). The entire test portion of the SemEval dataset contains 1700 annotated sentences for 170 target words. We filter this data to keep only sentences with one or more human-annotated substitutes that overlap our PPDB XXL paraphrase vocabulary. The resulting test set, which we use for evaluating SemEval targets, has 1178 sentences and 157 target words. We cluster each of the 157 targets, using the Co-InCo development data to optimize substitutability for the 32 SemEval targets that also appear in CoInCo. For the rest of the SemEval targets we choose a number of senses equal to its WordNet synset count.

2.6.2 Clustering Method Variations

We try all combinations of the following parameters in our clustering model:

- Clustering method: We try the basic clustering – clustering Paraphrases Only – and the WordNet Co-Clustering method.

- PPDB2.0 Score Threshold: We cluster paraphrases of each target having a PPDB2.0 Score above a threshold, ranging from 0-3.0.

- Masking: When clustering paraphrases only, we can either use the PP-PP mask or allow positive similarities between all words. When co-clustering, we try all combinations of the PP-PP, PP-SYN, and SYN-SYN masks.

For each combination, we evaluate the NMI substitutability of the resulting sense inventory over our CoInCo and SemEval test instances. The substitutability results are given in Tables 2 and 3.

3 Filtering Substitutes

3.1 A WSD oracle

We now question whether it is possible to improve the rankings of current state-of-the-art lexical substitution systems by using the optimized sense inventory as a filter. Our general approach is to take a set of ranked substitutes generated by a vector-based model. Then, we see whether filtering the ranked substitutes to bring words belonging to the correct sense of the target to the top of the rankings would improve the overall ranking results.

Assuming that we have a WSD oracle that is able to choose the most appropriate sense for a target word in context, this corresponds to nominating substitutes from the applicable sense cluster and elevating them in the list of ranked substitutes output by the state-of-the-art lexical substitution system. If sense filtering successfully improves the quality of ranked substitutes, we can say that the sense inventory captures substitutability well.

3.2 Ranking Models

Our approach requires a set of rankings produced by a high-quality lexical substitution model to start. We generate substitution rankings for each target/sentence pair in the test sets using a syntactic vector-space model (Thater et al., 2011; Apidianaki, 2016) and a state-of-the-art model based on word embeddings (Melamud et al., 2015).

The syntactic vector space model of Apidianaki (2016) (Syn.VSM) demonstrated an ability to correctly choose appropriate PPDB paraphrases for a target word in context. The vector features correspond to syntactic dependency triples extracted from the English Gigaword corpus [6] analyzed with Stanford dependencies (Marneffe et al., 2006). Syn.VSM produces a score for each (target, sentence, substitute) tuple based on the cosine similarity of the substitute's basic vector representation with the target's contextualized vector (Thater et al., 2011). The contextualized vector is derived from the basic meaning vector of the target word by reinforcing its dimensions that are licensed by the context of the specific instance under consideration. More specifically, the contextualized vector of a target is obtained through vector addition and contains information about the target's direct syntactic dependents.

The second set of rankings comes from the AddCos model of Melamud et al. (2015). AddCos quantifies the fit of substitute word s for target word t in context C by measuring the semantic similarity of the substitute to the target, and the similarity of the substitute to the context:

$$AddCos(s,t,W) = \frac{|W| \cdot cos(s,t) + \sum_{w \in W} cos(s,w)}{2 \cdot |W|}$$

(1)

The vectors s and t are word embeddings of the substitute and target generated by the *skip-gram with negative sampling* model (Mikolov et al., 2013b; Mikolov et al., 2013a). The context W is the set of words appearing within a fixed-width window of the target t in a sentence (we use a window (cwin) of 1), and the embeddings c are context embeddings generated by *skip-gram*. In our implementation, we train 300-dimensional word and context embeddings over the 4B words in the Annotated Gigaword (AGiga) corpus (Napoles et al., 2012) using the gensim word2vec package

---

[6] http://catalog.ldc.upenn.edu/ LDC2003T05

(Mikolov et al., 2013b; Mikolov et al., 2013a; Řehůřek and Sojka, 2010).[7]

3.3 Substitution metrics

Lexical substitution experiments are usually evaluated using generalized average precision (GAP) (Kishida, 2005). GAP compares a set of predicted rankings to a set of gold standard rankings. Scores range from 0 to 1; a perfect ranking, in which all high-scoring substitutes outrank low-scoring substitutes, has a score of 1. For each sentence in the CoInCo and SemEval test sets, we consider the PPDB paraphrases for the target word to be the candidates, and we set the test set annotator frequency to be the gold score. Words in PPDB that were not suggested by annotators receive a gold score of 0.001. Predicted scores are given by the two ranking models, Syn.VSM and AddCos.

3.4 Filtering Method

Sense filtering is intended to boost the rank of substitutes that belong to the most appropriate sense of the target given the context. We run this experiment as a two-step process.

First, given a target and sentence, we obtain the PPDB XXL paraphrases for the target word and rank them using the Syn.VSM and the AddCos models.[8] We calculate the overall *unfiltered* GAP score on the test set for each ranking model as the average GAP over sentences.

Next, we evaluate the ability of a sense inventory to improve the GAP score through filtering. We implement sense filtering by adding a large number (10000) to the ranking model's score for words *belonging to a single sense*. We assume an oracle that finds the cluster which maximally improves the GAP score using this sense filtering method. If the sense inventory corresponds well to substitutability, we should expect this filtering to improve the ranking by downgrading proposed substitutes that do not fall within the correct sense cluster.

We calculate the maximum sense-restricted GAP score for the inventories produced by each variation on our clustering model, and compare

this to the unfiltered GAP score for each ranking model.

3.5 Baselines

We compare the extent to which our optimized sense inventories improve lexical substitution rankings to the results of two baseline sense inventories.

- **WordNet+**: a sense inventory formed from WordNet 3.0. For each CoInCo target word that appears in WordNet, we take its sense clusters to be its synsets, plus lemmas belonging to hypernyms and hyponyms of each synset.

- **PPDBClus**: a much larger, abeit noisier, sense inventory obtained by automatically clustering words in the PPDB XXL package. To obtain this sense inventory we clustered paraphrases for all targets in the CoInCo dataset using the method outlined in Cocos and Callison-Burch (2016), with PPDB2.0 Score serving as the similarity metric.

We assess the substitutability of these sense baseline inventories with respect to the human-annotated substitutes in the CoInCo and SemEval datasets, and also use them for sense filtering.

Finally, we wish to estimate the impact of the NMI-based optimization procedure (Section 2.4.3) on the quality of the senses used for filtering. We compare the performance of the optimized CoInCo sense inventory, where the number of clusters, k, for a target word is defined through NMI optimization (called 'Choose-K: Optimize NMI'), to an inventory induced from CoInCo where k equals the number of synsets available for the target word in WordNet (called 'Choose-K: #WN Synsets).

4 Results

We report substitutability, and the unfiltered and best sense-filtered GAP scores achieved using the paraphrase-only clustering method and the co-clustering method in Tables 2 and 3.

The average unfiltered GAP scores for the Syn.VSM rankings over the CoInCo and SemEval test sets are 0.528 and 0.673 respectively.[9] All

---

[7]The `word2vec` training parameters we use are a context window of size 3, learning rate *alpha* from 0.025 to 0.0001, minimum word count 100, sampling parameter $1e^{-4}$, 10 negative samples per target word, and 5 training epochs.

[8]For the SemEval test set, we rank PPDB XXL paraphrases having a PPDB2.0 Score with the target of at least 2.54.

[9]The score reported by Apidianaki (2016) for the Syn.VSM model with XXL PPDB paraphrases on CoInCo was 0.56. The difference in scores is due to excluding from our clustering experiments target words that did not have at least 10 sentences in CoInCo.

	$subst_{CoInCo}$	Syn.VSM		AddCos (cwin=1)	
		Unfiltered GAP	Oracle GAP	Unfiltered GAP	Oracle GAP
PPDBClus	0.254		0.661		0.656
WordNet	0.252		0.655		0.651
Choose-K: # WN Synsets (avg)	0.205		0.639		0.636
Choose-K: # WN Synsets (max, no co-clustering)	0.250*	0.528	0.695*	0.533	0.690*
Choose-K: # WN Synsets (max, co-clustering)	0.241**		0.690**		0.683**
Choose-K: Optimize NMI (avg)	0.282		0.668		0.662
Choose-K: Optimize NMI (max, no co-clustering)	0.331*		0.719 *		0.714 ***
Choose K: Optimize NMI (max, co-clustering)	0.314**		0.718 ****		0.710 **

Table 2: Substitutablity (NMI) of resulting sense inventories, and GAP scores of the unfiltered and best sense-filtered rankings produced by the Syn.VSM and AddCos models, for the CoInCo annotated dataset. Configurations for the best-performing sense inventories were: * Min PPDB Score 2.0, cluster PP's only, use PP-PP mask; ** Min PPDB Score 2.0, co-clustering, use PP-PP mask only; *** Min PPDB Score 1.5, cluster PP's only, use PP-PP mask; **** Min PPDB Score 2.0, co-clustering, use PP-PP, Syn-Syn masks only

	$subst_{SemEval}$	Syn.VSM		AddCos (cwin=1)	
		Unfiltered GAP	Oracle GAP	Unfiltered GAP	Oracle GAP
PPDBClus	0.357		0.855		0.634
WordNet	0.291		0.774		0.595
Average of all Clustered Sense Inventories	0.367	0.673	0.841	0.410	0.569
Max basic (no co-clustering) sense inventory	0.448*		0.917*		0.626*
Max co-clustered sense inventory	0.449**		0.906***		0.612****

Table 3: Substitutablity (NMI) of resulting sense inventories, and GAP scores of the unfiltered and best sense-filtered rankings produced by the Syn.VSM and AddCos models, for the SemEval07 annotated dataset. Configurations for the best-performing sense inventories were: * Min PPDB Score 2.31, cluster PP's only, use PP-PP mask; ** Min PPDB Score 2.54, co-clustering, use PP-SYN mask only; *** Min PPDB Score 2.54, co-clustering, use PP-SYN mask only; **** Min PPDB Score 2.31, co-clustering, use PP-SYN mask only.

baseline and cluster sense inventories are capable of improving these GAP scores when we use the best sense as a filter. Syntactic models generally give very good results with small paraphrase sets (Kremer et al., 2014) but their performance seems to degrade when they need to deal with larger and noisier substitute sets (Apidianaki, 2016). Our results suggest that finding the most appropriate sense of a target word in context *can* improve their lexical substitution results.

The trend in results is similar for the AddCos rankings. The average unfiltered GAP scores for the AddCos rankings over the CoInCo and SemEval test sets are 0.533 and 0.410 respectively. The GAP scores of the unfiltered AddCos rankings are much lower than after filtering with any baseline or cluster sense inventory, showing that lexical subsitutition rankings based on word-embeddings can also be improved using senses.

To assess the impact of the NMI-based optimization procedure on the results, we compare the performance of two sense inventories on the CoInCo rankings: one where the number of clusters (k) for a target word is defined through NMI optimization and another one, where k is equal to the number of synsets available for the target word in WordNet. We find that for both the Syn.VSM and AddCos ranking models, filtering using the sense inventory with the NMI-optimized k outperforms the results obtained when the inventory with k equal to the number of synsets is used.

Furthermore, we find that the NMI substitutability score is a generally good indicator of how much improvement we see in GAP score due to oracle sense filtering. We calculated the Pearson correlation of a sense inventory's NMI with its oracle GAP score to be 0.644 (calculated over all target words in the CoInCo test set, including GAP results for both the Syn.VSM and AddCos ranking models). This suggests that NMI is a reasonable measure of substitutability.

We find that for all methods, applying a PPDB-Score Threshold prior to clustering is an effective way of removing noisy, non-substitutable paraphrases from the sense inventory. When we use the resulting sense inventory for filtering, this effectively elevates only high-quality paraphrases in the lexical substitution rankings. This supports the finding of Apidianaki (2016), who showed that the PPDB2.0 Score itself is an effective lexical substitution ranking metric when large and noisy paraphrase substitute sets are involved.

Finally, we discover that co-clustering with WordNet did not produce any significant improvement in NMI or GAP score over clustering paraphrases alone. This could suggest that the added structure from WordNet did not improve overall substitutability of the resulting sense inventories, or that our co-clustering method did not effectively incorporate useful structural information from WordNet.

5 Conclusion

We have shown that despite the high performance of word-based vector-space models, lexical substitution can still benefit from word senses. We have defined a substitutability metric and proposed a method for automatically creating sense inventories optimized for substitutability. The number of sense clusters in an optimized inventory and their contents are aligned with lexical substitution annotations in a development set. Using the best fitting cluster in each context as a filter over the rankings produced by vector-space models boosts good substitutes and improves the models' scores in a lexical substitution task.

For choosing the cluster that best fits a context, we used an oracle experiment which finds the maximum GAP score achievable by a sense by boosting the ranking model's score for words *belonging to a single sense*. The cluster that achieved the highest GAP score in each case was selected. The task of finding the most appropriate sense in context still remains. But the improvement in lexical substitution results shows that word sense induction and disambiguation can still benefit state-of-the-art word-based models for lexical substitution.

Our sense filtering mechanism can be applied to the output of any vector-space substitution model at a post-processing step. In future work, we intend to experiment with models that account for senses during embedding learning. The models of Huang et al. (2012) and Li and Jurafsky (2015) learn multi-prototype, or sense-specific, embedding representations and are able to choose the best-fitted ones for words in context. These models have up to now been tested in several NLP tasks but have not yet been applied to lexical substitution. We will experiment with using the embeddings chosen by these models for specific word instances for ranking candidate substitutes in context. The comparison with the results presented in this paper will show whether it is preferable to account for senses before or after actual lexical substitution.

Acknowledgments

This material is based in part on research sponsored by DARPA under grant number FA8750-13-2-0017 (the DEFT program). The U.S. Government is authorized to reproduce and distribute reprints for Governmental purposes. The views and conclusions contained in this publication are those of the authors and should not be interpreted as representing official policies or endorsements of DARPA and the U.S. Government.

This work has also been supported by the French National Research Agency under project ANR-16-CE33-0013.

We would like to thank our anonymous reviewers for their thoughtful and helpful comments.

References

Marianna Apidianaki. 2016. Vector-space models for PPDB paraphrase ranking in context. In *Proceedings of EMNLP*, pages 2028–2034, Austin, Texas.

José Camacho-Collados, Mohammad Taher Pilehvar, and Roberto Navigli. 2015. NASARI: a Novel Approach to a Semantically-Aware Representation of Items. In *Proceedings of NAACL/HLT 2015*, pages 567–577, Denver, Colorado.

Anne Cocos and Chris Callison-Burch. 2016. Clustering paraphrases by word sense. In *Proceedings of NAACL/HLT 2016*, pages 1463–1472, San Diego, California.

Katrin Erk, Diana McCarthy, and Nicholas Gaylord. 2013. Measuring word meaning in context. *Computational Linguistics*, 39(3):511–554, 9.

Manaal Faruqui, Jesse Dodge, Sujay Kumar Jauhar, Chris Dyer, Eduard Hovy, and Noah A. Smith. 2015. Retrofitting Word Vectors to Semantic Lexicons. In *Proceedings of NAACL/HLT*, Denver, Colorado.

Christiane Fellbaum, editor. 1998. *WordNet: an electronic lexical database*. MIT Press.

Juri Ganitkevitch, Benjamin VanDurme, and Chris Callison-Burch. 2013. PPDB: The Paraphrase Database. In *Proceedings of NAACL*, Atlanta, Georgia.

Eric Huang, Richard Socher, Christopher Manning, and Andrew Ng. 2012. Improving Word Representations via Global Context and Multiple Word Prototypes. In *Proceedings of the ACL (Volume 1: Long Papers)*, pages 873–882, Jeju Island, Korea.

Ignacio Iacobacci, Mohammad Taher Pilehvar, and Roberto Navigli. 2015. SensEmbed: Learning Sense Embeddings for Word and Relational Similarity. In *Proceedings of the ACL/IJCNLP*, pages 95–105, Beijing, China.

Adam Kilgarriff. 1997. I don't believe in word senses. *Computers and the Humanities*, 31(2):91–113.

Kazuaki Kishida. 2005. *Property of average precision and its generalization: An examination of evaluation indicator for information retrieval experiments*. National Institute of Informatics Tokyo, Japan.

Gerhard Kremer, Katrin Erk, Sebastian Padó, and Stefan Thater. 2014. What Substitutes Tell Us - Analysis of an "All-Words" Lexical Substitution Corpus. In *Proceedings of EACL*, pages 540–549, Gothenburg, Sweden.

Jiwei Li and Dan Jurafsky. 2015. Do Multi-Sense Embeddings Improve Natural Language Understanding? In *Proceedings of the EMNLP*, pages 1722–1732, Lisbon, Portugal.

M. Marneffe, B. Maccartney, and C. Manning. 2006. Generating Typed Dependency Parses from Phrase Structure Parses. In *Proceedings of LREC-2006*, Genoa, Italy.

Diana McCarthy and Roberto Navigli. 2007. SemEval-2007 Task 10: English Lexical Substitution Task. In *Proceedings of SemEval*, pages 48–53, Prague, Czech Republic.

Oren Melamud, Omer Levy, and Ido Dagan. 2015. A Simple Word Embedding Model for Lexical Substitution. In *Proceedings of the 1st Workshop on Vector Space Modeling for Natural Language Processing*, pages 1–7, Denver, Colorado.

Tomas Mikolov, Kai Chen, Greg Corrado, and Jeffrey Dean. 2013a. Efficient estimation of word representations in vector space. *arXiv preprint arXiv:1301.3781*.

Tomas Mikolov, Ilya Sutskever, Kai Chen, Greg S Corrado, and Jeff Dean. 2013b. Distributed representations of words and phrases and their compositionality. In *Advances in neural information processing systems*, pages 3111–3119.

Courtney Napoles, Matthew Gormley, and Benjamin Van Durme. 2012. Annotated Gigaword. In *Proceedings of the Joint Workshop on Automatic Knowledge Base Construction and Web-scale Knowledge Extraction (AKBC-WEKEX)*, pages 95–100, Montreal, Canada.

Ellie Pavlick, Pushpendre Rastogi, Juri Ganitkevitch, Benjamin Van Durme, and Chris Callison-Burch. 2015. PPDB 2.0: Better paraphrase ranking, fine-grained entailment relations, word embeddings, and style classification. In *Proceedings of ACL/IJCNLP*, pages 425–430, Beijing, China.

Radim Řehůřek and Petr Sojka. 2010. Software Framework for Topic Modelling with Large Corpora. In *Proceedings of the LREC 2010 Workshop on New Challenges for NLP Frameworks*, pages 45–50, Valletta, Malta.

Joseph Reisinger and Raymond J. Mooney. 2010. Multi-Prototype Vector-Space Models of Word Meaning. In *Proceedings of HLT/NAACL*, pages 109–117, Los Angeles, California.

Alexander Strehl and Joydeep Ghosh. 2002. Cluster ensembles—a knowledge reuse framework for combining multiple partitions. *Journal of machine learning research*, 3(Dec):583–617.

Stefan Thater, Hagen Fürstenau, and Manfred Pinkal. 2011. Word Meaning in Context: A Simple and Effective Vector Model. In *Proceedings of IJCNLP*, pages 1134–1143, Chiang Mai, Thailand.

Nguyen Xuan Vinh, Julien Epps, and James Bailey. 2009. Information theoretic measures for clusterings comparison: is a correction for chance necessary? In *Proceedings of the 26th Annual International Conference on Machine Learning*, pages 1073–1080. ACM.

Stella X. Yu and Jianbo Shi. 2003. Multiclass spectral clustering. In *Proceedings of International Conference on Computer Vision (ICCV 03)*, pages 313–319. IEEE.

Supervised and Unsupervised Word Sense Disambiguation on Word Embedding Vectors of Unambiguous Synonyms

Aleksander Wawer
Institute of Computer Science
PAS
Jana Kazimierza 5
01-248 Warsaw, Poland
axw@ipipan.waw.pl

Agnieszka Mykowiecka
Institute of Computer Science
PAS
Jana Kazimierza 5
01-248 Warsaw, Poland
agn@ipipan.waw.pl

Abstract

This paper compares two approaches to word sense disambiguation using word embeddings trained on unambiguous synonyms. The first one is an unsupervised method based on computing log probability from sequences of word embedding vectors, taking into account ambiguous word senses and guessing correct sense from context. The second method is supervised. We use a multilayer neural network model to learn a context-sensitive transformation that maps an input vector of ambiguous word into an output vector representing its sense. We evaluate both methods on corpora with manual annotations of word senses from the Polish wordnet.

1 Introduction

Ambiguity is one of the fundamental features of natural language, so every attempt to understand NL utterances has to include a disambiguation step. People usually do not even notice ambiguity because of the clarifying role of the context. A word *market* is ambiguous, and it is still such in the phrase *the fish market* while in a longer phrase like *the global fish market* it is unequivocal because of the word *global*, which cannot be used to describe physical place. Thus, distributional semantics methods seem to be a natural way to solve the word sense discrimination/disambiguation task (WSD). One of the first approaches to WSD was context-group sense discrimination (Schütze, 1998) in which sense representations were computed as groups of similar contexts. Since then, distributional semantic methods were utilized in very many ways in supervised, weekly supervised and unsupervised approaches.

Unsupervised WSD algorithms aim at resolving word ambiguity without the use of annotated corpora. There are two popular categories of knowledge-based algorithms. The first one originates from the Lesk (1986) algorithm, and exploit the number of common words in two sense definitions (glosses) to select the proper meaning in a context. Lesk algorithm relies on the set of dictionary entries and the information about the context in which the word occurs. In (Basile et al., 2014) the concept of overlap is replaced by similarity represented by a DSM model. The authors compute the overlap between the gloss of the meaning and the context as a similarity measure between their corresponding vector representations in a semantic space. A semantic space is a co-occurrences matrix M build by analysing the distribution of words in a large corpus, later reduced using Latent Semantic Analysis (Landauer and Dumais, 1997). The second group of algorithms comprises graph-based methods which use structure of semantic nets in which different types of word sense relations are represented and linked (e.g. WordNet, BabelNet). They used various graph-induced information, e.g. Page Rank algorithm (Mihalcea et al., 2004).

In this paper we present a method of word sense disambiguation, i.e. inferring an appropriate word sense from those listed in Polish wordnet, using word embeddings in both supervised and unsupervised approaches. The main tested idea is to calculate sense embeddings using unambiguous synonyms (elements of the same synsets) for a particular word sense. In section 2 we shortly present existing results for WSD for Polish as well as other works related to word embeddings for other languages, while section 3 presents annotated data we use for evaluation and supervised model training. Next sections describe the chosen method of calculating word sense embeddings, our unsuper-

Proceedings of the 1st Workshop on Sense, Concept and Entity Representations and their Applications, pages 120–125,
Valencia, Spain, April 4 2017. ©2017 Association for Computational Linguistics

vised and supervised WSD experiments and some comments on the results.

2 Existing Work

2.1 Polish WSD

There was very little research done in WSD for Polish. The first one from the few more visible attempts comprise a small supervised experiment with WSD in which machine learning techniques and a set of a priori defined features were used, (Kobyliński, 2012). Next, in (Kobyliński and Kopeć, 2012), extended Lesk knowledge-based approach and corpus-based similarity functions were used to improve previous results. These experiments were conducted on the corpora annotated with the specially designed set of senses. The first one contained general texts with 106 polysemous words manually annotated with 2.85 sense definitions per word on average. The second, smaller, WikiEcono corpus (http://zil.ipipan.waw.pl/plWikiEcono) was annotated by another set of senses for 52 polysemous words. It contains 3.62 sense definitions per word on average. The most recent work on WSD for Polish (Kędzia et al., 2015) utilizes graph-based approaches of (Mihalcea et al., 2004) and (Agirre et al., 2014). This method uses both plWordnet and SUMO ontology and was tested on KPWr data set (Broda et al., 2012) annotated with plWordnet senses — the same data set which we use in our experiments. The highest precision of 0.58 was achieved for nouns. The results obtained by different WSD approaches are very hard to compare because of different set of senses and test data used and big differences in results obtained by the same system on different data. (Tripodi and Pelillo, 2017) reports the results obtained by the best systems for English at the level of 0.51-0.85% depending on the approach (supervised or unsupervised) and the data set. The only system for Polish to which to some extend we can compare our approach is (Kędzia et al., 2015).

2.2 WSD and Word Embeddings

The problem of WSD has been approached from various perspectives in the context of word embeddings.

Popular approach is to generate multiple embeddings per word type, often using unsupervised automatic methods. For example, (Reisinger and Mooney, 2010; Huang et al., 2012) cluster contexts of each word to learn senses for each word, then re-label them with clustered sense for learning embeddings. (Neelakantan et al., 2014) introduce flexible number of senses: they extend sense cluster list when a new sense is encountered by a model.

(Iacobacci et al., 2015) use an existing WSD algorithm to automatically generate large sense-annotated corpora to train sense-level embeddings. (Taghipou and Ng, 2015) prepare POS-specific embeddings by applying a neural network with trainable embedding layer. They use those embeddings to extend feature space of a supervised WSD tool named IMS.

In (Bhingardive et al., 2015), the authors propose to exploit word embeddings in an unsupervised method for most frequent sense detection from the untagged corpora. Like in our work, the paper explores creation of sense embeddings with the use of WordNet. As the authors put it, sense embeddings are obtained by taking the average of word embeddings of each word in the sense-bag. The sense-bag for each sense of a word is obtained by extracting the context words from the WordNet such as synset members (S), content words in the gloss (G), content words in the example sentence (E), synset members of the hypernymy-hyponymy synsets (HS), and so on.

3 Word-Sense Annotated Treebank

The main obstacle in elaborating WSD method for Polish is lack of semantically annotated resources which can be applied for training and evaluation. In our experiment we used an existing one which use wordnet senses – semantic annotation (Hajnicz, 2014) of Składnica (Woliński et al., 2011). The set is a rather small but carefully prepared resource and contains constituency parse trees for Polish sentences. The adapted version of Składnica (0.5) contains 8241 manually validated trees. Sentence tokens are annotated with fine-grained semantic types represented by Polish wordnet synsets from plWordnet 2.0 plWordnet, Piasecki et al., 2009, http://plwordnet.pwr.wroc.pl/wordnet/). The set contains lexical units of three open parts of speech: adjectives, nouns and verbs. Therefore, only tokens belonging to these POS are annotated (as well as abbreviations and acronyms). Składnica contains about 50K nouns, verbs and adjectives for annotation, and 17410 of them belonging to 2785 (34%) sentences has been already annotated. For 2072 tokens (12%), the lexical unit appropriate in the context has not been found in plWordnet.

4 Obtaining Sense Embeddings

In this section we describe the method of obtaining sense-level word embeddings. Unlike most of the approaches described in Section 2.2, our method is applied to manually sense-labeled corpora.

In Wordnet, words either occur in multiple synsets (are therefore ambiguous and subject of WSD), or in one synset (are unambiguous). Our approach is to focus on synsets that contain both ambiguous and unambiguous words. In Skadnica 2.0 (Polish WordNet) we found 28766 synsets matching these criteria and therefore potentially suitable for our experiments.

Let us consider a synset containing following words: 'blemish', 'deface', 'disfigure'. Word 'blemish' appears also in other synsets (is ambiguous) while words 'deface' and 'disfigure' are specific for this synset and do not appear in any other synset (are unambiguous).

We assume that embeddings specific to a sense or synset can be approximated by unambiguous part of the synset. While some researchers such as (Bhingardive et al., 2015) take average embeddings of all synset-specific words, even using glosses and hyperonymy, we use unambiguous words to generate word2vec embedding vector of a sense.

During training, each occurrence of unambiguous word in corpus is substituted for a synset identifier. As in the provided example, each occurrence of 'deface' and 'disfigure' would be replaced by its sense identifier, the same for both unambiguous words. We'll later use these sense vectors to distinguish between senses of ambiguous 'blemish' given their contexts.

We train word2vec vectors using substitution mechanism described above on a dump of all Polish language Wikipedia and 300-million subset of the National Corpus of Polish (Przepiórkowski et al., 2012). The embedding size is set to 100, all other word2vec parameters have the default value as in (Řehůřek and Sojka, 2010). The model is based on lemmatized (base word forms) so only the occurrences of forms with identical lemmas are taken into account.

5 Unsupervised Word Sense Recognition

In this section we are proposing a simple unsupervised approach to WSD. The key idea is to use word embeddings in probabilistic interpretation and application comparable to language modeling, however without building any additional models or parameter-rich systems. The method is derived from (Taddy, 2015), where it was used with a bayesian classifier and vector embedding inversion to classify documents.

(Mikolov et al., 2013) describe two alternative methods of generating word embeddings: the skip-gram, which represents conditional probability for a word's context (surrounding words) and CBOW, which targets the conditional probability for each word given its context. None of these corresponds to a likelihood model, but as (Taddy, 2015) note they can be interpreted as components in a composite likelihood approximation. Let w = $[w_1 \ldots w_T]$ denote an ordered vector of words. The skip-gram in (Mikolov et al., 2013) yields the pairwise composite log likelihood:

$$logp_\mathcal{V}(w) = \sum_{j=1}^{T} \sum_{i=1}^{T} \mathbb{1}_{[1 \leq |k-j| \leq b]} logp_\mathcal{V}(w_k|w_j)$$

(1)

We use the above formula to compute probability of a sentence. Unambiguous words are represented as their word2vec representations derived directly from corpus. In case of ambiguous words, we substitute them for each possible sense vector (generated from unambiguous parts of synsets, as has been previously described). Therefore, for an ambiguous word to be disambiguated, we generate as many variants of a sentence as there are its senses, and compute each variant's likelihood using formula 1. Ambiguous words which occur in the context are omitted (although we might also replace them with an averaged vector representing all their meanings). Finally, we select the most probable variant.

Because the method involves no model training, we evaluate it directly over the whole data set without dividing it into train and test sets for cross-validation.

6 Supervised Word Sense Recognition

In the supervised approach, we train neural network models to predict word senses. In our experiment, neural network model acts as a regression function F transforming word embeddings provided at input into sense (synset identifiers) vectors.

As the network architecture we selected LSTM (Hochreiter and Schmidhuber, 1997). Neural network model consists of one LSTM layer followed by a dense (perceptron) layer at the output. We train the network using mean standard error loss function.

Input data consists of the sequences of five word2vec embeddings: of two words that make left and right symmetric contexts of each input word to be disambiguated, and the word itself represented by the average vector of vectors representing all its senses. Ambiguous words for which there are no embeddings are represented by zero vectors (padded). Zero vectors are also added if the context is too short. This data is used to train LSTM model (Keras 1.0.1 `https://keras.io/`) linked with the subsequent dense layer with sigmoid activation function.

At the final step, we transform the output into synsets rather than vectors. We select the most appropriate sense from a set of possible sense inventory, taking into account continuous output structure. In this step, neural network output layer (which is a vector of the same size as input embeddings, but transformed) is compared with each possible sense vector. To compare vectors, we use cosine similarity measure, defined between any two vectors.

We compute cosine similarity between neural network output vector nnv and each sense from possible sense inventory S, and select the sense with the maximum cosine similarity towards nnv.

To test each neural network set-up we use 30-fold cross-validation.

7   Results

In this section we put summary of the results obtained on our test set, as well as two baseline results. The corpus consisted of 2785 sentences and 303 occurences of annotated ambiguous words which could be disambiguated by our algorithms, i.e. there were unambiguous equivalents of its senses and there were appropiate word embeddings for at least one of the other senses of this word. There were 5571 occurences of words which occurred only in one sense.

Table 1 presents precision of both tested methods computed over the Skladnica dataset. The

set contains 344 occurrences of ambiguous words which were eligible for our method. For the unsupervised approach we tested a window of 5 and 10 words around the analyzed word.

The ambiguous words from the sentence other than the one being disambiguated at the moment are either omitted or represented as a vector representing all their occurrences. The *uniq* variant omit all other ambiguous words from the sentence while in the *all* variant we use not disambiguated representation of these words.

Method	Settings	Precision
random baseline	N/A	0.47
MFS baseline	N/A	0.73
pagerank	N/A	0.52
unsupervised	5 word, all	0.507
	5 word, uniq	0.507
	10 word, uniq	0.529
	10 word, all	0.513
supervised	750 epochs	0.673
	1000 epochs	0.680
	2000 epochs	0.690
	4000 epochs	0.667

Table 1: Precision of word-sense disambiguation methods for Polish.

In the supervised approach the best results were obtained for 2000 epochs but they did not differ much from these obtained after 1000 epochs. For comparison, we include two baseline values:

- random baseline select random sense from uniform random probability distribution,

- MFS baseline use most frequent sense as computed from the same corpus (There is no other available sense frequency data for Polish, that could be obtained from manually annotated sources.)

The table also includes results computed using pagerank WSD algorithm developed at the PWR (Kędzia et al., 2015). These results were obtained for all the ambiguous words occurring within the sample, so cannot be directly compared to our results.

As the results indicate, unsupervised method performs at the level of random sense selection.

Below there are two examples of the analyzed sentences.

- *lęk przed nicością łączy się z doświadczeniem pustki* 'fear of nothingness combines with the experience of emptiness': in this sentence, Polish ambiguous words 'nothingness' and 'emptiness' were resolved correctly while an ambiguous words 'experience' does not have unambiguous equivalents.

- *na tym nie kończą się problemy* 'that does not stop problems': in this example ambiguous word 'problem' was not resolved correctly, but this case is difficult also for humans.

The low quality of the results might be the effect of a relatively short context available as the analysed text is not continuous.

It might have also pointed out to the difficulty of the test set. Senses in plWodnet are very numerous and hard to differentiate even for human. But the results of the supervised method falsify this assumption.

Our supervised approach gave much better results although they are also not very good as the amount of annotated data is rather small. In this approach more epochs resulted in a slight model over-fitting.

8 Conclusions

Our work introduced two methods of word sense disambiguation based on word embeddings, supervised and unsupervised. The first approach assumes probabilistic interpretation of embeddings and computes log probability from sequences of word embedding vectors. In place of ambiguous word we put embeddings specific for each possible sense and evaluate the likelihood of thus obtained sentences. Finally we select the most probable sentence. The second supervised method is based on a neural network trained to learn a context-sensitive transformation that maps an input vector of ambiguous word into an output vector representing its sense. We compared the performance of both methods on corpora with manual annotations of word senses from the Polish wordnet (plWordnet). The results show the low quality of the unsupervised method and suggest the superiority of the supervised version in comparison to the pagerank method on the set of words which were eligible for our approach. Although the baseline in which just the most frequent sense is chosen is still a little better, this is probably due to a very limited training set available for Polish.

Acknowledgments

The paper is partially supported by the Polish National Science Centre project *Compositional distributional semantic models for identification, discrimination and disambiguation of senses in Polish texts* number 2014/15/B/ST6/05186.

References

Eneko Agirre, Oier López de Lacalle, and Aitor Soroa. 2014. Random walks for knowledge-based word sense disambiguation. *Comput. Linguist.*, 40(1):57–84, March.

Pierpaolo Basile, Annalina Caputo, and Giovanni Semeraro. 2014. An enhanced lesk word sense disambiguation algorithm through a distributional semantic model. In *Proceedings of COLING 2014, the 25th International Conference on Computational Linguistics*, Dublin, Irleand. Association for Computational Linguistics.

Sudha Bhingardive, Dhirendra Singh, Rudra Murthy, Hanumant Redkar, and Pushpak Bhattacharyya. 2015. Unsupervised most frequent sense detection using word embeddings. In *DENVER*.

Bartosz Broda, Michał Marcinczuk, Marek Maziarz, Adam Radziszewski, and Adam Wardynski. 2012. KPWr: Towards a free corpus of polish. *Proceedings of LREC'12*.

Elżbieta Hajnicz. 2014. Lexico-semantic annotation of *składnica* treebank by means of PLWN lexical units. In Heili Orav, Christiane Fellbaum, and Piek Vossen, editors, *Proceedings of the 7th International Word-Net Conference (GWC 2014)*, pages 23–31, Tartu, Estonia. University of Tartu.

Sepp Hochreiter and Jürgen Schmidhuber. 1997. Long short-term memory. *Neural Comput.*, 9(8):1735–1780, November.

Eric H. Huang, Richard Socher, Christopher D. Manning, and Andrew Y. Ng. 2012. Improving word representations via global context and multiple word prototypes. In *Proceedings of the 50th Annual Meeting of the Association for Computational Linguistics: Long Papers - Volume 1*, ACL '12, pages 873–882, Stroudsburg, PA, USA. Association for Computational Linguistics.

Ignacio Iacobacci, Mohammad Taher Pilehvar, and Roberto Navigli. 2015. Sensembed: Learning sense embeddings for word and relational similarity. In *Proceedings of the 53rd Annual Meeting of the Association for Computational Linguistics and the*

7th International Joint Conference on Natural Language Processing of the Asian Federation of Natural Language Processing, ACL 2015, July 26-31, 2015, Beijing, China, Volume 1: Long Papers, pages 95–105.

Łukasz Kobyliński and Mateusz Kopeć. 2012. Semantic similarity functions in word sense disambiguation. In Petrand Horák Sojka, Alešand Kopeček, and Karel Ivanand Pala, editors, *Text, Speech and Dialogue: 15th International Conference, TSD 2012, Brno, Czech Republic, September 3-7, 2012. Proceedings*, pages 31–38, Berlin, Heidelberg. Springer.

Łukasz Kobyliński. 2012. Mining class association rules for word sense disambiguation. In Pascal Bouvry, Mieczysław A. Kłopotek, Franck Leprevost, Małgorzata Marciniak, Agnieszka Mykowiecka, and Henryk Rybiński, editors, *Security and Intelligent Information Systems: International Joint Conference, SIIS 2011, Warsaw, Poland, June 13-14, 2011, Revised Selected Papers*, volume 7053 of *Lecture Notes in Computer Science*, pages 307–317, Berlin, Heidelberg. Springer.

Paweł Kędzia, Maciej Piasecki, and Marlena Orlińska. 2015. Word sense disambiguation based on large scale Polish CLARIN heterogeneous lexical resources. *Cognitive Studies| Études cognitives*, 15:269–292.

Rada Mihalcea, Paul Tarau, and Elizabeth Figa. 2004. Pagerank on semantic networks, with application to word sense disambiguation. In *Proceedings of the 20th International Conference on Computational Linguistics*, COLING '04, Stroudsburg, PA, USA. Association for Computational Linguistics.

Tomas Mikolov, Wen-tau Yih, and Geoffrey Zweig. 2013. Linguistic regularities in continuous space word representations. In *Human Language Technologies: Conference of the North American Chapter of the Association of Computational Linguistics, Proceedings, June 9-14, 2013, Westin Peachtree Plaza Hotel, Atlanta, Georgia, USA*, pages 746–751.

Arvind Neelakantan, Jeevan Shankar, Alexandre Passos, and Andrew McCallum. 2014. Efficient nonparametric estimation of multiple embeddings per word in vector space. In *Proceedings of the 2014 Conference on Empirical Methods in Natural Language Processing, EMNLP 2014, October 25-29, 2014, Doha, Qatar, A meeting of SIGDAT, a Special Interest Group of the ACL*, pages 1059–1069.

Adam Przepiórkowski, Mirosław Bańko, Rafał L. Górski, and Barbara Lewandowska-Tomaszczyk, editors. 2012. *Narodowy Korpus Języka Polskiego*. Wydawnictwo Naukowe PWN, Warsaw.

Radim Řehůřek and Petr Sojka. 2010. Software Framework for Topic Modelling with Large Corpora. In *Proceedings of the LREC 2010 Workshop on New Challenges for NLP Frameworks*, pages 45–50, Valletta, Malta, May. ELRA. http://is.muni.cz/publication/884893/en.

Joseph Reisinger and Raymond J Mooney. 2010. Multi-prototype vector-space models of word meaning. In *Human Language Technologies: The 2010 Annual Conference of the North American Chapter of the Association for Computational Linguistics*, pages 109–117. Association for Computational Linguistics.

Hinrich Schütze. 1998. Automatic word sense discrimination. *Computational Linguistics*, 24(1):97–123.

Matt Taddy. 2015. Document classification by inversion of distributed language representations. *CoRR*, abs/1504.07295.

Kaveh Taghipou and Hwee Tou Ng. 2015. Semi-supervised word sense disambiguation using word embeddings in general and specific domains. In *Human Language Technologies: The 2015 Annual Conference of the North American Chapter of the ACL*, page 314–323. Association for Computational Linguistics.

Rocco Tripodi and Marcello Pelillo. 2017. A game-theoretic approach to word sense disambiguation. *Computational Linguistics*.

Marcin Woliński, Katarzyna Głowińska, and Marek Świdziński. 2011. A preliminary version of Składnica—a treebank of Polish. In Zygmunt Vetulani, editor, *Proceedings of the 5th Language & Technology Conference: Human Language Technologies as a Challenge for Computer Science and Linguistics*, pages 299–303, Poznań, Poland.

Author Index